HUMAN RIGHTS
as PRACTICE

HUMAN RIGHTS *as* PRACTICE

DALIT WOMEN SECURING LIVELIHOOD ENTITLEMENTS IN SOUTH INDIA

JAYSHREE P. MANGUBHAI

OXFORD
UNIVERSITY PRESS

OXFORD
UNIVERSITY PRESS

Oxford University Press is a department of the University of Oxford.
It furthers the University's objective of excellence in research, scholarship,
and education by publishing worldwide. Oxford is a registered trademark of
Oxford University Press in the UK and in certain other countries

Published in India by
Oxford University Press
YMCA Library Building, 1 Jai Singh Road, New Delhi 110 001, India

© Oxford University Press 2014

The moral rights of the author have been asserted

First Edition published in 2014

ISBN-13: 978-0-19-809545-3
ISBN-10: 0-19-809545-7

Typeset in Berling LT Std 9.5/13
by The Graphics Solution, New Delhi 110 092

CONTENTS

ACKNOWLEDGEMENTS

During the three years of this research, one point that has been reinforced for me is that research is as much about the topic as it is about the relationships you build throughout the process. I am indebted to numerous people who made this book possible, of whom I must mention a few. I owe an enormous debt of gratitude to my research colleague, mentor, and friend, Aloysius Irudayam S.J. (Institute of Development Education, Action and Studies [IDEAS], Madurai), for planting the seeds of this research idea and for providing invaluable guidance during my fieldwork. A number of people then helped crystallize this research topic, not least Paul Gready (Professor at the Centre for Applied Human Rights, University of York), Rachel Kurian (Senior Lecturer at the Institute of Social Studies, the Hague), Kirrily Pells, and my father, Francis Mangubhai (retired Associate Professor at the University of Southern Queensland).

Three people warrant special mention and thanks for having teamed together so well in guiding this doctoral research: Bas de Gaay Fortman and Jenny Goldschmidt (Professors at the Netherlands Institute of Human Rights, Utrecht University); and Lorraine Nencel (Associate Professor at the Faculty of Social Sciences, Free University of Amsterdam). The lifeworld of a lawyer is so different from that of an anthropologist, and they became my essential 'knowledge brokers' to forge the links between human rights law and ethnographic research. I must especially appreciate Nencel for constantly challenging my ideas and normative understandings, making me more self-aware of my position and responsibilities in writing about the lives of others.

Without a doubt, the major contribution to my learning process has come from the Dalit women in the villages in Tamil Nadu. I cannot thank them enough for allowing me into their lives, to get to know them, to ask my endless questions, and participate in the daily flow of their lives as well as functions and events. Gandhi from Vettriyur village asked me when I first interviewed her, 'What can you learn from us? We only can learn from you.' And in this she was mistaken, as time spent with these women showed me that knowledge from experience, from sufferings and joys that come in taking collective action to change a situation of exclusion, has as much value as knowledge gained from formal education. Understanding their lives brings me that one step closer to understanding human rights as practice suited to local contexts, and my role in that practice.

I am also deeply indebted to A.M. Veronnika (Director, Vidiyal Mahalir Membāttu Sangam), D. Kalvikkarasi (Tamil Nadu Dalit Women's Movement member), N. Fatima Burnad (Coordinator, Society for Rural Education and Development), and A. Magimai (Coordinator, Tamil Nadu Dalit Women's Movement) for sharing their rich experiences working with Dalit women and for all their help with the logistics of fieldwork in the villages. Veronnika and Fatima Burnad also generously allowed me to use their staff to undertake the quantitative survey part of my research. My gratitude further goes to all the Dalit men, other caste villagers, government officials, and social activists and movement leaders who gave time to me for interviews and discussions.

I could not have done this work without A.E. Anushiya, P. Jeevitha, Jenifer Fercy, S. Jaya Sophia, M. Shalini, and R. Thilagam, who became my companions and translators throughout the many days spent in the villages and the long hours of patiently transcribing interviews. The Jesuit fathers in IDEAS also never failed to welcome me to interact with them as I worked through my data, and to stay during the last stages of writing up this research.

Crossing the oceans back to the Netherlands as I wrote up this research, my colleagues at the Netherlands Institute of Human Rights were invaluable in sharing their academic and other knowledge and ideas. I also thank my father and Joel G. Lee (PhD candidate at Columbia University) for patiently going through my draft chapters and giving me feedback. Further, I had the privilege of having my research examined by academics from a wide range of disciplines, whose comments and suggestions have found a way into this book: David Mosse (Professor of Social Anthropology, School of African and Oriental Studies, University of London); Cees Flinterman (Honorary Professor of Human Rights, the Netherlands Institute of Human Rights); Titia Loenen (Professor of Legal Theory, Utrecht University); Barbara Oomen (Professor at Law, Utrecht University); Rachel Kurian (Senior Lecturer in International Labour Economics, Institute of Social Studies); and Maarten Bavinck (Associate Professor, Department of Human Geography, Planning and International Development Studies, University of Amsterdam).

I also thank Cordaid for providing me with the financial support to undertake this research.

Finally, but not least, I express my gratitude to my parents, Francis and Linda Mangubhai, and my sister, Sangeeta, for all their support, encouragement, and inspiration throughout the lengthy and sometimes difficult period of my research. They have never ceased to amaze me for their patience and love in all my endeavours, and I am proud to present this book to them.

ABBREVIATIONS

AFHRD	Asian Forum for Human Rights and Development
AHRC	Asian Human Rights Commission
ANNI	Asian NGO Network on National Human Rights Institutions
AWID	Association for Women's Rights in Development
CEDAW	Convention on the Elimination of All Forms of Discrimination against Women
CERD	Committee on the Elimination of Racial Discrimination
CHRGJ	Centre for Human Rights and Global Justice
CESCR	Committee on Economic, Social and Cultural Rights
CRZ	Coastal Regulation Zone
DFID	Department for International Development
DRDA	District Rural Development Agency
DRO	district revenue officer
FAO	Food and Agricultural Organization
GDP	gross domestic product
GDI	gender development index
HDI	human development index
HRW	Human Rights Watch
ICCPR	International Covenant on Civil and Political Rights
ICERD	International Convention on the Elimination of All Forms of Racial Discrimination 1965
ICESCR	International Covenant on Economic, Social and Cultural Rights 1966

ICHRP	International Council on Human Rights Policy
ICJ	International Commission of Jurists
IDEAS	Institute of Development Education, Action and Studies
IDS	Institute of Development Studies
IHRIP	International Human Rights Internship Programme
IIPS	International Institute for Population Sciences
MGNREGS	Mahatma Gandhi National Rural Employment Guarantee Scheme
MHRD	Ministry of Human Resource Development
MLA	Member of the Legislative Assembly
MPEDA	Marine Products Export Development Authority
MPPGP	Ministry of Personnel, Public Grievances and Pensions
MRD	Ministry of Rural Development
MSJE	Ministry of Social Justice and Empowerment
MWCD	Ministry of Women and Child Development
NCEUS	National Commission for Enterprises in the Unorganized Sector
NCRB	National Crimes Records Bureau
NCW	National Commission for Women
NGO	non-governmental organization
NHRC	National Human Rights Commission
NSSO	National Sample Survey Organization
OBCs	other backward castes/classes
OHCHR	Office of the High Commissioner for Human Rights
PDS	public distribution system
PIL	public interest litigation
PT	Puthiya Thamizhagam
PWESCR	Programme on Women's Economic, Social and Cultural Rights
RDPRD	Rural Development and Panchayati Raj Department
SC	Scheduled Caste
SCP	Special Component Plan
SHG	self-help group
SRED	Society for Rural Education and Development
ST	Scheduled Tribe
TASMAC	Tamil Nadu State Marketing Corporation

TNCDW	Tamil Nadu Corporation for the Development of Women
TNDWM	Tamil Nadu Dalit Women's Movement
UDHR	Universal Declaration of Human Rights
UN	United Nations
UNDP	United Nations Development Programme
VCK	Viduthalai Chiruthaigal Katchi

INTRODUCTION
Situating Dalit Women Within Rights and Development

The authorship of human rights rests with communities in the struggle against illegitimate power formations and the politics of cruelty.

Baxi (1998: 148)

Dialectics of Social Exclusion and Collective Agency

Dalit[1] women collectives across the villages in the south Indian state of Tamil Nadu reiterated a Tamil saying again and again during the course of my interactions with them: 'If only one hand claps, no one will hear. But if ten hands clap, the sound will be heard by others.' On the one hand, it spoke of the women's sense of exclusion, the feeling that no one listened to their individual voices. On the other hand, it alluded to their sense of power and voice that came from the collective. As Asha, a woman from Vettriyur village, put it: 'We have changed in a positive way since joining the *sangam* (women's association). We are no longer like our mothers, silent.'

The dialectics of social exclusion and collective power, expressed in collective action to obtain access to and command over livelihood[2] resources, became a recurrent theme during conversations and discussions over the months I spent with these women between 2009 and 2010. These interactions revealed that despite a historical and enduring context of social, economic, and political exclusion resulting in livelihood deprivation, Dalit women often are at the forefront of struggles for livelihood resources and opportunities. In part, this can be traced to the substantial contribution these women make daily to sustaining their families through labour both inside and outside the home. Their place thus lies at the centre, and not at the periphery, of rural livelihood strategies. By making claims to livelihood resources, these women contribute to the socio-economic changes taking place in Indian villages today. Their role, however, is little acknowledged, researched, or understood.

Under India's hierarchical caste system, Dalits in general are subjected to widespread discrimination and exclusion on the basis of their birth into particular castes, to which historically prescribed, degrading occupations linked to death, dirt, and menial labour are attached. They are spatially and socially segregated from mainstream Indian society, and commonly denied equality and basic rights in practice. This includes denial of equal access to and command over resources, ranging from land to decent employment to education. All these resources are required in order to have a decent livelihood and to fully participate in society. The graded inequality among castes inherent to this social system vests resources, power, and social status with so-called 'higher' castes in a hierarchical ranking order. This enables these castes to exploit the labour of the 'impure' 'lower' castes dependent on them for their livelihood (Irudayam et al. 2011). Caste and class thus are seen to generally converge, making Dalits one of the poorest and systematically disempowered social groups in India today (see Desai et al. 2010). Caste is also embedded in institutions of the state, society, and family. It manifests itself in the social norms and practices of state officials and dominant castes[3] vis-à-vis Dalits. Thus, despite the legal prescription of equal citizenship rights, social norms engender collective prejudice against 'low caste', 'polluted' Dalits, and often result in discrimination and/or violence against them.

Within the Dalit community, Dalit women have been described as bearing a double burden of subordination due to both their caste and their gender (Parliamentary Committee on the Welfare of Scheduled Castes and Scheduled Tribes 2005). Gender subordination is, in fact, built into the caste system because social norms and institutions interlink caste and gender, and make control over women crucial to the maintenance of boundaries between castes. Examples are the social norms of endogamy, 'untouchability', and patrilineal inheritance, which emphasize caste hierarchy and gender inequality. In the case of Dalit women, they are set apart from other caste women as 'polluted' and are actively excluded from livelihood resources (see Chapter 2). They experience lower education and health levels than other caste women, limiting their access to knowledge, employment, and to decent and healthy lives. Caste and gender discriminations in terms of access to resources such as land or credit, or in terms of employment opportunities, operate to limit their occupational mobility. The majority of Dalit women are effectively ghettoized into 'unskilled', manual work where they receive lower wages as compared to their male counterparts and dominant castes. Moreover, their relative independence and freedom of movement as they engage in such work, as compared to their dominant caste counterparts who are more secluded within the home, is balanced by continuing discrimination and violence that often arises from that independence (Gorringe 2005; Irudayam *et al.* 2011). They also, increasingly, carry the burden of maintaining livelihoods and traditional caste occupations in rural areas due to factors such as the increasing feminization of agricultural operations and male outmigration to urban areas in search of work. With little political voice, then, Dalit women have little power to alter their socio-economic conditions and those of their families and communities.

Compounding this situation, violence is often targeted towards them in order to reinforce structural inequalities and/or to punish those who assert their entitlement to resources (Irudayam *et al.* 2011). This is particularly the case because women are perceived as embodying the honour of their caste community (Kannabiran and Kannabiran 2003). Thus, for instance, Dalit women who attempt to access common water sources in villages, or who assert their rights to land granted by the government to their families, are vulnerable to attacks from dominant caste women and men. At the same time, they face gender discrimination from Dalit men, which prevents their equal access to what little livelihood resources their families and communities possess.

The key problem thus is 'structural violence' (Galtung 1969; Winter and Leighton 2001): historical and enduring structural inequalities place Dalit women at a perpetual disadvantage vis-à-vis other social groups. Constraints on their socio-economic progress, political voice, and agency are normalized through social relations and institutions.

Through cultural violence (Galtung 1980: 291–2), socio-cultural norms and practices render direct and structural violence against some people legitimate and acceptable in society. Structural violence, as a form of everyday, 'invisible', and widespread harm, predicated on structural and relational factors, often lies at the root of more sporadic physical manifestations of violence. This harm further reduces their ability to escape physical violence, and, in fact, is often further entrenched through such violence. For these reasons, this research concentrates on Dalit women overcoming exclusion from livelihood resources and realizing their social and economic rights, and not on atrocities.[4]

Their experiences of structural (and physical) violence notwithstanding, the growth of Dalit women's movements, organizations, and grassroots groups in recent years attests to a small but significant counter-trend. These women are mobilizing the few resources they do possess, namely, 'their capacity to resist and transform through collective strength' (Kabeer 1994: 150–1). National and state-level Dalit women's networks have emerged in the mid-1990s, including the National Federation of Dalit Women and the Tamil Nadu Dalit Women's Movement. These networks have focused on organizing Dalit women independently, articulating an autonomous identity for Dalit women and building their leadership potential. Their aims have been to empower these women to assert their rights in the face of the state's manifest inability or unwillingness to fulfil those rights, as well as the sidelining of their voices and concerns by both the Dalit and women's movements (Smith 2008; Subramaniam 2006). More locally, smaller Dalit women's organizations have started to organize Dalit women separately. Some have facilitated the women's involvement in microcredit activities alone, while others have encouraged their collective action to secure specific entitlements and freedoms. Examples of the latter are seen in Chapters 3–5, and are struggles that often involve negotiation and contestation with the state at the local level.

Both levels of organization of Dalit women are responses to trends wherein gender and caste inequalities have not automatically declined with the process of economic growth. In fact, in many cases, new manifestations of inequalities have emerged in pace with the changing village economy. For instance, the women find themselves excluded from new employment opportunities or new 'untouchability' norms emerge in spaces for engagement such as women's savings and credit self-help groups (SHGs). Dalit women thus are increasingly moving outside the 'private' sphere of the family today to collectively engage in micro-political processes such as the securing of entitlements to livelihood resources. By moving into public–political spaces from which they are traditionally excluded, 'natural' or unquestionable social norms and practices that perpetuate their exclusion are being questioned. Women are frequently entering into arenas of contestation over resources, pow-er, and status with multiple actors ranging from Dalit men to dominant caste villagers to state officials. In doing so, they push at the overlapping structural boundaries of caste and gender and thus create the potential to transform the power relations that produce their disentitlement to resources and opportunities.

The increasing visibility of Dalit women's collective action amidst social movements striving for social change in India is complemented by the growing recognition of difference arising from multiple, intersecting identities. Most studies to date have focused on Dalit *or* women's movements in general, and their processes of empowerment and the establishment of particularly civil–political claims to security and a dignified identity (for example, Gorringe 2005; Omvedt 1995; and Purushothaman 1998). Many Dalit and women's movements have placed less emphasis on the economic development of these two social groups. Most have directed their efforts to combatting endemic violence. Additional focus has lain on eradicating 'untouchability' prac-tices and struggles to construct a dignified identity in the case of Dalits, while for women, action has been taken to reform gender inequitable personal laws and demand equal political representation. Some of this research has noted Dalit women's lesser participation or the marginal-ization of their voices in processes aimed at social mobility (Dietrich 2003; Gorringe 2005; Mosse 1994). Little or no emphasis, however, has been placed on examining the heterogeneity within these movements and particularly, the different needs, perspectives, and agency of Dalit women members. Consequently, these movements tend to promote the unnamed perspective and concerns of Dalit men and dominant caste women respectively. Such movements thereby reproduce the power relations the other seeks to combat (see Makkonen 2002).

Increasingly, several feminists have articulated demands that the Indian women's movements recognize difference and focus on the processes by which gender, caste, and class mutually construct each other (Dietrich 2003; Rege 1998; Subramaniam 2006). An equivalent demand has been extended to the Dalit movements to overcome resistance to the understanding and articulation of the gender dimensions of caste (Thorat 2001). One argument is that adopting the viewpoint of those located in the most disadvantageous position within intersecting social axes arguably yields a deeper understanding of the complexities of exclusion and subordination. This can lead to more effective strategies for inclusive and equitable development. Another argument is that one cannot afford to overlook the role of caste in women's development, nor gender in Dalits' development, if one wants to generate lasting change in Dalit women's lives (Govinda 2009). At the same time, differences among Dalit women along lines such as (sub)caste and class also have to be acknowledged and factored into collective action strategies.

A focus on Dalit women's collective action therefore aims to enrich the small but growing literature on these women's rights. In particular, I move away from the current research trend of marking these women as 'victims' of human rights violations. Exclusive attention to this aspect often reduces Dalit women's subjectivity to mere recipients of discrimination and violence. This is not to deny or diminish their intolerable situation of exclusion, discrimination, and violence in any way. Rather, it is to balance structural analysis of their situation with an acknowledgement of their subjectivity, cultural resources, and agency. It is also to recognize that social exclusion processes provide the framework of meanings and motivation for Dalit women's collective action. At the same time, I avoid any allusion that all Dalit women are agents of social change. Nor do I assume that those women who do not engage in collective action are passive and unaware of their subordination. This research instead concentrates on examining the structural and political opportunities, as well as constraints, for their organizing and collectively acting to acquire livelihood resources.

Opportunities and Limitations in Development and Rights-based Approaches

Analysis of the process by which Dalit women secure access to and command over livelihood resources as entitlements is set against the backdrop of discourses on development and human rights. These discourses have shaped a host of different approaches and strategies ostensibly to resolve the problem of structural violence. Traditionally, development has encompassed national industrialization and modernization, with the narrow goals of improving incomes, productivity, and consumption linked to economic growth. These goals translate into strategies promoting employment, market freedom, and the expansion of exports facilitated by political institutions. By increasing the income of the poor, individuals arguably are able to satisfy their basic livelihood needs and develop their capabilities. At the same time, contestations over the meaning of development have occurred where the state's economic priorities conflict with the development interests of local communities. Examples are the development-induced displacement of local villagers or export-driven commercial shrimp farming damaging local livelihoods (see Chapter 5). Moreover, 'development hazards' have resulted from state-driven development projects, allowing minimal participation by the intended beneficiaries in their design, and negatively affecting the ability of beneficiaries to sustain their livelihoods (Hadiprayitno 2009).

With poverty reduction becoming a central plank in development policy from the 1990s (see World Bank 1990), development discourses have broadened their focus. There is now an emphasis on livelihoods, vulnerability, and livelihood security (Lipton and Maxwell 1992). The development paradigm is centred on people and their contexts, and people's participation in decision making on improving their own lives and livelihoods (Friedmann 1992). Livelihood and rural development approaches, particularly sustainable livelihood approaches emerging from the late 1990s, view livelihood security as the essential element in human development and economic growth. A number of development strategies accordingly have been implemented in India, with the primary aim of ensuring livelihoods and simultaneously mitigating livelihood risk factors. These are to be achieved through enhancing people's human, social, economic, natural, and physical resources or assets, which then can be combined in pursuit of various livelihood strategies. At the same time, efforts are made to improve the institutional and policy contexts that affect claims and access to these resources (Department for International Development [DFID] undated; Ellis 2006; Scoones 1998).

In the implementation of these strategies, however, there has often been a narrow focus on developing the economic productivity and livelihood security of poor individuals through enhancing their asset base and capacity to manage livelihood resources. Considerably less focus has been placed on transforming the structures and institutions that determine resource distribution and entitlements, and which perpetuate inequality, exploitation, and injustice (Wilson 2008). In other words, livelihoods are abstracted from their socio-economic and political contexts and also, issues of resource redistribution among social groups are neglected. Structural or social factors are viewed as merely mediating the link between assets and the pursuit of livelihood activities. The result is that there is a tendency to construct a linear notion of causality regarding livelihood development (Rew and Rew 2003). This supports a managerial 'project mode' of functioning by development agencies that marginalizes people's knowledge and active participation in decision making (Mosse 2003a). It also ignores the fact that the contexts in which Dalit women live—complicated by unequal power relations producing livelihood deprivation, economic dependency on others, and unresponsive local political institutions—determines to a great extent the effectiveness of development interventions (Pattendon 2011).

Another common approach to development arising from the mid-1990s is the rights-based approach. Several basic elements constitute this approach: an express linkage to human rights as both the means (tools, legitimate claims) and end (benchmark indicators) of development; greater accountability from state actors[5] and development interveners; a stronger focus on empowerment and people's participation in determining their own development; and stress on non-discrimination, equality, and attention to vulnerable groups (Office of the High Commissioner for Human Rights [OHCHR] 2004). Proponents of this approach claim that it politicizes development by viewing the subjects of development as rights holders. Moreover, its focus on equality should promote strategies for structural change, challenging the power relations which produce subordination, disentitlement, and lack of voice for excluded social groups (Chapman *et al.* 2005; VeneKlasen *et al.* 2004). There is an emphasis on strengthening the ability of rights holders to make claims on the state, as duty bearer, so as to establish socially and legally protected entitlements to resources. It is argued that this contributes to making people citizen–subjects and not just passive objects of development. They should be empowered to negotiate equal access to development resources alongside promoting state account-ability and responsibility. Beyond adding legitimacy to individual resource claims based on international human rights standards, this approach also enables wider political claims to laws, policies, and insti-tutions which ensure citizens' development-related rights (Association for Women's Rights in Development [AWID] 2002; United Nations Development Programme [UNDP] 2000).

A number of authors (for example, Bradshaw 2006 and Rajagopal 2003), however, have questioned the extent to which current rights-based strategies are oriented towards promoting agency and trans-forming unequal power relations. There has been a tendency towards top-down strategies, which apply universal rights-based legal or policy rules to influence changes to social norms and perceptions. Important as legal and policy measures and legal rights claims are, the wider eco-nomic and political factors which define the context and shape the process and outcomes of local livelihood struggles are not taken into account. An underlying assumption has been that law is the most influ-ential set of rules structuring social activity as opposed to the myriad of social norms and practices. Superficial approaches therefore are applied to politics and power, favouring legal and technical solutions. These fail to adequately contend with the dynamic nature of power in determin-ing who participates, whose voices get heard, and who benefits under current institutional rules (Miller *et al.* 2006; VeneKlasen *et al.* 2004). Empowerment, accordingly, is often translated into capacity building on legal rights to initiate formal claims. Lesser emphasis is placed on the utilization of rights to legitimize people's struggles for resources and to alter the structural conditions which influence the claims pro-cess. Nor are inhibitions on women's capacity to make certain claims due to their positioning within multiple power relations taken into account. The potential then lies for legal claims to generate unexpected outcomes such as more social conflict or the reinforcement of power relations. All the above critiques have formed the basis for arguments that rights-based strategies add nothing new to existing development approaches. Instead, they further legitimize social inequalities and hier-archical relationships of power (Uvin 2002).

In addition, the focus on strengthening legal rights provisions and people's recourse to litigation to promote compliance with human rights law and social change obscures the fact that many excluded and subordinated people engage in non-legal, political struggles on a daily basis to realize their rights (SLSA Team 2003; Stammers 1999). In doing so, they construct their own understandings of rights based on what they perceive they are entitled to as a matter of justice and fairness (Institute of Development Studies [IDS] 2003). Legal strategies further do not account for the challenges, based on the integrated nature of legal and social norms, that many socially excluded groups, such as Dalit women, face in accessing the law and experiencing legal processes (Griffiths 2005). Such challenges include problems of access to adequate financial resources for what are often protracted legal struggles, or coercive pressures applied by other social actors to prevent these women from accessing their legal rights. Legal remedies are also compromised by state institutions and actors reproducing social biases and often failing to be accountable for respecting, protecting, and fulfilling Dalit women's rights. In such a situation, the realization of rights for Dalit women requires non-legal *as well as* legal strategies, where rights are *both* political and legal tools utilized to challenge unequal power relations. There is, therefore, an emphasis on extra-institutional forms of mobilization around rights (collective action) which can effectively support the observance of formal (legal) institutional norms (Rajagopal 2003: 235).

Through this research, I seek to address some of these critiques or gaps in development and rights-based approaches in order to support their translation into practical, operational strategies enabling social change. I also strive to show how top-down approaches which encourage states to establish legal and policy norms and benchmarks for progressive realization of socio-economic rights can and should be complemented by bottom-up approaches. Bottom-up approaches focus on strengthening the processes by which people construct and give meaning to their rights as concrete entitlements and undertake strategic action to secure such entitlements. Both top-down and bottom-up approaches are required to answer the challenge of making development inclusive in the sense of promoting redistribution of resources *and* social equality. S.D.J.M. Prasad, convener of the National Dalit Movement for Justice, New Delhi, stated in this regard:

> Social inclusion is not related to any type of resource achievement. It is a question of achieving equality. I distinguish between growth and development. Development is my freedom, including my equality and

dignity. Growth is my wages, food and education...People think social inclusion will come with growth alone, but it is not enough. Social inclusion is not only growth, but also comes with development if you ensure my fundamental freedoms.[6] This means viewing development policy in a much broader framework, and tailoring schemes to address this framework.[7]

The framework I develop involves grounding an understanding of livelihoods and development in a contextualized analysis of local power relations and structural inequalities, and their interface with politics and the economy. Ensuring formal equality or equality of opportunity, therefore, is not enough. Formal and informal (social) institutional rules and practices require transformation so as to ensure equality of (structural) condition, which may lead to equality of outcomes (Devlin 1993; Kabeer 1994).[8] Complementing this analysis is an orientation towards actors and a wider definition of politics and the political as extending beyond formal political arenas into the arena of local struggles over entitlements. The focus is on the ways in which people interpret their situation and engage with the socio-cultural norms, social relations, and institutional arrangements which influence the realization of rights (Kapur and Duvvury 2006).[9] The proposed approach is elaborated next.

Mapping a Contextualized and Actor-oriented Approach

This book is about Dalit women in rural Tamil Nadu and their struggles to secure basic livelihood entitlements. Rights are understood as acknowledgements of a legitimate claim to resources, based primarily on international human rights law as well as national laws. Hence, all Dalit women have a right to housing, food, education, health, work, and so on. De jure rights, however, become realized through a concrete act of acquisition or claiming as 'entitlements', referring to actual protected access to resources: an example of an entitlement is a specific house to which one has legitimate title deeds. Access to resources is then complemented by the ability to make decisions regarding those resources. This analytical distinction between rights and entitlements is necessary because it highlights that people's agency is required to translate a universal right into a concrete, secure entitlement. Agency here is understood as 'the ability to define one's goals and act on them'

(Kabeer 2001: 21). It encompasses Dalit women's ability to define their entitlements and make choices to deliberately engage in collective action in pursuit of the goal of a secure entitlement (Kabeer 2001). These are choices shaped by the social relations and existing socio-cultural norms, not independent of them.

The approach taken in this research centres on analysing the processes of these women's collective action to claim livelihood resources in specific socio-historical contexts and the extent to which they challenge the structural inequalities that lead to their livelihood resource deprivation (see Chapter 1). Such a challenge foregrounds the power dynamics between these women and state and non-state actors implicit in the concept of entitlement. The premise is that their rights cannot be realized without transforming power relations in order to remove injustices. These power relations are reflected through the various strategies that the Dalit women devise to secure entitlements. Their strategies range from accommodation or negotiation of gender and caste interests, to confrontation and protest. They use strategies of both working within and outside of formal and informal institutions. These strategies are examined as they evolve primarily through contact with Dalit women attached to non-governmental organizations (NGOs), who play a mediatory role to outside agencies and resources. Knowledge of different strategies of the Dalit women 'development brokers', in turn, is developed through their history of social activism and the social networks to which they are connected. The constraints of this mediatory role by outside 'development brokers', however, is examined both in terms of antecedent models of patronage and the sustained attention that is required to building a wider range of capabilities and access to symbolic and material resources that sustain livelihood entitlement struggles.

The research also highlights the links between rights and entitlements sourced from different institutional arrangements such as national laws, state schemes, and human rights norms as the basis for the women's political struggles. Rights here are conceived as political tools of a transformational nature related to challenging and (re)distributing power, a means of resisting domination and exploitation (de Gaay Fortman 2011; Devlin 1993). They are socially constructed based on the perceptions and politico-legal meanings Dalit women attribute to just entitlements and freedoms required to enjoy a dignified life in a given context and at a given point in time.[10] It is from these perceptions and meanings that their actions to secure entitlements arise. Their struggles then transform the established normative parameters of rights, by expanding the range of claims to livelihood resources based on rights in a local context (Nyamu-Musembi 2002: 17).

Ethnographic data on three collective struggles by Dalit women to secure or protect entitlements with the support of external development interveners—that is, NGO staff who operate outside the village—form the core of the book. Each case study, however, presents a different context, sets of relationships, and dynamics of negotiation, contestation, and conflict. Their entitlement struggles are analysed in terms of the women's representations and interpretations of their agency in order to unearth the underlying meanings and values behind entitlements and their actions. These representations are understood as the consequence of their relational community context of social exclusion and their location within multiple social axes (described later). The focus is on Dalit women's ability, limited or otherwise, to manoeuvre within social structures and rules and seize opportunities to challenge social exclusionary norms and practices. Scrutiny also falls on overlapping formal (state) and informal (social) institutions which often establish conflicting rules regarding resource distribution and entitlement. It is around these institutions that entitlement struggles are enacted and caste, class, and gender structures (re)produced.

An examination of these processes of struggle exposes the women's changing perceptions and actions as they encounter other social actors during their claim making, and provides insights into the extent to which they are prepared to seek the support and protection of the Indian state and its institutions (Khare 1998). These processes further indicate the complex array of relational, institutional, and contextual factors which both constrain and enable these women's agency. It is through the interactions between these factors that women's perceived choices during the course of struggle are formed and decisions made. Beyond the women's subjective experiences of struggle for resources, simultaneously cultural struggles are shown to be taking place over socially constructed meanings and identities as poor Dalit women. These relate to both the delineation of entitlements and their social status in their families, community, and wider society, and thus are inherently political.

The assertion of Dalit women's agency embodies multiple caste, class, and gender meanings which cannot be neatly separated or reduced to one dominant thread. A key concept utilized throughout the book thus is intersectionality,[11] meaning Dalit women's exclusion and agency are viewed from their specific location within intersecting social axes such as caste, class and gender. Intersectionality accords with an understanding that the universality of rights does not imply that all people's experiences, social location, and material circumstances from which they construct political consciousness, make choices, and take action are the same (Bunch 2002). Hence, rights must be contextualized and their multiple local interpretations and meanings from different, overlapping, and sometimes conflicting social positions unearthed. Consequent strategies to secure entitlements and freedoms become adapted to people's specific social location and the relevant factors which mediate their experiences. An intersectional analysis applied to the process of Dalit women's collective action thus draws attention to how caste, class, and gender mutually construct each other and shape social relations of power within the women's specific contexts. It reveals the unequal power dynamics between Dalit women and Dalit men, dominant caste women, dominant caste men, and state officials with conflicting interests centred on these three interlocking structures. These dynamics both condition and are conditioned by Dalit women's participation in livelihood entitlement struggles, determining to a great degree the success of their actions.

In sum, this research seeks to answer the following question: 'how do Dalit women in rural South India secure livelihood entitlements, thereby overcoming social exclusion and transforming power relations?' This can be further broken down into three sub-questions.

1. What are Dalit women's perceptions of basic livelihood needs and priorities, entitlements and freedoms, constructed from their specific social location within power relations, and influencing their organization for collective action?
2. What are the social, economic, and political strategies Dalit women utilize, and the counter-strategies they develop in response to reactions from other actors, to manoeuvre around power relations as they collectively secure livelihood entitlements?
3. How do social exclusion processes, arising from intersecting structures and embedded in the Indian state and society, impact on Dalit

women's strategies and ability to acquire livelihood entitlements within existing entitlement systems?

The challenge is to come to grips with these dynamics of collective action and explore their broader implications in answering a second question: 'what insights can Dalit women's experiences and actions provide for obtaining human rights-based entitlements and freedoms?' By drawing upon entitlements, gender, social exclusion, agency, and social movement theories, I argue that it is possible to conceptualize human rights as practice. Rajagopal (2003) asserts that a contextualized understanding of resistance to oppression and structural injustices shifts the focus of human rights discourse from the sole arena of the state to the praxis of social movements. It also draws attention to the roles that state and non-state actors can play in facilitating and strengthening Dalit women's livelihood entitlement strategies, built on a reflexive understanding of these women's perceptions and interests. The framework provided in this research uncovers the general enabling factors and context-driven conditions for effective strategies for inclusion and securing entitlements by Dalit women. At the same time, a process-oriented understanding of entitlement strategies indicates a more open-ended and non-linear approach, which does not seek to determine in advance the consequences of supporting a particular strategy.

Translating Framework into Research Method

Adopting a contextualized and actor-oriented approach means my focus is on particular case studies at the micro level. Case studies enable one to move beyond legal norms and quantified measures of enjoyment of rights to comprehend the complex interplay of factors that influence Dalit women's agency to realize their rights. Accordingly, a number of techniques, primarily ethnographic, are outlined in the production of three case studies of rural Tamil Dalit women's livelihood struggles. Here, the ways in which Dalit women understand and explain their livelihood struggles and relations with others, and the meanings and beliefs behind their explanations, are as important as the actual exchanges. Their discursive practices and strategies reveal how their reasoning changes when they deal with entitlement deprivation and external development interventions. This approach helps one to understand the factors that inspire and enable the women to become politically conscious, and those factors that translate political consciousness into collective action with concrete aims. The approach also gives an insight into the factors that work against these transformations. At the same time, it helps one to understand the ways in which processes at the local level not only reflect larger socio-political processes, but may contribute to them (Gledhill 2000: 128).

The challenge, therefore, was to interpret Dalit women's views by situating myself as far as possible in the position and complex set of relations in which these women are located. Based on the women's experiences as they were shared over time, I was able to follow different strands of inquiry as they emerged and thereby discover the organization of social relations in their lives and the impacts on their agency. Throughout this process, my effort was to ensure that the women remained the subjects and knowledge bearers who transformed my understandings, and not to objectify their knowledge. I could then map that organization of social relations and its impacts 'beyond the local of the everyday' (Smith 2005: 11), always taking care not to subordinate the knowledge of Dalit women to my own. At the same time, Dalit women's perspectives and agency need to be situated in relation to other actors—Dalit men, dominant castes, state officials, development interveners—who offer different interpretations of, and responses to, the women's actions. This allows one to understand Dalit women's perceptions of other actors' actions, as well as the extent to which the women's actions alter the perceptions of other actors. It also draws attention to power relations and the continual negotiations over interests, expectations, and meanings taking place between the different actors (Long and van der Ploeg 1989).

The translation of the given framework into a practical research strategy required the use of multiple, primarily qualitative research techniques of an ethnographic nature. These techniques were exploratory, contextual, and experiential, and aimed to capture the complexity and dynamics of collective action in particular circumstances. Ethnographic techniques allowed me to uncover and interpret the processes underlying the women's collectivization and action, including social practices, discourses, and strategies. In particular, ethnography exposed the interactional relationship between caste, class, and gender structures and their agency (Herbert 2000).

A reflexive process was used, by which fieldwork and analysis mutually informed each other and then, provided the basis for theory building (not theory testing). This process meant that theory was grounded in Dalit women's experiences and understandings of their lifeworlds (Strauss and Corbin 1990). My rationale was to avoid closing off any issues for investigation. Given my focus on how collective action happens, the three case studies provide a detailed situational analysis of various organizing and collective action strategies. Each study is embedded in contextual conditions of culture, history, and political economy. As well as being interesting in themselves, the case studies provided plenty of opportunities for comparison and contrast. With collective action processes as the unit of analysis, each case study is exemplary of specific entitlement outcomes: a successful securing of livelihood entitlements; an ongoing struggle; and an unsuccessful attempt to protect existing entitlements.

The construction of these case studies involved my tracing the perspectives, strategies, and actions of Dalit women, individually and as a group, over an extended period of time. I was able to capture their multiple realities as well as ongoing social changes wrought by their actions and by changing external contexts (van Velsen 1967; see also O'Donoghue 2007). However, as this research was interdisciplinary and applied diverse data collection techniques (see subsection titled 'Fieldwork Process and Techniques'), the time period per field site was shorter than in traditional ethnography. Nonetheless, the year of fieldwork meant that I was able to see the livelihood cycle of Dalit women. For the majority, this means survival on seasonal labour such as agriculture or fishing. Detailed discussions with multiple actors took place over this period, which I interpreted separately and in relation to each other to arrive at my analysis.

Further, an extended fieldwork period allowed me to build relationships of trust with the women and others in the village. This was crucial given my understanding that all knowledge is relative, being dependent on one's perspective. It cannot, therefore, be considered as independent of the researcher. Rather, the construction of knowledge occurs *between* the researcher and the researched as a dialogical process (Madison 2005: 8–9). Moreover, the power imbalances in a research situation,[12] especially one involving socially excluded groups and an outsider–researcher, meant that I had to pay constant attention to issues of positionality and representativity. By this I refer to, first, my different background and structural location in relation to Dalit women, and the meanings we both attach to this difference. Second, writing about other people's lives cannot be separated from the question of whether or not one is speaking for them (Ackerly and True 2010; Moore 1994).

This research, therefore, represents an attempt to bring to the fore the perspectives and experiences of rural Dalit women through a process involving constant reflexivity and checking of my interpretations with the women. I had to be aware of how my own subjectivity affected how I construed perspectives and lives very different to my own. At the same time, I acknowledge that I share a Dalit feminist standpoint emphasizing structural power relations and inequalities (see Rege 1998). Accordingly, my value-based commitment to the goals of the Dalit women's sangams, and of supporting grassroots initiatives towards caste and gender equality in general, influenced how I interpreted these women's actions. However, one must distinguish between 'objectivity' based on commitment to the research problematic and techniques, and 'neutrality' (Omvedt 1979: 375). While I was not a neutral observer, my objectivity stemmed from a determination to reveal the complexities of analysing human rights as practised through Dalit women's struggles. Following this understanding of objectivity, my position as researcher, and not social activist, meant that I had to make the difficult decision not to intervene in ongoing livelihood struggles where it would damage my credibility, as a researcher, with other communities in the area.

Selecting the Struggles and Subject–Participants

The three livelihood entitlement struggles that form the basis for the case studies are located in the south Indian state of Tamil Nadu (see Figure 1). Tamil Nadu was chosen for several reasons, not least because of my familiarity with the socio-political context and the language, and the contacts I have there. Its high levels of economic growth, being currently the fourth largest contributor to India's gross domestic product (GDP), mean that it has resources available for livelihood development. Its political culture, moreover, has been noted as supportive of redistributive state policies and programmes, though these have often been implemented in clientelist and populist ways without the language of

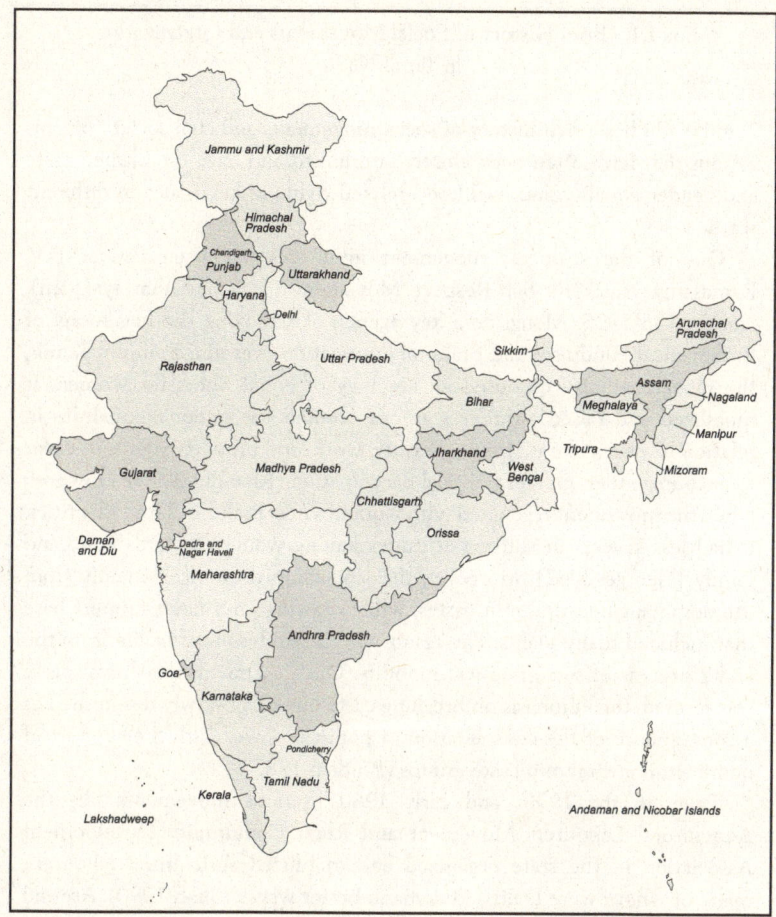

Figure 1   India Map Indicating the State Covered in the Research
Source: Available at d-maps.com/carte.php?num_car=24868&Lang=en.

entitlements (Harriss-White 2004b). Tamil Nadu is also the fifth most
Dalit populated state in India, making Dalits a (potentially) significant
political force. According to the 2001 national census data, the 11.9
million Scheduled Castes (SCs) (5.9 million of whom are women)
are made up of 76 notified castes and constitute 19 per cent of the
state's population. Tamil Nadu was the first state to implement reservations (affirmative action) for SCs and has strong social movements
and NGOs working for Dalit and women's livelihoods (see Box I.1).

Box I.1   Brief History of Social Movements and Organizations
in Tamil Nadu

Tamil Nadu has a rich history of social movements and civil society organizations that have often been closely interlinked and have established caste
and gender equality and livelihood-related rights as key issues in different
ways.

One of the strongest movement influences has been Periyar E.V.
Ramasamy Naicker's Self-Respect Movement (Suyamariāthai Iyakkam),
launched in 1926. Alongside a key agenda of removing the hegemony of
Brahmanical Hinduism and Brahmin domination over non-Brahmin Tamils,
the movement also espoused an ideology of equal rights for women. It
mobilized and raised awareness among women on gender inequalities in
relation to issues like marriage, chastity, work, and property rights, in order
to encourage their greater political participation (Anandhi 2003). However,
while the movement resonated with women's non-Brahmin Tamil identities,
it had less success in shifting attitudes among women towards caste and
family (George 2002). Moreover, the leadership drew itself mainly from
the dominant non-Brahmin castes, while drawing on a large support base
that included many Dalits. The result was the exclusion of Dalits from the
wider process of socio-political mobility. Once a Dravidian political party
was formed, the emphasis on breaking caste hierarchy slowly diminished as
a consequence of the consolidation of political power with the support of
dominant non-Brahmin caste groups (Pandian 1987).

Then, in the 1970s and early 1980s, various movements like the
Agricultural Labourers Movement and Rural Community Development
Association in the state organized and mobilized agricultural labourers,
many of whom were Dalits, to demand better wages (Shah 1990). Around
the same time in the 1970s, a number of Dalit movements and community-
based organizations emerged, many in response to the series of caste riots
and large-scale atrocities that took place. These were often led by Dalits
with links to Left movements, or the Communist Party, or to Christian
institutions that promoted liberation theology. The politicization of Dalit
women and men in the villages was around atrocities, but also around
access to land and common property resources. Additionally, then Ramnad
district witnessed political mobilization around religious rights in temples,
aided by the presence of the Communist Party of India. While these Dalit
movements and organizations implied inclusion and were ideology based
(Gorringe 2005), gender equality was rarely addressed as part of the struggle
against caste oppression. The late 1990s, then, witnessed the emergence of
two Dalit political parties, Viduthalai Chiruthaigal Katchi (VCK) and the

Puthiya Thamizhagam (PT), representing Dalits from different regions of the state.

Meanwhile, from the 1980s, a number of NGOs shifted focus to women's empowerment through organizing women into local sangams (village-level associations) to take up livelihood issues. This was also the period when NGOs, and also the state government, shifted into microcredit provisioning, especially among women of different castes. Women's groups across the state became involved in a widespread anti-liquor movement, which resulted in rising political awareness among these women (Sivakumar 2009). Gender equality, however, was rarely linked to caste equality in any of these group formations. Only some organizations like the Society for Rural Education and Development, which later spearheaded the Tamil Nadu Dalit Women's Movement, focused on the needs of rural women labourers in ways that began to address caste discrimination. This gender–caste linkage then crystallized in the form of the state-level Dalit Women's Movement in 1996. Moreover, with the passage of the 73rd and 74th Constitutional Amendments in 1992, large numbers of women entered into the panchayats throughout the state, including many Dalit women via primarily the SC women's quota. While panchayat political participation has shown mixed results as far as women are concerned, some have taken up livelihood issues such as clean water and minimum wages (Gorringe 2005).

The state also has two Dalit political parties. In terms of gender indicators, positive trends are its high sex ratio among SCs (999:1000); a high work participation rate among SC women (40 per cent as compared to 32 per cent for women in general); as well as literacy rates higher than the national average for SC women (53 per cent as compared to 42 per cent) (Government of India 2001). In sum, in the Tamil Nadu context, one would expect high development and low levels of livelihood deprivation for Dalit women. One would also expect to see strong examples of collective action.

Tamil Nadu, however, also evidences highly uneven distribution of livelihood entitlements. The National Planning Commission reported that 31.2 per cent of the state's SC rural population lives below the official state rural poverty line of Rs 351.86 per capita monthly income (Planning Commission 2005). It is also the state with the highest disparities in poverty and vulnerability levels between SCs and other castes (Kannan 2008). Further, in 2009, it ranked eighth highest among the 28 states for reported crimes against SCs and twelfth for crimes against women (National Crimes Records Bureau [NCRB] 2010). In other words, despite positive economic growth and a strong civil society presence, rural Tamil Dalit women continue to experience a disadvantaged livelihood entitlements position. It is this seeming contradiction which makes the state an interesting place to conduct this research. Further, my focus on rural and not urban areas stems from the fact that, despite strong trends towards urbanization in the state, over two-thirds of Dalit women still reside in rural areas where agriculture is a key employment sector.

Two districts within the state were chosen because of the presence of two Dalit women's organizations/movements. Both districts are identified by the state government as atrocity-prone districts, meaning caste tensions between Dalits and dominant castes are prevalent (Ministry of Social Justice and Empowerment [MSJE] 2011). What distinguish these districts are their geographical location and a number of socio-economic and political features that generate diverse livelihood dynamics. Dry, landlocked, Sivagangai district in south-east Tamil Nadu contrasts with the more fertile, coastal district of Kanchipuram in the north-east close to the state capital, Chennai (see Figure 2). Sivagangai is officially considered an 'economically backward' district dependent primarily on agriculture. It has few industries, and one of the lowest per capita incomes. The more urbanized Kanchipuram district has a high concentration of industries and is among the top five districts measured by per capita income. Kanchipuram thus ranks second highest in the state by human development index (HDI) and gender development index (GDI) indicators, as compared to Sivagangai's middle ranking (18th out of 29 states) (Government of Tamil Nadu 2003).

Caste configurations are likewise very different. Sivagangai district has a small SC population, a major proportion of which are Pallars, with a lower district concentration (16.4 per cent of total district population) compared to the state concentration (19 per cent)(Government of India 2001). The backward caste Thevar caste grouping, dominates the district both socially and politically. Kanchipuram district, by contrast, is home to one of the highest concentrations of SCs (25.1 per cent of total district population), predominantly Paraiyars, in the state. Nonetheless, backward caste Vanniyars exercise socio-political power(Government of India 2001). Dalit women's socio-economic

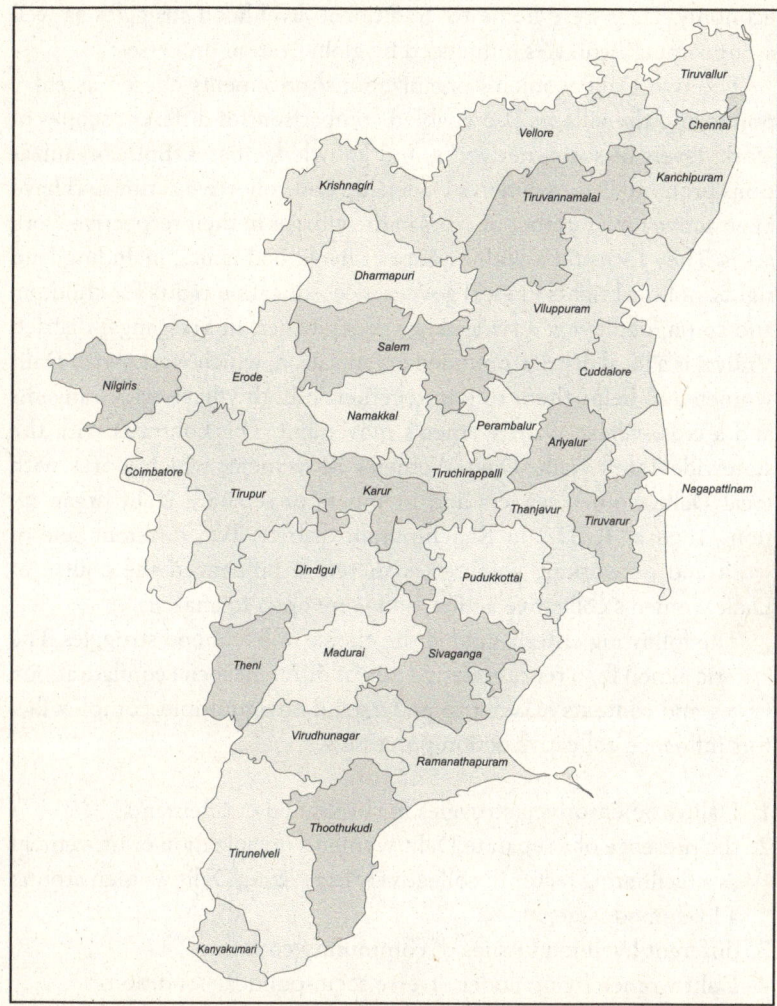

Figure 2 Tamil Nadu Map Indicating Districts Covered in the Research
Source: Available at d-maps.com/carte.php?num_car=32346&Lang=en.

status, gauged by literacy, sex ratios, and work participation rates, however, is roughly the same in both districts. These contrastive features of the two districts offered opportunities to determine the influence of different socio-political environments on Dalit women's collective action strategies. These environments ranged from semi-feudal to new economy. They were home to 'traditional' livelihood struggles as well as 'upcoming' struggles influenced by globalization processes.

The two Dalit women's organizations/movements chosen as entry points into the villages also enabled comparisons of different scopes of work, levels of social networks, and knowledge bases. Both organizations promote Dalit women's leadership and collective action and have been active for a number of years in the villages in their respective work areas. They focus on a wide variety of livelihood issues, including land rights, political rights in local governance, education rights for children, and so on, deploying a wide range of strategies. In Sivagangai district, Vidiyal is a local district-bounded organization, which works with Dalit women and helps them to join together in both village-wide sangams and a cross-village Dalit women's movement. This contrasts with the statewide Tamil Nadu Dalit Women's Movement, which works with local Dalit women leaders and members of separate Dalit organizations, such as RADA in Kanchipuram district. Two different sets of work and networking parameters therefore influenced the course of Dalit women's collective action, and were open to analysis. .

The following criteria guided the choice of livelihood struggles. The criteria aimed for a representative mix of different social configurations, issues, and contexts in order to understand how multiple, complex factors influence collective action processes:

1. Dalit women-driven struggles for livelihood entitlements;
2. the presence of a separate Dalit women's organization or movement as a facilitating factor in collectively organizing Dalit women around a livelihood issue;
3. different livelihood issues of community concern;
4. Dalit women living under diverse socio-political conditions;
5. issues allowing overall representation of the three main Dalit caste groups in Tamil Nadu—Arunthathiyars, Paraiyars, and Pallars;
6. issues involving different types of opposition from state and non-state actors; and
7. issues in which a number of Dalit women were willing to share their experiences.

Dalit women villagers were the primary subject–participants of this research, particularly those affiliated to women's sangams. Recognizing the heterogeneity among Dalit women, however, I chose my interviews through purposive sampling with the help of the Dalit women's organization/movement and sangam leaders. This was accompanied by snowball sampling as I came to know the women in each village. This sampling method aligned with my research in three ways. It answered my research question because most of the subject–participants had participated in collective action. It matched my theoretical position and analytical framework, which are based on intersectionality and coverage of multiple realities. And it aided my development of an actor-oriented account of the process to secure entitlements (Mason 1996). Hence, at one level, I sought to ensure that there was a fair representation of the main Dalit castes in the village concerned, along with women of different occupational statuses, where such economic differentiation was present. Additionally, I chose women of different marital statuses, to whom different gender norms applied. These norms affected their freedoms of movement and expression, how much free time they had, and the social recognition they received. At a second level, the sampling focused on women sangam members, and ensured coverage of all sangam leaders, who tended to be more articulate about sangam activities. The aim of this sampling process was to continue collecting information until a saturation point was reached and there was no new information being provided. This would create a sample that was representative at the level of socio-structural relations (Bertaux 1981). Balancing the issue of representativity, however, were pragmatic considerations of the time available to undertake this research.

I was also concerned with analysing how other people interpreted and responded to Dalit women's livelihood entitlement struggles. These people may have been bystanders, supportive or opposing stakeholders, or targets of the women's strategic actions. This created a second tier of subject–participants, which illuminated the complexity of power relationships determining entitlements. Included in this group were Dalit male villagers, Dalit women of neighbouring villages, dominant castes in or around the village who were implicated in the livelihood entitlement struggle, and government officials either targeted by, or supporting, the women. The problem with interviewing government officials, however, was that many involved in the livelihood struggles had since been transferred out of the area and were difficult to trace. In order to understand the dynamics of organizing these women from

the other side, I also undertook extensive interviews with both of the
key development interveners in the struggles, and was a participant
observer in several movement meetings outside the villages. I also interviewed Dalit movement and organization leaders and other Dalit rights
activists in both districts. They supplemented my knowledge on the
socio-political context and the specificities of Dalit women's livelihood
exclusion, agency, and position within local social movements.

A third tier of supplementary interviews involved other Dalit/wom-
en/human rights activists who focus on Dalit women's rights at least to
some extent. These interviews aimed to reveal more about how prevalent norms, beliefs, and entitlement systems operate in a rural Indian
context. From these interviews, I gained a stronger understanding of
key livelihood entitlement strategies and the factors that influence the
transformation of unequal power relations between Dalit women and
others in broader contexts.

Fieldwork Process and Techniques

Fieldwork was carried out from May 2009 to July 2010. It started with
an exploratory phase of interactions with Dalit women in a number of
villages suggested by the local NGO/movement leaders. Based on these
interactions, the sample was defined, and three villages and entitlement
struggles selected. The draft interview guide was refined accordingly. The
multiple research techniques employed were primarily qualitative—
participant observation alongside a series of semi-structured individual
and focus group interviews. This was accompanied by documentary
analysis and a small quantitative livelihood survey. Diverse techniques,
a noted feature of case studies, enhanced data credibility (Baxter and
Jack 2008; Yin 1993). Credibility also came from my objectively interpreting patterns and interrelationships formed by multiple information
sources, alongside my own observations as researcher (Sunstein and
Chiseri-Slater 2007). The outcome was an integrated understanding
of livelihood survival and livelihood change patterns. That is, I came
to understand how women explained and attached meaning to daily
livelihood activities and experiences of exclusion and livelihood deprivation. I also learnt how they handled caste, class, and gender norms
and practices when they decided to adopt collective action to change
their livelihood entitlements position.

The influence of both Dalit women's and my socio-structural positions on the fieldwork process itself was inescapable. I met most women in the afternoons or early evenings, after they arrived home from labouring outside. The timing was ideal in one sense because often men were not present, yet, it also made plain the women's double burden of labour. Interviews were often conducted around women cooking evening meals, collecting water or firewood, or washing clothes. Interruptions were frequent, whether due to the needs of children, or men later coming to sit nearby and altering the social dynamics. During the agricultural season, women might return from labouring in others' fields to work in their own or sharecropped fields. They could only be met in the late evenings, therefore, and then only for a short while, owing to their physical tiredness. When I interviewed government officials, by contrast, I discovered for myself the difficulties and frustrations Dalit women face in accessing the state. I experienced the long waits to meet officials, the cancelled meetings when officials did not show up or were detained by official work. The caution with which officials greeted my questions, moreover, was often shown in the extreme care they took not to proffer any comments or critical analysis of the implementation of such schemes, or comments on Dalit women's livelihood situation. As participant observer, all these found their way into my understanding and analysis.

Participant observation involved sustained attention to relational patterns, and extended interaction with particularly Dalit women villagers. I not only interacted with Dalit women and men in informal interviews and discussions but also participated in village daily events. I spent days accompanying the women around their homes, talking to them in their fields, as well as celebrating their festivals and family functions with them. I also got to know other caste villagers and Dalit women from neighbouring villages through casual encounters and through using the entry point of other women's sangams established in the villages. There, I both observed and discussed about their own lives, how the sangams helped women, as well as their opinions on the action by the Dalit women who were the focus of my research. I also attended several Dalit women's movement meetings in Sivagangai district in order to observe the dynamics of interactions between the women. All this revealed how Dalit women move between public and private spaces in which caste, class, and gender roles and norms are continually produced and reproduced, and the ways in which the women negotiate their daily livelihoods within these spaces. Further shown were the interrelations among these women, as well as between them and Dalit men, dominant caste women and men. From these observations, I discovered systems of knowledge and meaning that stimulated these women's organization and agency (Herbert 2000).

Participant observation also allowed me to map access to, and control over, livelihood resources by social group, as well as within social groups. I was able to map spaces of inclusion and exclusion in the villages; for example, those temples or water sources closed to Dalits. It further indicated to me the problems of access that female researchers, in particular, face in undertaking fieldwork in the villages and the substantial effects that the discourse of protecting women's sexuality engenders. In my case, my desire to live in the villages was overridden by others' concerns for my safety as a single, young female and how male villagers might react to my continual presence. Even travelling regularly into the villages with my female translators revealed the gender and class structuring of the villages and how I stood socially there. All this increased my awareness of the gender boundaries and insecurity these women negotiate in their daily lives.

Participant observation data were supported by women's statements in individual, semi-structured informal interviews. Considered as another type of observed behaviour, informal interviews generated interpretations of events based on the women's opinions or value judgements (van Velsen 1967: 134). Steinar and Brinkmann (2009) characterize interview knowledge as socially constructed, interrelational, and intersubjective, requiring a negotiation of meaning. As such, the interview guide I developed was flexible. The predetermined, open-ended questions were modified from one interview to the next as I synthesized new knowledge on the research topic.

These characteristics of interviews were also reflected in what women felt about me and the research process, as well as about the possible consequences of their responses. Initially, what they feared might happen led them to respond with what they felt I would want to hear. This slowly changed over time as I gained their trust. The clearest example came from Sivagangai district where women were initially wary of talking with me, despite an extensive introduction about me, the purpose of my research, and the confidential nature of any information shared. This stemmed from the absence of previous contact with researchers and a lack of understanding of what research meant. Hence, in Kovilur village, initial mention of their securing housing land title without conflicts slowly changed only once women became more confident that I would not be exposing their actions to other villagers, the media, or government officials. In itself, this reluctance to speak highlighted the underlying tensions in social (caste) relations that the women negotiate daily. In Mallibakkam village, by contrast, the influx of NGOs in the wake of the 2004 tsunami led to expectations that a researcher would bring material help. Again, time and regular accompaniment by the local NGO leader was required for women to become comfortable with sharing information and their viewpoints with me.

Aside from the meanings women attributed to their context, resources, organization, and actions, interviews also enabled mapping of the interrelations between Dalit women and other social actors in their habitats. From this mapping, key power holders could be identified, including informal social institutions. This involved investigating with the women the interests and circumstances of these power holders, the patterns and contexts of their interaction with the women, and an assessment of their power and potential roles in livelihood claims (Mayers 2005). Where possible, these interrelations were examined further in independent meetings with power holders, after I assessed the risk to the women of such inquiries.

Focus group interviews, by contrast, are noted as a useful method to explore the joint construction of collective identity, understanding, and action. They also expose the process of interaction, negotiation, and affirmation through which these three factors are produced and sustained within the group (Munday 2006: 90). I used these interviews, one per village with Dalit women, to understand the dynamics of interactions between the sangam women. I also wanted to understand the ongoing process by which exclusion and unequal power relations shape their identities, organizational patterns, and agency. Focus group interviews aimed to encourage the verbalization of diverse perspectives and opinions on issues shared by women in the same livelihood position. Nonetheless, I was aware of the tendency in group interviews towards uniformity of opinions. This was very evident in all three villages, where sangam members consistently deferred to the opinions of sangam leaders. The counterbalance was then found in individual interviews with the women (Pösö *et al.* 2008).

Finally, two further sources of data generation moved away from qualitative techniques. First, documentary sources substantiated the process of collective action and the types of discourses women evoked when they presented their claims to government officials. This data source consisted of copies of petitions that Dalit women, and occasionally Dalit men, had written to various officials, as well as copies of official replies and court orders. Unfortunately, language limitations precluded access to a wealth of Tamil writings. Second, a small survey questionnaire, developed and field tested in Tamil Nadu, was undertaken among Dalit households[13] by Dalit NGO staff following a two-day training session. This survey quantified the extent to which Dalit women have access to livelihood resources[14] in each village, the intra-household distribution of livelihood resources and roles, and women's perceptions of livelihood needs and priorities. This information pointed to the interconnections between different resources that together constitute livelihood deprivation. The recording of women's resource priorities indicated the types of issues around which they wanted to organize to secure entitlements. The representative Dalit women in the survey thus reinforced the qualitative analysis, besides generating a picture on the overall status of livelihood entitlements. Where villages had very small Dalit populations, such as in Kovilur and Vettriyur, the survey was conducted in all households. By contrast, in Mallibakkam village, which has a large Dalit population, a stratified (colony) circular random sampling method was followed to cover a sample of 20 per cent of Dalit households.

Analysing the Data and Presenting the Findings

While data collection and initial broad analysis were carried out concurrently, detailed coding of the data occurred later. Manual coding revealed patterns and divergences in the data, and identified the key concepts around which to organize an explanation of the women's collective action. Data were read in terms of the collective action processes the women described as well as the perspectives implied, discursive strategies deployed, and power dynamics suggested (Hammersley and Atkinson 2007). Often, women narrated changes in their local contexts as collective action progressed. The impact of those changes on women's agency had to be interpreted. Certain ideas common to all case studies were confirmed, but there were significant context-specific divergences to be analysed comparatively. My commitment to intersectional analysis, moreover, meant stressing where the perspectives of the Dalit women differed, as well as what they had in common. Participant observation, coupled with my working knowledge of the community, also illuminated how I should interpret what people said in interviews, sometimes enabling me to unearth meanings that might not otherwise have been obvious.

The emphasis of these case studies lay on the diversities in Dalit women's agency and the complexities of each livelihood struggle. At the same time, it is possible to generalize or transfer some of the emerging principles and factors to other contexts, because these case studies are very detailed about the factors they describe (O'Donoghue 2007). The generalization I aimed for, therefore, was not empirical in the sense that these case studies were never intended to be representative of a wider population of Dalit women. Instead, I expected to produce an explanation of the types of collective action processes that were possible in order to suggest a framework directing relevant inquiries about entitlement struggles in other contexts (Mason 1996). The implications of my research extend to rights-based approaches to development, which are discussed in the Conclusion.

In order to help the reader to understand the argument built in each of the three case studies detailed in Chapters 3–5, the analysis is broken down into three broad sections. First, an introduction to the village setting establishes the conditions under which Dalit women's livelihood struggles are enacted. This introduction includes a brief history of the operation of entitlement systems and changing power relations. Second is a descriptive analysis of the process of Dalit women's organization and collective action, including the effects of their actions on power relations. Third, the main themes or implications thrown up by the women's struggle are analysed. The analytical themes in each of the chapters are then synthesized in the Conclusion.

Finally, in these empirical chapters, confidentiality of data is preserved at all times. To ensure anonymity, pseudonyms are used throughout for the village names and the names of all subject–participants. Additionally, after the names of specific subject–participants, indications are given of gender, marital status, and age in order to aid the non-Indian reader gain a picture of the people involved. Only in the case of government officials has their official designation been mentioned, without indicating their territorial jurisdiction, except where district-level officials are involved. References to individual caste names have also been reduced to avoid confusion for the non-Indian reader, with the term 'dominant caste' used as much as possible to indicate relative power position.

Dalit Women Securing Entitlements: Construction of the Argument

Examination of the process, outcomes, and implications of rural Tamil Dalit women's collective action regarding livelihood entitlements is carried out in three parts over six chapters. The first part establishes the backdrop for the research, examining existing theory in order to provide a methodological and conceptual framework for the empiri-cal research. This framework is set against the general context of Dalit women in India and state discourses and practices regarding these women's entitlements, freedoms, and agency.

This chapter introduced the dialectics of structural violence result-ing in Dalit women's chronic resource deprivation and their collective agency to secure livelihood resources as entitlements. It showed that these dialectics, when located within prevailing discourses on poverty reduction, development, and human rights, raise questions regarding current approaches to development. The reality of structural non-implementation of rights arising from complex power configurations in specific socio-historical contexts demands a more contextual and actor-oriented approach. The focus thus shifts to how excluded and discrimi-nated social groups are able to transform power relations in claiming the livelihood resources to which they feel justly entitled. In doing so, they give meaning to human rights. The examination of micro-political processes necessitates primarily qualitative, ethnographic methods, enabling the production of case studies of Dalit women's livelihood struggles.

Chapter 1 details an analytical framework to study the practice of human rights. Central is an understanding of entitlement systems, the arrangements through which people acquire protected access to resources. Social exclusion explains why certain social groups fail to secure entitlements in terms of the power dynamics and institutional practices that shape Dalit women's sense of entitlement and agency. Dalit women's agency is understood in relation to structural power expressed in social norms, practices, and discourses. Their agency is further complicated by the intersections of caste, class, and gender axes, generating multiple and often conflicting experiences of exclusion and power expressed in action. Positing collective action processes as a key analytical category to study entitlements then brings focus to the enabling and constraining factors shaping these women's agency in particular contexts.

Chapter 2 forms a bridging chapter between theoretical concepts and the reality of Dalit women's entitlement struggles that follows in the next part of the book. Available research and statistics are used to trace the multidimensional exclusions Dalit women face. This is counterpoised against the Indian state's attempt to redress the situation through a host of laws, policies, and targeted development schemes. A large accountability gap, however, exists due to the state's consistent failure to adequately implement its measures to respect, protect, and fulfil Dalit women's rights. Further, state measures generate particular discourses on rural livelihood needs, entitlements, and women's empowerment, which shape in specific ways the perceptions of socially excluded Dalit women regarding entitlements and agency. The argument for an orientation towards the micro-politics of Dalit women's collective action is thus strengthened.

The second part of this book offers descriptive analysis based on fieldwork in three villages in Tamil Nadu, delving into the empirical complexities of Dalit women's lifeworlds. Chapter 3 presents a successful struggle by Dalit women to secure housing entitlements in a general mixed-caste context. It shows how these women's perspectives and agency, informed by structural conditions of disentitlement, are reshaped by external development interventions organizing these women to secure livelihood entitlements. This is achieved by introducing new knowledge and discourses that disturb dominant, disempowering discourses and thus transform the women's understandings of entitlements and agency. The spaces created by exclusion then facilitate their collective action. Equally important as these struggles for material resources are struggles for symbolic resources and recognition that enable Dalit women to construct a positive collective identity and interests. Nonetheless, successful acquisition of livelihood entitlements does not necessarily end the process of dislodging gender inequalities embedded in social customs surrounding control over those resources.

Chapter 4 shifts to a semi-feudal context marked by an informal governance system controlled by a dominant caste community. Dalit women cultivators here are engaged in an ongoing struggle to secure agricultural land title. The struggle demonstrates the interaction between formal and informal institutions, which produces competing notions of rights, entitlements, and obligations. In particular, informal power holders seek to preserve patronage relations within a shifting socio-political context by influencing state entitlement arrangements. This creates distinct strategic pathways for Dalit women to secure entitlements: they turn to state institutions in order to advance their claims while simultaneously delinking from informal institutions. An analysis of the organizational and collective action strategies in this adverse environment indicates the ways in which women negotiate multiple layers of relations and interactions in claiming value-laden resources such as land. In order to do this, external brokerage is necessary to overcome the women's knowledge/power limitations.

Chapter 5 examines an unsuccessful struggle Dalit fisherwomen undertook to protect their existing entitlements to traditional fishing work, good health, and decent living standards by stopping the operation of a shrimp farm in their coastal village. It shows how these women's collective strategies are not only continuously (re)shaped by their encounters with state and non-state actors, but also play out on an unequal political and economic terrain. Their relative lack of power and economic resources obstructs their ability to protect their meagre entitlements when these entitlements conflict with the state's macroeconomic policies. The disjuncture between state laws/policies and state practices, especially corruption, ingrains Dalit women's exclusion and social inequalities in new ways. Concurrently, multiple interventions by NGO development brokers generate shifting entitlement discourses among the women, with consequences for the meanings women attribute to collective action.

The final part of the book draws together the analysis within the previous chapters to derive concluding observations on the insights Dalit women's livelihood entitlement struggles provide for operationalizing development strategies to secure rights-based entitlements and freedoms (see Conclusion). The central implication explored is the reorientation of human rights from pure law to the inclusion of action-oriented practice. Insights also are developed regarding the indivisibility of rights in real life, and the need to factor issues of culture, status, and identity into entitlement struggles.

Notes

1. Dalits are defined in this research by the criterion of the social practice of 'untouchability'—the imposition of social disabilities on persons by reason of their birth into certain 'polluted' castes—irrespective of their religious affiliation or formal legal identity as 'Scheduled Caste'.
2. Livelihood here is understood in a broad sense, in keeping with the literal translation of the Tamil word *vazhvādhāram*, proof of life. It thus comprises the material, human, and social resources people require in order to have choices and to enjoy a decent and dignified life.
3. Throughout this book, the term 'dominant caste' is used to refer to those castes, irrespective of religious affiliation, which are socially, politically, and economically dominant from the perspective of Dalits. In most cases, everyone in a village who is not a Dalit or Adivasi—that is, both 'forward' and 'backward' castes—wields real socio-economic and political power over Dalits and, therefore, is dominant vis-à-vis Dalits. This definition is more expansive than that of M.N. Srinivas (1987), for whom a combination of numerical, ritual, political, and economic criteria qualifies certain castes as 'dominant' in a given region.
4. Atrocity is a legal term used to denote any offence under the Indian Penal Code committed against Scheduled Castes or Scheduled Tribes by persons not belonging to a Scheduled Caste or Scheduled Tribe. For such offences, caste consideration, as a motive, is not necessary to evidence such an offence (National Human Rights Commission [NHRC] 2004: 28).
5. Article 2(1) of the International Covenant on Economic, Social and Cultural Rights 1966 commits each state party to take steps, to the maximum of its available resources, with a view to achieving progressively the full realization of the rights recognized in the Covenant by all appropriate means.
6. These freedoms have been articulated as freedoms: from discrimination; from want; to develop and realize one's human potential; from fear; from injustice and violations of the rule of law; of thought and speech and to participate in decision making and form associations; and for decent work United Nations Development Programme (UNDP 2000: 1).
7. Interview with Dr S.D.J.M. Prasad, General Secretary, National Dalit Movement for Justice—National Campaign on Dalit Human Rights, New Delhi, 9 July 2010.

8. The Committee on Economic, Social and Cultural Rights (CESCR) (2009) specifies a focus on *both* substantive equality and formal equality, the former requiring state measures to eliminate the conditions and attitudes that cause or perpetuate substantive or de facto discrimination.

9. Kapur and Duvvury (2006: 12) propose a feminist redefinition of rights-based approaches to development. This redefinition emphasizes the social as opposed to individual nature of rights and shifts focus to strengthening the ability of formal institutions to carry out their obligations. It further recognizes the communal and relational contexts in which individuals pursue rights, and also rights bearers with respect to their multiple identities.

10. This perspective aligns with a social constructivist approach to human rights, which examines rights in their specific history and context as means of challenging existing power relations and structures (Stammers 1999).

11. Note that international human rights law has started to incorporate more complex understandings of discrimination. The 2001 World Conference against Racism established focus on the intersections between gender and racial discrimination. The Committee on the Elimination of Racial Discrimination (CERD) (2002) specifies measures to eradicate multiple discrimination against women members of descent-based (caste) communities. Further, the Committee on Economic, Social and Cultural Rights (2009) specifically recognizes the need to remedy the multiple discrimination some groups experience that is cumulative and has a unique impact on individuals. Most recently, the Committee on the Elimination of Discrimination against Women (CEDAW) (2010) has explicitly recognized intersectionality as a basic concept for understanding the scope of state obligations to eradicate discrimination against women. This entails state parties undertaking specific measures to prohibit and eliminate intersectional discrimination.

12. These are power relations that relate to the respective structural positionings of researcher and researched, to the research process itself and who defines the research, and to the relationship during data collection processes (Wolf 1996, in Harding and Norberg 2005: 2012).

13. A household is considered to consist of a group of individuals unified by a common budget that arises from a greater or lesser degree of income pooling, common cooking quarters, and/or a common residence.

14. The survey covered aspects of occupation; annual household income; migration patterns; landownership and leasing; access to common property resources; basic amenities; housing status and type; asset ownership; current savings and loans; access to public distribution system (ration shop); main healthcare sources and status of health; main educational institutions accessed and educational status; and participation in social and political organizations.

1

COLLECTIVE ACTION, EXCLUSION, AND ENTITLEMENTS

I am conscious of the fact that if women are conscientised the [Dalit] community will progress. I believe that women should organise and this will play a major role in bringing an end to social evils...The progress of the Dalit community should be measured in terms of the progress made by its women.

Dr B.R. Ambedkar, speech to the Dalit Mahila Federation, Nagpur, 1942

Selvi from Mallibakkam village described how around a quarter of Dalit families in her village today do not own their house sites, and consequently do not enjoy electricity and cannot access loans or government housing schemes. Their houses instead rest on land on which they have lived for several generations in exchange for working for the dominant caste Reddiyars. Escalating land prices mean that none can afford to purchase the land today. After having lived on the land for so long Selvi feels, 'We have a right [to the land], but what can we do? The Reddiyar will not give us the land title unless we pay for it.' Notwithstanding the government scheme allotting legal title to Dalits in such circumstances, they fear that they might be evicted if they assert their right, thereby losing what little security they currently enjoy. This prevents her and others from acting together to secure this entitlement.

Women from Kovilur village, according to Chitra, collectively protested in 2009 against the lowering of daily wages from Rs 80 to Rs 40 per person, for work done under the National Rural Employment Guarantee Scheme. While this statutory scheme grants an entitlement to Rs 80 per day, the entitlement had been reduced owing to the large numbers of mainly women engaging in this work in the area. The 250 Dalit and other 'lower' backward caste women refused to accept these wages, and instead, after informing the police and District Collector's office, staged a road blockade. The police eventually brokered a compromise wherein the next day the women delivered their petition to the Collector, demanding their right to full wages for work done. In response, they received a promise of proper wages in future.

These two contrastive accounts from the villages in this research highlight a common theme. In both cases, there are government schemes that stipulate certain rights. For Selvi, however, livelihood insecurity prevents her from translating her right into a secure entitlement to housing land. By comparison, Chitra notes that only by collective protest were women able to secure the enforcement of their right to full wages. Taken together, the accounts endorse an understanding of human rights as instruments for the realization of concrete freedoms and entitlements that relate to people's dignity. Rights become realizable when people exercise their agency and assert claims in specific contexts. Human subjectivity and agency thus are at the core of bottom-up, actor-oriented approaches to human rights. These approaches look beyond Dalit women's lack of available resources as deprivation, to the structural causes. They also examine the power dynamics that condition these women's agency. Social change here means 'structural change of a society, its institutions and norms as part of more equitable sharing of resources and opportunities' (Guijt 2007: 13). Producing structural discontinuities through collective action becomes crucial to the progress Dr Ambedkar had in mind.

This chapter seeks to explain how one can analyse the processes by which Dalit women pursue resources for a decent livelihood, taking into account their greater disadvantage than others when it comes to access to the same resources. This is done by reconstructing Dalit women's perspectives and embedding them in a relational and power context. First, entitlement systems—the institutions behind actual entitlement positions—and social exclusion explain how and why livelihood deprivation occurs, in terms of institutional and relational power dynamics (see the following sections, 'From Declared Rights to Secured Entitlements' and 'Processes of Social Exclusion'). This forms the terrain on which livelihood entitlement struggles are fought. Second, this terrain exhibits the complex and dynamic interactions between power and agency, the understanding of which is deepened by an intersectional analysis (see the sections on 'Dynamics of Power and Agency' and 'Agency at the Intersections of Multiple Axes of Difference'). This analysis interrogates points at which multiple social axes, such as caste, class, and gender, intersect; it looks for their impact on the collective action undertaken by the women. Dalit women actors, their interpretations and relations with others, are foregrounded as drivers of collective action, ahead of external development interveners. It is through these women's interactions with other actors, and with their socio-political context, that predetermined strategies become redefined and reinterpreted over the course of struggles. Third, the examination is taken forward by framing the processes of developing and strategizing collective action (see 'Constructing Collective Action, Developing Strategies').

From Declared Rights to Secured Entitlements

Dalit women claim access to and command over livelihood resources as entitlements, in order to live with dignity and fulfilment as human beings. Livelihood security and sustainability are intrinsically linked to the realization of social and economic rights, particularly the rights to work under just and favourable conditions,[1] education,[2] health,[3] and an adequate standard of living.[4] Where these women live without such security, rights provide legitimacy to claims based on their entitlement to such resources. A distinction, however, can be drawn between rights as 'declared' in international human rights conventions as well as in domestic Indian laws, and rights that have been 'acquired'. Declared rights exist but may be systematically violated in a local context so as to create a right 'without' an entitlement (de Gaay Fortman 2006a). Taking the above-mentioned example of Selvi, she has a right to housing land under the government scheme but is unable to secure this as an entitlement. By contrast, acquired rights take the form of protected access to resources, goods, and services necessary for one's livelihood (de Gaay Fortman 2011: 25). In Selvi's case, an acquired right would imply that she had full possession of housing land legally granted to her by the government. While acquired rights are grounded in the political economy, they are intimately connected to 'actualized' or 'effective' rights grounded in the moral–cultural economy, which imply control over a resource in its use (Appadurai 1984). In other words, Selvi should both possess the land and be able to determine how it is used. It is the processes by which Dalit women secure actual entitlements and fulfil their rights in reality that this research aims to explain.

There are two key factors that condition the levels to which different social actors enjoy social and economic rights in practice. First, there is the 'availability' of resources, which is often the focus of conventional economic analysis, development, and poverty alleviation programmes. Second is a person's ability to establish effective command over resources through legitimate[5] means available in society, and thereby 'secure' entitlements. It is the latter, first elaborated by Sen (1981), which provides a framework for the analysis of poverty as an issue of inequality, manifested as relative entitlement deprivation. An entitlements approach examines *how* some people are deprived of livelihood resources, while others are able to access and gain control over resources to develop their livelihoods. In other words, processes of acquirement, and not just outcomes, are central. This approach confronts the heart of the problem as the 'distribution' of available resources. It explains why India ranks among the 10 largest world economies in terms of gross domestic product (GDP) and yet, also has the largest population of the poor; and why Dalit women continue to sit at the bottom of all development indicators despite progressive laws, policies, and development schemes (see Chapter 2).

The distribution of resources is determined by different entitlement systems, meaning different regularized, institutional arrangements for establishing legitimate claims to resources. Sen (1981) defined entitlements in terms of legally owned resources, as well as the goods and services that can be obtained through production, exchange, or transfer of those resources. Entitlements analysis, however, can be extended further to include other entitlement systems beyond legal ownership. These include state arrangements such as affirmative action, and development policies and programmes claimed on the basis of citizenship. They also include affiliation to socially sanctioned, informal institutions such as the family or traditional caste councils in India (de Gaay Fortman 1990, 1999, 2011). As will be seen in the following chapters, informal institutional rules, which establish local norms on entitlement based on caste and gender ideologies, often conflict with legal rules and state entitlement arrangements based on principles of equality and social justice.[6]

Legal, state-granted, and informal institutional entitlements are all helpful for understanding the entitlements that people *can* have command over.[7] A rights perspective, however, emphasizes the entitlements people *should* have command over to live with dignity. A further entitlement system thus is introduced, which comprises international human rights law, domestic laws (especially constitutional rights), and judicial decisions on social and economic rights (de Gaay Fortman 1990, 1999, 2011; Petchesky 1998). This entitlement system becomes particularly pertinent when Dalit women are structurally excluded from access to livelihood resources, and when formal and informal institutions both operate to entrench this exclusion. In this situation, rights discourse articulates a vision of how things might or should be. This vision, in turn, may inspire political action to secure entitlements and rewrite inequitable institutional rules (Hunt 1993: 247). Moreover, institutional rules sometimes conflict; for example, conflict between state entitlement arrangements and entitlements granted by informal (social) institutions. In this circumstance, human rights ideally become the basis for mediating claims based on universal principles (Leach *et al.* 1997).

These entitlement systems and interactions between them, including the array of social relationships established within these institutional domains, influence how different social actors gain access to and control over resources (Webster 2004). The operation of these systems often reproduces social relations of power and authority in determining resource claims (Gore 1993; Leach *et al.* 1997). That is, power relations strongly influence which rules apply and whose interests prevail in contestations over resources. At the same time, although established patterns of entitlement contestation and determination exist, and generate certain expectations, the final outcomes remain open. This is because informal institutional rules and power relations are subject to change. They change in local contexts because Dalit women negotiate and contest the power relations by drawing upon other entitlement arrangements such as rights (Bastiaensen *et al.* 2005). All this underscores the need to study Dalit women's entitlement struggles within their specific contexts, with due emphasis on the workings of institutions and social relations of power.

Processes of Social Exclusion

Entitlements analysis offers a broad approach to examining how different social actors gain access to and control over resources. But it does
not account for the structural and socio-historical 'causes' of such processes. Nor does it explain *why* certain actors, such as Dalit women, fail
to acquire entitlements from any of the given entitlement systems (Fine
1997). The concept of social exclusion complements this approach,
because it is concerned with the synergy between distributional (economic) and relational (socio-political) aspects of poverty (Bhalla and
Lapeyre 1997; de Haan 1999).[8] Social exclusion is constituted by
the social relations and dynamic processes through which individuals
or groups are systematically deprived, either partially or fully, of the
resources and recognition that would allow them to participate fully in
a given society. Attention is thus drawn to the processes that engender
persistent livelihood disadvantage for Dalit women, the wider structures and institutions in which these processes are embedded, and the
actors behind livelihood entitlement failure (Ruggeri Laderchi *et al.*
2003: 257–60; also, see Commins 2004; Hickey and du Toit 2007).
These are processes in which actors actively or deliberately exclude
Dalit women; or social practices that result in exclusion; or processes
in which Dalit women are unfavourably included so as to produce the
same adverse effects as exclusion (Hickey and du Toit 2007; Sen 2000).
The focus is thus on denied or restricted access to resource entitlements, rather than whether people choose to use that access.

Social exclusion explains the disadvantaged position (relative to
others) from which Dalit women struggle to secure livelihood entitlements. It brings to the fore the interests promoted by exclusion, as
well as the institutional mechanisms and practices that protect those
interests and perpetuate structural inequalities. Silver's (1995) charac-
terization of a monopoly paradigm of social exclusion aptly describes
the Indian hierarchical social order. Caste groups maintain their
exclusivity and domination through the monopolies they hold over
material and symbolic resources and by exercising coercive power over
excluded caste groups (Dalits). Gender exclusion of women, rooted in
patriarchy, cross-cuts all caste groups and creates another layer of male
monopoly and domination. Patriarchy, as a 'system of social structures
and practices in which men dominate, oppress and exploit women'
(Walby 1990: 20), is integrated into both the caste system and the

Indian state. It is manifested as women's exclusion from the ownership of critical resources, which is sometimes reflected in state laws and policies. It is also seen in their lacking a voice and the freedom to act in the public–political arena. Women also lack these same freedoms in the family, where they are excluded from participation in decision making (Hamadeh-Banerjee 2000).

Moreover, Dalit women's disadvantage from the viewpoint of social exclusion is much broader than material deprivation, judged in terms of income. Multiple dimensions—social, cultural, economic, political (Burchardt *et al.* 2002; Rodgers 1995; Saith 2001)—are captured. These dimensions of exclusion are interlocking and cumulative, indicative of the complex processes that shape exclusion and inequality. They often ensure that disadvantage is transmitted down the generations (Clert 1999; Kabeer 2006b). In particular, social exclusion focuses on the process of identity formation, which shapes meaning systems, cultural values, and Dalit women's confidence and sense of belonging. The ability to construct a socially acknowledged, dignified identity has implications for the likelihood of these women then asserting their agency to secure entitlements (Louis undated). The effects of these multidimensional exclusion processes likewise multiple. They include insecurity, vulnerability, the denial of access to resources and participation in decision making, and a lack of equality and justice. Such effects diminish a person's 'capacity to aspire' (Appadurai 2004, 2007). This capacity consists of the social interactions and contacts Dalit women are able to develop to extend their choices vis-à-vis livelihood resources and opportunities. The effects of exclusion may also extinguish the women's sense of entitlement, understood as a conviction of the moral rightness of their claim to resources necessary for eking out a decent livelihood (Petchesky 1998: 13).

At the same time, this research argues the limit of the exclusion–inclusion binary, implying either being outside and not participating or inside and participating in society, for conceptualizing complex power relations and agency therein.[9] The low socio-economic status of Dalits, as with women, in fact is characterized by their being simultaneously included and excluded. They are indispensable for the continuance of the caste system, by virtue of their productive role in providing essential services, yet they are excluded from resources and power to such an extent as to create durable structural inequalities (Deliege 1997; Pandey 2010).

Hence, a more nuanced understanding is instead developed, based on the following conceptualization of power in relation to agency.

Dynamics of Power and Agency

Modes of struggle against exclusion, domination, and other forms of power provide insights into the operation of power relations and structures of power (Okely 1991). Power in this context is understood as existing only in an action taken by some person(s) on others, which establishes certain relationships between different actors (Foucault 1980b, 1994). It is not, as livelihood approaches suggest (for example, Bebbington 1999), a resource that causes things to happen, such as socio-political networks that facilitate claims and access to opportunities to acquire livelihood resources. Instead, the focus is on power relations and the exercise of power made possible by factors such as caste, class, and gender differences, and laws and policies (Foucault 1994). This focus reveals how power relations within 'private' social institutions, such as the family, shape the subjectivity and agency of Dalit women, and has an impact on their entry into the public domain (Allen 2002). Further, all mechanisms of power, including formal authority and social institutions, are understood to play a mutually influencing role in determining entitlements. This view of power is thus both relational and dynamic. Power is vested both in actors and structures, and both constrains and facilitates agency. The dichotomy between powerful and powerless, which sees power as a zero-sum game, is thereby displaced by the more complicated reality of fluid power relations.

Adopting Foucault's analysis of power, Dalit women are produced by power relations, in that institutional and socio-cultural practices produce them, as well as social relations, discourses, and knowledge. At the same time, these women also are subjected to power relations through simultaneously experiencing and exercising power (Foucault 1980c: 119; also, Allen 2002, 2005). This problematizes the notion of the autonomous, free-willed individual as citizen and subject holding (legal) rights. Viewing the constitution of Dalit women through power relations enables analysis of the effects in terms of the creation of hierarchies among social identities, and the structural exclusion of, and discrimination against, them.[10] It also reveals how social exclusion, built around structural boundaries, affects the women's perceptions of agency and choice. For instance, Dalit women may 'choose' not to demand equal access to common village resources, such as wells, owing to operative 'untouchability' norms and purity/pollution discourses limiting their access. This is in addition to the actions of various actors that significantly constrain the women's possible actions (Hayward and Lukes 2008). Such actors include dominant castes who establish practices preventing Dalit women from gaining equal access to drinking water, or state officials whose failure to protect the women's entitlement to water entrenches their exclusion.

The possibility of agency, however, is not eliminated by a conception of power as structural and productive. Power dynamics both condition, and are conditioned by, Dalit women's participation in livelihood entitlement struggles to overcome exclusion. This is because no single group or institution controls all heterogeneous power relations in a society. Embedded in every power relationship is the potential for those with less power to counter domination and structural and other constraints (Foucault 1994; also, Heller 1996; Sawicki 1991).[11] In exercising power via collective action, Dalit women seek to reshape the structural boundaries that define their possible actions (Hayward 1998) as well as the values behind structural differences. Action to secure livelihood entitlements, for instance, involves these women's circulating alternative discourses, such as gender and caste equality, to legitimize their resource claim when they interact with non-state and state actors. In these spaces of interaction or 'critical social interfaces' (Long 2001), there will be differences in interests, knowledge, resources, and power. This may create a disjunction between social norms that deny Dalit women material resources and the women's practical actions. This disjunction may then transform these norms and reconfigure power relations. Long-lasting change requires shifts in the meaning of interrelations between Dalit women and others (Eyben *et al.* 2006), the discourses that frame their actions, and ultimately, the boundaries of resource control. Perceptions of all concerned actors should move towards a greater sense of entitlement for Dalit women.

Thus, in circumstances where power is exercised over them and structures of inequality perpetuate social exclusion, Dalit women are capable of exercising power by using their knowledge and abilities to negotiate any constraints and collectively assert claims to livelihoods resources. In the process, they may reshape structural boundaries. This fact forms the basis for locating power in relation to agency. A basic definition of agency, therefore, is 'not as a synonym for resistance to relations of domination, but as a capacity for action that historically specific relations of subordination enable and create' (Mahmood 2009: 15). In other words, agency cannot be reduced to the exercise of autonomous free will to resist conditions of subordination and pursue one's interests (Madhok 2007). This reduction presupposes that all actions are intentional, and that individuals are able to make autonomous, meaningful choices outside of power relations.[12] Instead, accounts of agency move away from over-scrutinizing the intentions of actors. Agency is better understood in relation to structural power. It is seen in specific socio-historical contexts, in terms of social norms, practices and discourses (Mahmood 2001; Ringrose 2007), as well as political interactions (Lovell 2003). It is these contextual factors and workings of power that influence Dalit women's perceptions of entitlements and determine the range of actions they might take to secure entitlements. All this represents a move away from liberal human rights theory and its notion of the autonomous, free-willed individual as citizen and political subject holding (legal) rights.

A second move away from liberal rights theory is from an emphasis on individual capacities and rights-based obligations and outcomes. Instead, this research invites a contextualized analysis of human sociality and power relations in the processes of realizing rights. Social connectedness has important implications for what agency means, since experience and, therefore, action are social and not individual processes. Beteille (1999) highlighted the unusually long period over, and the unusual extent to, which the Indian social order has established the group (joint family, caste, village) and not the individual as the basic unit. Women, in particular, view their own interests as bound up with those of caste, kin, and family, notwithstanding the fact that these groups do not treat women equally. Because individual identity is intimately linked to caste identity, social mobility within the caste system is then group based as opposed to individual based (Liddle and Joshi 1986). Moreover, women must balance their desires with what their families or society will give them. The understanding of agency that I propose encompasses subjectivity embedded in kinship and other social relations. It includes perceptions of interests, entitlements, and actions that do not conform to the idea of a woman acting autonomously in fulfilment of her gender interests (Apffel-Marglin and Simon 1994; Sangari 1996).

My analysis of Dalit women's agency also highlights the false dichotomy between power as resistance and power as domination, the latter correlating with submission or accommodation by the less powerful. Haynes and Prakash (1991) noted that domination is rarely eradicated by acts of resistance; resistance is constantly conditioned by structures of power. This is particularly the case where interdependence underlies social and economic relations, as has been true of Dalits and other castes: resistance often coexists with dependency. Dalit women, thus, may choose to avoid outright resistance and settle for actions that could entail modest changes in their subordinate status (Charrad 2010). Their choices often reflect counterbalancing considerations of the livelihood and personal security, stability, and belonging provided by existing social arrangements (Eyben *et al.* 2006). In reality, therefore, a vast continuum of actions exists between total submission/domination and total resistance, and these require analysis to unearth their meanings and implications within specific socio-historical contexts (Haynes and Prakash 1991; Petchesky 1998).[13]

It is thus important to examine the processes that create a subjective sense of entitlement and the desire to resist dominant social norms and practices, rather than limiting agency simply to acts of resistance. One must also analyse all forms of action that reiterate or revalue social norms, or that reveal how such norms are experienced. These actions draw attention to the ways in which Dalit women modify constraints imposed by practices of subordination, thereby negotiating a space for manoeuvre within power relations that transect the public and private domains (Villarreal 1994). They may therefore choose to reproduce, or acquiesce, to certain norms in order to gain the freedom to manoeuvre around others, given their dependence on others. It is only by 'wielding and yielding power' that women can engage with the available socio-cultural, economic, and discursive resources to secure livelihood entitlements in the most appropriate way (Villarreal 1992).

Agency at the Intersections of Multiple Axes of Difference

Dalit women's location within multiple axes of difference, such as caste, class, and gender, further complicates this picture of their agency. A number of Indian feminists (for example, Chakravarti 2003; Kapadia

1995; Rege 1998, 2000; Sangari 1995, 1996; and Subramaniam 2006) have noted that gender cannot be understood in isolation from caste, class, religion, and other axes of difference. The focus on Dalit women actors therefore draws upon a deeper understanding of the complex interactions between intersecting axes of difference. These interactions produce different experiences of subordination and privilege, exclusion and agency (Association for Women's Rights in Development [AWID] 2004),[14] and form part of the resources by which Dalit women exercise power and agency.

Difference here is distinguished from the notion of diversity, which is often used to explain the experiences of heterogeneous, fixed social groups as though these groups were detached from their socio-historical context and power relations (Andersen 2005; Andersen and Collins 2007/2010; Pandey 2010). This leads to treating caste, class, and gender as independent variables that can be added together—caste *plus* class *plus* gender—to bring to light Dalit women's position, identity, and extra burden of exclusion. Dalit women's experiences of social exclusion, however, are not neatly divided into those suffered as a Dalit, as a poor person, and as a woman. Adding them together, moreover, assumes that these different axes are alike: it ignores their different organizing logics, power relations, and dynamics (Verloo 2006; Yuval-Davis 2006). Such addition also essentializes the types of subordination each axis produces by reducing Dalit women's position to how identity politics would label them—as a Dalit or a woman. Their politics and political values according are narrowed to those of the unmarked categories of each identity (Yuval-Davis 2006), namely, Dalit men or dominant caste, middle-class women. This identity politics erases Dalit women's experiences and perspectives, as well as the workings of power relations that structure resource distribution.

Instead, these multiple axes of difference are mutually constitutive. Each axis develops in the context of the other to become inextricably intermeshed; it assumes meaning in relation to the other(s). As such, these distinctive axes form part of one overarching 'matrix of domination' (Collins 1990: 222) that is dynamic and shifting, affecting all social life. The effects, however, are different for diverse social groups. This is because the hierarchical structuring of axes of difference allows power to accumulate at certain intersections to certain social groups. Together, these axes simultaneously structure Dalit women's positions, individual consciousness, identities, and power relations in a specific time and place, and impact on their access to institutional power (Andersen and Collins 2007/2010; Brah and Phoenix 2004; Crenshaw Williams 1994; Norris *et al.* 2010). At the same time, they create contradictions in these women's positioning within the power structures that determine the operation of entitlement systems. Hence, despite exclusion and subordination, Dalit women differ from Dalit men in the spaces they have in which to manoeuvre and exercise their agency, as the empirical chapters will show.

This approach is particularly relevant to the operation of the caste system and its impact on entitlements. The foundations of the system are reproduction and production control: caste, class, and gender structures are interlinked. First, the principle of endogamy marks women as the symbolic and genetic gatekeepers of their caste community. Endogamy structures the gendered distribution of resources and property rights (via patrilineage), as well as control over female sexuality, in order to preserve caste purity and identity (Ambedkar 2002; Dietrich 2003; Dube 2003). Gender, in this sense, is crucial to the production of caste hierarchy and community identity. Second, the caste division of labour promotes a dominant caste monopoly over resources and knowledge in order to sustain labour exploitation (Chakravarti 2003; Rao 2003a). This links with the gender division of labour: the higher status of dominant caste women is signalled by their not having to labour outside the family. Women's going about in public (for labour, implying lesser control over their sexuality) is viewed as marking low status. In comparison, Dalit women's relative poverty leads to their being less secluded,[15] to their having greater freedom of movement for labour and relative autonomy in household decision making, but consequently, a heightened vulnerability to sexual violence.

A Dalit feminist framework becomes relevant here. It shifts the focus from the identity politics of naming difference (Dalit woman–dominant caste woman) to the structural power relations that convert this difference into oppression (Rege 1998: WS40). It sees patriarchy in India as structured by and embedded in the caste system, and manifested in the varying degrees of female subordination by caste and compensatory structures that 'upper'caste women enjoy. The unique matrix of domination formed by these intersecting axes of difference has been termed 'Brahmanical patriarchy'.[16] This denotes a set of interlinked caste and gender norms and practices differentially applied to women (and men) of different, hierarchically ranked castes (Chakravarti 2003: 34). Hence, mutually constitutive axes of difference entail varying degrees of subordination for Dalit women vis-à-vis Dalit men, dominant caste men, and dominant caste women. Given this complex interweaving of power relations, agency by Indian women towards securing entitlements and realizing their rights must necessarily encompass 'all' the structural inequalities in which patriarchy is embedded. This draws attention to sexual politics—the control over female sexuality and reproduction—as well as the material basis of patriarchy, thereby rejecting any dichotomy between material and symbolic struggles (Rege 1998, 2000).

At the same time, this emphasis on a single group, Dalit women, should not be mistaken for an identity politics that reifies categorical boundaries and conflates differences among Dalit women collective actors. Dalit women may be primarily analysed as a social group located at the intersections of caste, class, and gender. These are the most prominent axes through which their social position and identities are defined, their livelihood resource base is constrained, and their subjectivities and agency to claim livelihood resources are shaped. They draw upon their common history of oppression, which is based on these axes, when they interpret new situations, development interventions, and discourses that facilitate entitlement struggles. However, this analysis does not essentialize their identity in ways that conceal internal differences among them of age, marital status, and so on. Rather, it tries to take into account the ways in which different Dalit women interpret and respond to the same structural conditions and negotiate claims to livelihood resources as entitlements. Moreover, the perspectives of Dalit men and dominant caste women and men, shaped by caste, class, and gender in different ways, are included insofar as their power and agency affect Dalit women's entitlement struggles.

Finally, the influence of multiple, intersecting axes of difference on entitlement struggles also draws one's attention to the political and economic context. Dalit women's subjectivity and agency are affected by the state's making laws to protect the rights of Dalits and women separately, and development policies with also separately target these groups. These laws and policies thereby render invisible Dalit women's specific livelihood needs, priorities, and experiences of intersectional discrimination (see Chapter 2). This invisibility can occur through under-inclusion of one axis, such as gender, where an issue is viewed only as a Dalit issue and not a gender issue. Invisibility also stems from over-inclusion. For example, an issue may be seen only as a gender issue and not one of caste (Crenshaw 2000; Norris *et al.* 2010). In addition, some economic and livelihood policies and practices of the state threaten or exploit Dalit women's vulnerable livelihood entitlement situation. These policies are influenced by wider processes of globalization (see Chapter 5). Again, though, this overall structure of domination, and the social, economic, and political institutions that sustain it, is amenable to change through collective action. The dynamics of such action by Dalit women are broken down in the next section.

Constructing Collective Action, Developing Strategies

In situating Dalit women's collective livelihood entitlement struggles within a complex web of power relations and interlocking structures, I adopt a constructivist perspective based in social movement theory.[17] This combines the strengths of other, more structural social movement theories[18] by taking into account structural conditions, resources, political opportunities, and constraints on collective action. More attention, however, is paid to the processes through which these women interpret their situation of entitlement deprivation, construct common interests based on a collective identity, and make strategic choices as to how to claim resources (Klandermans 1992). Collective action to secure entitlements is thus a complex and continual process of interaction and negotiation between Dalit women and their socio-economic and political environment. The analysis of collective action is organized around three interwoven points: collective identity construction, political consciousness, and motivation; discourses and claim framing; and strategic repertoires and dilemmas.

Collective Identity, Political Consciousness, and Motivation

As mentioned, an individual Dalit woman is socially located by her caste, class, and gender group identities. This shapes her cultural reasoning, sense of entitlement, and what she expects will change as a result of her actions. These group identities include both caste identity and an identity formed by kinship relationships within her caste. A Dalit woman draws upon her own personal characteristics as well as group identities when she interprets the deprivation she shares with other Dalit women (Gamson 1992).

The process of collective identity formation explains how structural inequalities get translated into subjective discontent (Polletta and Jasper 2001: 288). This process demands that women reach a position where they view as changeable both the identity ascribed to them and their social relations. They must learn to define themselves as 'Dalit women' and develop discursive consciousness of the situation they share. This happens in four ways: (i) the women must all understand that the problem(s) and causes of entitlement deprivation are externally induced; (ii) they must mutually perceive the resources at their disposal and the structural opportunities to take action that exist within their context; (iii) they must have common interests and goals; and (iv) they must share opinions about the effectiveness of collective action to change their situation (Kelly and Breinlinger 1996; Klandermans 1992; Ryan and Gamson 2006). For Dalit women, this consciousness would take the form of discontent with their status and power vis-à-vis other social groups, together with an understanding that their status is linked to their poor livelihood situation and that securing entitlements requires action on *their* part. The process also has social implications for solidarity, that is, the development and maintenance of commitment to the group and collective action.

Several internal factors and/or external circumstances create openings for identification and discursive consciousness processes. Joe Arun (2007) argued that caste conflicts centred on livelihood issues are the source and driving force that makes Dalits conscious of their 'low' identity as poor Dalits. Conflicts motivate them to join in collective action to correct perceived injustices. The acquisition of educational and informational resources further contributes to this process. These aside, external interventions can be critical for encouraging discursive consciousness of structural inequalities and promoting collective identities. At the same time, internal factors often influence the process. One example is Dalit women's inherent drive for personal dignity and respect, for upholding family or community honour, or for recognition of their equal right to survive (Khare 1998: 216). This is similar to Scott's (1985) findings that the will of excluded people to resist structural injustices is formed in their everyday struggles for survival with dignity, along with the perceived needs and interests associated with those efforts.

Notably, creating a collective identity as Dalit women represents a paradox. On the one hand, mobilizing around an ascribed identity—in this case, as 'untouchable', 'poor', and 'female'—reinforces that identity. On the other hand, asserting rights as Indian 'citizens' is an attempt to change or eliminate that stigmatized identity (Jasper 2008). In a rigidly stratified caste society where group identity and mobility are heavily circumscribed, however, subordinated social groups like Dalits often have little alternative but to mobilize around their group identity. One way around this issue is to build a sense of pride and positive group identity among Dalit women by getting them to value their actions, rather than see themselves as victims. Perceptions of success would increase their motivation and strengthen collective identity, lessening the power of negative identity discourses.

The process of defining collective identity is not linear. It continues to be negotiated and to develop as collective action evolves, resources become available, and opportunities open up. Individual women's views and preferences must be balanced to arrive at a consensus on collective identity that mobilizes the women to take action (Melucci 1988). The role of leaders is to give stability to this process. External mobilizing organizations can also play a role by instituting legitimate decision-making and resource aggregation processes and accountability structures (Ganz 2000). Both leadership and organizational structure feed into the strategizing process, facilitating collective identification and solidarity.

Discourses and Claim Framing

The ways in which Dalit women interpret their situation, assess the solutions available through exercising agency, and express their claims have a bearing on collective action processes and outcomes (Snow and Benford 1988). They achieve a consensus on livelihood needs and entitlements that justify action by drawing on a number of alternative discourses. These discourses often emphasize values of caste and gender equality that differ from the dominant discourse; they therefore promote emerging new norms (Gamson 1992). Alternative discourses link symbols and arguments in defining the terms of an entitlement struggle, the relational positions of various actors, and the rationale, objectives, and strategies for action. Deciding which discourse to deploy is an ongoing process of negotiation among the women and the external intervening organization (Hilhorst 1997). The internal dynamics of decision-making power within the collective then determines who has the greater say in this process.

The success of collective action depends partially on Dalit women establishing links between how they frame their actions, and dominant beliefs and values. They must be able to engage with the worldview of those wielding the power to grant them entitlements. Engaging involves aligning their demands with formal institutional rules and principles, such as equal access and non-discrimination. Ideally, it also requires analysing the dominant discourses that legitimate injustice against them. Such analysis would open up to critique the given 'truths' within discourses of hierarchy and disentitlement, and introduce new interpretations and new values such as equality (Hunt 1993).[19] It is then that a politically contested claim to livelihood resources becomes both socially and formally legitimized and therefore secure.

Strategic Repertoires and Dilemmas

The continuous negotiation and choices around collective identity and discourses are connected with the strategies Dalit women adopt to reach their goals. Identity and discourses inform which strategies are chosen, and are themselves influenced by the strategies. Strategy here is defined as 'the conceptual link we make between the places, the times and the ways we mobilise and deploy our resources, and the goals we hope to achieve' (Ganz 2000: 1010). Encompassed in this definition are, first, the principles that govern the methods one uses to reach one's goal (such as violence or non-violence). Second is the action taken, which presumably leads to a particular outcome (Wilson 1973). Dalit women's interactions with other actors who take up supportive, opposing, or neutral stances on their actions influence the dynamic process of making strategic choices throughout collective action. These are choices as to the tactics, the targets, and the timing of the action (Ganz 2000; McAdam 1983).

Dalit women's livelihood strategies can be distinguished by their institutional location. They often deploy both formal institutional and extra-institutional tactics, depending on the opportunities they perceive within their political contexts (King and Cornwall 2005; Tarrow 1994). Conventional methods of securing entitlements rely on formal state institutions. They include petitioning government officials, women's entering into local governance institutions, and individual and representative litigation. By contrast, extra-institutional or confrontational tactics constitute a continuum along the lines of legality and violence. They range from non-violent methods within democratic norms (such as official strikes and public demonstrations) to non-violent but illegal methods (such as occupations of government land) and violent and illegal methods that cause damage to property and persons (Taylor and van Dyke 2007; Wilson 1973). Protests using extra-institutional tactics are the common political resource of subjugated social groups due to their lack of access to formal institutions and support from power holders for their claims. Instead, they rely on mobilizing large numbers of people in order to influence the wider public and state authorities to grant them livelihood resources. Furthermore, by disrupting normal life, they draw attention to their underlying moral message of the need to change both cultural and political values (della Porta and Diani 1999).

Jasper's (2004) concept of strategic dilemmas helps one to examine the types of strategic choices that Dalit women make during the course of collective action. One is that the 'depth of the challenge' posed by the socio-political context has to be balanced against the 'breadth of appeal' to movement members, potential allies, and the wider public (Downey and Rohlinger 2008). Tactics must be chosen that both appeal to Dalit women and help to maintain their collective identity and solidarity. Concurrently, the women must gauge the potential impact of their actions on the authority figures who are able to grant their demands, as well as the reactions of current and potential opponents. The latter include the risks of negative repercussions, such as physical and livelihood insecurity.

Another consideration is that tactics also have an impact on the relations between collective actors and bystanders. In response to the transition of Dalit women to more active public–political roles, their communities and families may seek to suppress their voices and collective action. The framing of the resource claim itself also invites dilemmas: for example, whether to shift from voicing the substantive claim (for example, claiming government land as an entitlement) to highlighting a procedural complaint (for example, how the land complaint was handled by district authorities). It is by comparing these strategic dilemmas, and the choices made at different points during collective action, that a more accurate comparison and explanation of collective action trajectories and outcomes emerges (Jasper 2004).

Finally, Dalit women's livelihood entitlement strategies can be assessed by their effectiveness in securing the entitlements that formed the basis for the actions, as well as their structural impact. Structural impact will have occurred if new or modified structures and contexts emerge as the intended and unintended consequences of collective action. This invites the following questions: do the women's strategies influence the broader context of power relations and social interactions, and if so, does this result in equal opportunities and inclusion? Moreover, if new structures, interactions, and meanings come into existence, do emerging forms of leadership among Dalit women ensure the sustainability of the change they have brought about? Do these new contexts make any easier collective action to attain other entitlements?

***

This chapter elaborated a broad conceptual framework by which one can understand and study the process of Dalit women's collective action to secure livelihood entitlements. The conceptual framework consists of three layers of explanatory factors, which are linked to a fourth layer that details the key processes within collective action. The first layer interlinks entitlement systems and social relations of power manifested in exclusion. The second layer focuses on the dialectics of power and agency. It ties together an understanding of power as relational and dynamic, vested in actors and structures, which both constrains and facilitates agency. Power relations are shown to be central to determining the process and outcomes of entitlement struggles; this includes power operative at multiple levels, namely, those of the family, society, and the state. Dalit women's subjectivities and agency are produced by structures of power. At the same time, they are subjected to these structures as the women concede and exercise power.

Agency is thus understood as a capacity for action that historically specific relations of subordination enable and create. Socio-historically situated and socially connected individuals manoeuvre within the spaces available to them at their location in power relations. At times, they may generate those structural discontinuities and challenge power relations; at other times, they may reinforce existing power relations. Their actions depend on power and the institutional opportunities within their specific contexts.

The third explanatory layer complicates the workings of power and agency by drawing attention to the intersections of multiple structural axes of difference. These intersections create diverse positions for different social groups within the field of power relations. Dalit women are thus uniquely positioned to bear the brunt of social exclusion, disentitlement, and discrimination in ways different from those experienced by Dalit men and dominant caste women. At the same time, viewing Dalit women's agency in intersectional ways complicates the binary of exclusion–inclusion; an intersectional view captures the contradictions in the women's positioning within intersecting structures of power. These contradictions enable them, through organization and collective action, to reshape power relations in ways that may improve both their entitlement and social positions.

The fourth layer concerns the heart of the research: the process of organizing and engaging in collective action. It highlights the interweaving and simultaneity of several processes. One is discursive consciousness raising, which enables Dalit women to analyse and critique their situation, and increases their desire to take autonomous action. Consciousness raising is linked to the construction of a collective identity as Dalit women. Their identity comes to be marked by a sense of entitlement, shared understandings of collective power and institutional opportunities, and mutual expectations that their actions will be successful in securing entitlements. These understandings find expression in the discourses that Dalit women deploy in their interactions with other non-state and state actors. These discourses aim to legitimize, secure, and protect their entitlements. Collective identity and discursive formation, moreover, both shape and are shaped by the set of strategies perceived as available to Dalit women. These strategies must be examined in relation to the 'strategic dilemmas' that Dalit women are forced to negotiate throughout their process of struggle.

The empirical chapters that follow reflect this conceptual base. Each case study deals with all three process factors of collective identity, discourses, and strategies formation in collective action, though each case study emphasizes a different factor. By analysing the women's perspectives and actions, I develop an intersectional perspective on power and agency, which unearths a more complex understanding of the enabling and constraining factors in Dalit women's collective entitlement struggles.

Notes

1. Articles 6(1) and 7, International Covenant on Economic, Social and Cultural Rights 1966 (ICESCR); Article 11(1), Convention on the Elimination of Discrimination against Women 1979 (CEDAW); Article 5(e)(i), International Convention on the Elimination of All forms of Racial Discrimination 1965 (ICERD).
2. Article 13, ICESCR; Articles 10 and 14(2)(d), CEDAW; Article 5(e)(v), ICERD.
3. Article 12, ICESCR; Articles 12 and 14(2)(b), CEDAW; Article 5(e)(iv), ICERD.
4. Article 11, ICESCR; Article 14(2)(h), CEDAW (for rural women); Article 5(e)(iii), ICERD (housing).
5. Legitimacy here is judged in terms of the right institutions and principles, the right procedures, and normatively acceptable outcomes of the exercise of power. That is, in terms of fairness built into structures of the political system, due process in enforcing rules and regulations, and fulfilment of the ideal of justice (Klein Goldewijk and de Gaay Fortman 1999: 130).
6. In this regard, Falk Moore (1978) discusses the indeterminacy of law due to concurrent processes of regularization and situational adjustment, and therefore the need to study law within social contexts and how it is implemented.
7. Note, though, that some of Sen's later work (for example, Dreze and Sen 1989) does talk interchangeably about entitlements and a normative description of rights (Leach et al. 1997).
8. Bhalla and Lapeyre (1997) argue that both the lack of resources and lack of social ties to one's society and its institutions are relevant, because adequate income does not translate into people's having access to basic needs.
9. This corresponds with the critiques of social exclusion theory from a gender and development perspective (Daly and Saraceno 2002; Jackson 1999).
10. Stammers (1993) notes this concept of productive, systemic power as a contested dimension of the interrelation between human rights and power.
11. At the same time, Foucault has been rightly critiqued because his model of power does not account for or articulate the exercise of agency and

subjective processes of empowerment (Deveaux 1994). It is for this reason that I turn to a host of other writers to develop the link between Foucault's ideas on power and power exercised by socially excluded women via collective action.

12. Wilson (2008) critiques the notion of agency as the exercise of rational choice and action (see Giddens 1984) based on unfettered free will. Wilson's argument indicates how women's agency has been appropriated and transformed by neoliberal discourses. A linked argument concerns the removal of power relations from this notion of agency, thereby depoliticizing the notion of empowerment (Sardenberg 2007). Competing discourses on women's empowerment are discussed further in the next chapter.

13. In this regard, Haynes and Prakash (1991: 5) note how researchers have often discounted as resistance common South Asian tactics of social avoidance, such as small acts of foot-dragging, ignoring intrusive laws, and so on, which they use to express discontent with the social order. This has often led to South Asians being mischaracterized as passive, with factors such as caste or patriarchy being used to explain why they have not developed the capacity to resist.

14. Norris *et al.* (2010) distinguish between an intersectional perspective such as this, and mere intersectional data analysis. The latter frames social axes as demographic variables rather than as relations of inequality and power.

15. It has been suggested that Dalits' traditional landlessness and lack of property meant that Dalit men did not have to control Dalit female sexuality via seclusion in order to protect male inheritance (Kapadia 1991).

16. Brahmanism or Brahmanical Hinduism refers to the dominant form of Hinduism practised today in India, with a spiritual base in the Vedas (sacred Hindu texts containing religious and ethical philosophy) and the Brahmins ('highest' caste group of religious leaders), and a material base in the village production system based on (lower) caste exploitation. At the same time, Brahmanism today also encompasses wide-ranging values that go beyond Hinduism and permeate a social system structured around traditional caste hierarchies and economic exploitation of labouring castes.

17. My research considers grassroots women's sangams engaged in public–political action and engaging with wider movement networks as social movements, though these are often left out of the social movement literature.

18. Resource mobilization theory suggests that collective action is spurred by the awareness that one has interests in common with others (for example, collective deprivation) when a sufficient aggregation of human and material resources exists to outweigh the costs of taking action. The type of resources mobilized by self-appointed organizers or 'movement entrepreneurs' then determines movement strategies (della Porta and Diani 1999;

Foweraker 1995). Political process theory builds on resource mobilization theory. It advocates the investigation of the political and institutional environment in which movements are located to uncover the political processes that present opportunities and incentives for engaging in collective action (Tarrow 1994). New social movement theory, by contrast, focuses on the structural origins of conflicts due to which social movements emerge. These social movements mobilize around forms of exploitation and domination based on identity, lifestyles, and values; that is, they challenge dominant normative codes, such as gender (della Porta and Diani 1999).

19. Many Dalit and women's movements in India, for example, have combined political struggles for material resources with symbolic resistance against dominant caste or male oppression, or Brahmanical patriarchy. This has been achieved through critiques of the *Manusmriti*—the chief authority on Hindu jurisprudence which contains strong strictures on women and Dalits—and the reinterpretation of Hindu epics, such as the Ramayana, as legitimizing male domination and discourses of female honour/shame (Omvedt 1993).

2

POLITICAL RESPONSES TO SOCIAL EXCLUSION AND DISCRIMINATION
State Discourses and Practices

The Committee is deeply concerned that in spite of the Constitutional guarantee of non-discrimination as well as criminal law provisions punishing acts of discrimination, widespread and often socially accepted discrimination, harassment and/or violence persist against members of certain disadvantaged and marginalized groups, including women, scheduled castes...

Committee on Economic, Social and Cultural Rights (CESCR)
Concluding Observations on India Report (2008)

Fifty year old Ponni lives in Vettriyur village with her husband, four daughters and one son. Both she and her husband are illiterate. They cultivate rice paddy on 1 acre of wet land for which her husband has title, and more recently on 2 acres of government common land. Paddy sales enable them to repay loans taken out to purchase farming inputs and her husband's tab at the local liquor shop. But what is left over is insufficient to sustain the family. During the agricultural season, therefore, Ponni exchanges her labour in the fields for loans from local dominant caste moneylenders, receiving Rs 100–Rs 120 as daily wages. Men, by comparison, receive Rs 200 per day for similar work. Ponni recently also started working in a local brick kiln in order to repay loans from the dominant caste kiln owner, though she jokes about the number of bricks she broke while learning the skills for this work. Her four daughters also work to support the family. Two engage in daily wage labour alongside their mother, while the other two are live-in domestic servants for dominant castes outside the area. As domestic help, they receive Rs 1,500 per month for work from 5 am to around 10.30 pm with little rest in between. A combination of poverty, work burden—all the girls worked in the fields and looked after cattle before and after school—and beatings meted out by teachers led the daughters to stop their education after Standard 8. Ponni's son, by contrast, is spared most of the work and currently studies in the local middle school.

Aside from cultivation, Ponni's husband sets up firecrackers for festivals and functions. She describes his main work, however, as drinking in the nearby town. He rarely contributes money to the running of their family, only once in 10 days going to the market to purchase vegetables for them. Despite the family's daily maintenance deriving mainly from Ponni's income, her husband has final say on most large family decisions.

Ponni's daily routine, therefore, consists of rising early to do all the household work and cooking. In the afternoons, on returning from work outside, she grazes her cattle, washes clothes, prepares dinner with the help of her daughters, and collects firewood and water. She consequently rarely leaves the area, only occasionally going into town to buy medicine or cattle feed. Lack of time means she also finds it difficult to join in the women's *sangam* activities, though she regularly pays in Rs 50 as monthly savings. Her current savings of Rs 4,000 are matched by average annual loans of Rs 50,000 at 36 per cent annual interest. One daughter's marriage dowry and expenses alone, she estimates, will require loans that will take five years to repay. They also have to allocate money annually to repay loans, pay for school fees, medical costs, socio-religious functions, and the construction of a new one-room house.

Ponni's story illustrates the multiple, interlocking deprivations Dalit women contend with in daily life, most of which are rooted in a history of exclusion from resources on the basis of caste and gender (see Chapter 4). It also reveals the discriminatory practices and division of labour that accord Dalit women a central role/burden in maintaining rural livelihoods today (cf. Harriss-White 2004a). This role, combined with household duties and her lack of education, alternative skills, and resources, confines Ponni to daily wage labour in the immediate neighbourhood. Her husband, by contrast, has the freedom to do other labour work outside the area. The only other work her daughters have found outside the area is poorly remunerative and exploitative non-farm labour. Her narrative substantiates the argument that female employment, while important, is not enough by itself to foster women's autonomy and agency. To bring about substantial changes, structural inequalities have to be addressed.

The previous chapter pointed to structural inequalities within the patriarchal caste system that negatively affect Dalit women's ability to secure livelihood entitlements. This chapter examines that reality in concrete terms. The following section maps the wider context of exclusion and intersectional discrimination in which the livelihood entitlement struggles discussed in Chapters 3–5 will be located. Despite their inherent limitations, I have had to rely partly on studies or data that are about Dalits or women. There are simply very few empirical studies of Dalit women, and most data are not disaggregated by both gender and caste. The next section describes the workings of formal institutional arrangements—legal, policy, and welfare measures—through which the Indian state attempts to redress these structural inequalities and entitlement deprivations. It explores the accountability gap in which Indian state actors fail to discharge their obligations to respect, protect, and fulfil Dalit women's rights, and thereby reproduce these women's exclusion. The penultimate section focuses on one key aspect of state development planning for the empowerment of poor women, namely, microcredit provisioning through self-help groups (SHGs). I discuss the extent to which the discourses generated by this scheme reiterate, or transform, structural inequalities and shape Dalit women's perceptions of entitlements and agency.

Experiences of Exclusion and Discrimination

In 2006, Indian Prime Minister, Manmohan Singh, noted in his address at the Dalit–Minority International Conference: 'Dalits have faced unique discrimination in our society that is fundamentally different from the problems of minority groups in general.... The only parallel to the practice of "untouchability" was *Apartheid* in South Africa' (Singh 2006b). The uniqueness he refers to includes forms of social exclusion that are based on ascriptive, rather than achieved, characteristics (Thorat and Newman 2007: 4121). 'Untouchability' is the imposition of disabilities on people based on their having been born into a caste that is deemed to be 'polluted'. It promotes particularly intense and durable forms of social exclusion. This durability is reflected in the lower human development index (HDI) for Dalits (officially known as Scheduled Castes or SCs) compared with other castes (not belonging to SCs or Scheduled Tribes [STs], herein referred to as dominant castes) (Thorat 2007). Deshpande (2003: 121) noted that when examining rates of representation for millions of members of a social group like the SCs, the differences in abilities and resources of individual members are averaged out. Hence, the only reasonable explanation for SCs as a group to enjoy consistently lower development levels is in terms of social mechanisms of durable, systematic discrimination.

Dalits thus continue to constitute a substantial section of India's poor, one that is out of proportion to their numbers: in 2004–2005, 32 per cent of SCs, who represent only 16 per cent of the population, lived below the poverty line[1] as compared to 20 per cent of dominant castes in rural areas (National Sample Survey Organization [NSSO] 2005).[2] The fact that levels of Dalit poverty and vulnerability are the same in nearly every Indian state, moreover, reveals that social inequality overcomes regional differences (Kannan 2008). Forms of exclusion and discrimination likewise persist for those few Dalits who surmount the caste barriers that obstruct their equal access to livelihood resources and opportunities.

Transecting caste-based exclusion and discrimination are comparable gendered forms. Kannan (2008) argues, based on government data, that social inequalities between Dalit and dominant caste women are, in fact, more pronounced than between men of these two groups. This section, therefore, examines the specific features of social exclusion and intersectional discrimination that Dalit women face in the economic, political, and socio-cultural spheres. Where possible, I compare Dalit women to Dalit men and dominant caste women in order to further distinguish the entitlement deprivations that flow from Dalit women's specific positioning within caste, class, and gender relations.

Economic Exclusion

Economic exclusion refers to Dalit women's being denied the means and abilities to participate in land, labour, credit, factor input, and consumer market exchanges, as well as non-market transactions (Thorat 2007). Thorat and Sabharwal (2010: 14–15) distinguish four methods by which Dalits are excluded. First, they are denied access to market-based livelihood resources such as land and credit. Second, their access to economic opportunities is on unfavourable terms: they are discriminated against in the conditions under which they work; or they receive lower prices than others would for the goods they sell. Third, they are adversely included in work based on traditional caste obligations, such as bonded labour (debt servitude or forced labour). Fourth, they are associated with traditional 'polluting' occupations, such as leather tanning or sanitary work, and are thus barred from other jobs. The value of women's productive work is therefore strati-fied according to caste status (Lingam 1994). Cross-cutting caste-based exclusion are norms of female seclusion, gender divisions of productive and household labour, and the consistent devaluation of women's work in comparison to men's. For Dalit women, however, more important than gender seclusion is the issue of their physical safety in access-ing workplaces and at work. All the stated factors effectively restrict Dalit women's occupational mobility and ensure that the Indian labour market remains highly segmented by caste and gender (Nayak 1995).

Abundant evidence of this continuing exclusion can be found in official data and extensive surveys (Das 2006; Desai *et al.* 2010). These show that Dalits remain restricted to caste-based manual labour occu-pations or congregate around the bottom rung of government services.[3] They also form the majority (62 per cent) of bonded labourers (National Commission for Enterprises in the Unorganized Sector [NCEUS] 2007). A higher percentage of Dalit women than dominant caste women are in the labour market, but the push factors are poverty and lack of land-ownership.[4] Despite their concentration in rural areas, Dalit women's significantly lower levels of landownership, either in their names[5] or the names of their families,[6] means that far fewer cultivate land compared with dominant caste women.[7] The majority of Dalit women instead eke out their livelihoods through casual labour. They work primar-ily for dominant castes in the unorganized or informal sector, a sector that is synonymous with low wages and lack of employment or social security (NCEUS 2007).[8] They are primarily agricultural labourers,[9] but they also take on non-farm labour, including 'polluted' tasks such as manual scavenging[10] (the manual removal of human excreta from dry pit latrines) and sweeping. Casual labour is also distinguished by high gender differentials in wages, which are only partially linked to skills and resources, and are more likely due to discrimination (Das 2006).

Some attribute the large gaps between Dalits and dominant castes more to differences in resource endowments that are rooted in historical discrimination, and less to ongoing discrimination that affects returns on those endowments (Gaiha *et al.* 2007). In doing so, they highlight a pattern of caste and class covariance particular to Dalits (Colatei and Harriss-White 2004; Sengupta *et al.* 2008). However, the emphasis on historical rather than current discrimination, and therefore on inequality of opportunity over inequality of outcome, is contested by others. They show that caste persists in defining both the opportunity structure and the outcomes for the majority of Indians. Today, Dalits are less likely to be landed, educated, financially secure, and socially connected than dominant castes, and social and market discrimination contributes to these outcomes (Desai *et al.* 2010). An examination of rural 'untouchability' practices across 11 states, including Tamil Nadu, revealed current economic discrimination at high levels (20–45 per cent of villages surveyed). For example, Dalits were denied entry into shops, discriminated against in waged work and wages, denied access to common property resources, and prevented from selling goods in local markets (Shah *et al.* 2006: 95). Active discrimination also prevails in the urban job market. Thorat and Attewell (2007) studied patterns of decision making among private sector employers. Their results showed that job applicants with 'high'-caste Hindu names were more likely to succeed than similarly well-qualified applicants with Dalit names.

Moreover, dominant castes, but not Dalits, have seized new economic opportunities that have opened up in the past 30 years, such as small- and medium-scale industries (Heyer 2007), shrimp farming, and contract farming (Mangubhai 2004). This is due to, inter alia, Dalits' comparatively low levels of education and health, lack of financial capital, non-labour skills, and lesser social networks (Heyer 2007). The market economy has so far failed to transform traditional institutions, such as caste; rather, a re-visioning of caste has occurred. Hence, new forms of caste-based economic exclusion operate to keep Dalits in the same socio-economic position *relative* to dominant castes. This is despite urban migration, the move among some Dalits into non-traditional occupations, and the reduction in their dependence on dominant caste landlords.[11] Dalits continue to be less successful than dominant castes in moving into new salaried, non-farm employment, despite their growing education levels (Das 2006).

Issues of gender difference interlinked with caste are often ignored in explanations of social changes that have occurred because of the market economy. Today, Dalit women assume de facto responsibility for continuing caste-based occupations, while Dalit men find limited opportunities to take up non-traditional labour occupations in urban areas (Dube 2003; Heyer 2007). Deshpande (2007) confirmed that significantly more 'high'-caste women are entering into high-level occupations than Dalit women, and such disparities are increasing, especially in Tamil Nadu. She further argued that whereas dominant caste women always enjoyed greater material entitlements but suffered from greater seclusion, and Dalit women always suffered from material deprivation but enjoyed greater autonomy, now both groups of women enjoy less autonomy, while the economic gap between them has widened (Deshpande 2002). In other words, they continue to diverge economically, but converge more on the level of autonomy. One explanation is that Dalit male outmigration and improvements in Dalit men's economic position are matched by an increasing emphasis on dominant gender norms, thereby decreasing Dalit women's status and freedoms (see Chapter 5).

Similar patterns of exclusion are evident in non-market transactions. Although Dalits are no longer barred from education, Dalit women's educational levels lag far behind those of Dalit men and dominant caste women. In 2001, literacy rates were 42 per cent for SC women compared with 54 per cent for women in general and 73 per cent for SC men (Government of India 2001).[12] Moreover, Dalit girls continued to drop out of schooling at higher rates than dominant caste girls and Dalit boys.[13] This situation is fuelled by dysfunctional government schools,[14] and poverty and discrimination, which is practised by both teachers and dominant caste students (Shah *et al.* 2006). Research in urban Maharashtra demonstrates that Dalit girl students are unfairly disciplined, both overtly and covertly. They are publically humiliated by teachers, who ignore their positive achievements while praising dominant caste students (Paik 2009). Structural inequalities therefore reproduce educational deprivation across generations. At the same time, even with educational parity between SCs and dominant castes, SCs are less likely to escape poverty and vulnerability (Sengupta *et al.* 2008).

Another area of exclusion is access to adequate health care and nutrition. The Asian Human Rights Commission (AHRC 2010: 33–4)

noted the prevalence of child malnourishment among predominantly
Dalit- and Adivasi-populated villages in Madhya Pradesh. The commission traced this back to poor access to potable water, bonded labour,
and landlessness, which leads to labour exploitation by dominant caste
landlords. Added to this picture are the considerable health risks Dalit
women endure, owing to a lack of, or caste discrimination in, access
to sanitation facilities (Programme on Women's Economic, Social and
Cultural Rights [PWESCR] 2007). The state provisioning of medical
(and education) services in rural areas, moreover, is biased: the higher
the percentage of rural SCs in a district population, the lower the level
of public services (Betancourt and Gleason 2000). The outcomes are
higher rates of mortality, morbidity, and undernourishment among SC
children compared with dominant caste children (Thorat and Sadana
2009). Similarly, SC women suffer from higher rates of anaemia and
undernourishment compared with dominant caste women (International
Institute for Population Sciences [IIPS] and Macro International 2007).

Political Exclusion

Political exclusion for Dalit women entails non-enjoyment of citizenship rights to justice, physical security, social protection, and political
participation, including participation in setting development agendas
(Bhalla and Lapeyre 1997; Figueroa *et al.* 1995). Such exclusion arises
because India's democratic governance system, with its impartial standards and rules of enforcement, is constructed upon a social system
in which caste and kinship relationships are highly valued. Power,
therefore, tends to be exercised on behalf, and for the benefit of, one's
caste group (Kumar and Rai 2006). The influence of castes extends
into the political sphere through the 'politicisation of castes' (Kothari
2004[1970]: 5), which refers to how politicians mobilize caste identities in political organizing and how caste groups seize political opportunities to augment socio-economic power. This exposes, as false, the
idea that law and state entitlement arrangements are insulated from the
influence of dominant social norms and institutions.

   In the political sphere, it is argued that Dalits' 'impure' status
makes them incapable of governing. This serves to deny them any
political status, which thereby stops them accessing resources needed
for their development (Irudayam *et al.* 2011). The effects are often

more intense for women, who are massively under-represented (2 per cent) in the current Indian Lower House of the Parliament (15th Lok Sabha). Moreover, despite the existence of formal institutional rules that promote inclusive governance through affirmative action quotas,[15] the Committee on the Elimination of Racial Discrimination (CERD 2007: 4) has noted: 'Dalit candidates, especially women, are frequently forcibly prevented from standing for election or, if elected, forced to resign from village councils or other elected bodies or not to exercise their mandate, [and] that many Dalits are not included in electoral rolls or otherwise denied the right to vote.'

Dalit women's exclusion from political participation is also evident when one looks at the operation of local governance institutions (panchayats). Research in Gujarat and Tamil Nadu (Mangubhai *et al.* 2009) revealed that only around one-third of elected Dalit women panchayat representatives were able to exercise their political authority. Most acted as proxies for dominant caste men or, to a lesser extent, their husbands. Moreover, 90 per cent of the women experienced discriminatory treatment from other panchayat representatives. This exclusion was then reproduced by government officials' refusing to address discrimination or proxy representation in their monitoring of panchayat performance. All these obstacles compromised the women's ability to deliver more caste- and gender-responsive development outcomes.

Another effect of the concentration of political power within the dominant caste majority is to help both non-state and state actors to make life less secure for Dalit women (Jacob and Bandhu 2009; Ravikumar 2005). Social exclusion is reinforced through coercive mechanisms, such as violence; Dalits who assert their rights are punished.[16] Failure to perform the duties attached to one's Dalit caste invites culturally legitimized penalties, including assault and destruction of property. The impunity with which much of this violence takes place reinforces a culture of fear, which diminishes Dalit women's freedoms and agency. Research covering 500 Dalit women across four states, including Tamil Nadu, revealed that the most common forms of violence (experienced by over 20 per cent of women) were verbal abuse, physical assault, sexual harassment or assault, rape, and domestic violence. The primarily dominant castes perpetrators were often not punished because they used their greater socio-political power to threaten Dalit women victim–survivors into silence or to influence the women's ability to obtain legal remedies. Police officers, who are primarily dominant caste, also neglected to investigate or prosecute such crimes (Irudayam *et al.* 2011).

A clear link between exclusion and violence emerges when one examines the causes of violence. In the same research, Dalit women identified four overlapping factors that triggered violence against them in the general community (Irudayam *et al.* 2011). These were, first, the perception that they lacked sexual integrity, which was linked to their low caste–class identity. This meant that they were deemed sexually available to dominant caste men. Second, violence was used to reinforce their gender and caste inequality, such as when women attempted to access common water sources on equal terms. Third, violence was used to deny Dalit women and their families access to economic or productive resources, thereby preventing their economic independence or upward mobility. Fourth, violence accompanied denials or backlashes against assertions of Dalits' civil and political rights, such as freedom of expression or political participation. Compounding these rights violations were experiences of violence in the family, which were driven by poverty and caste-based gender norms.

The ability of Dalit women to appeal for legal protection against violence, or to influence the state's development agenda, however, partly depends on their political visibility and the access they have to information on laws and entitlements. The media plays an important role when it comes to political visibility. A 2006 survey of decision makers in 37 print and television media networks, however, found that 90 per cent in the English print media and 79 per cent in television were 'high' castes, who constitute only 16 per cent of the Indian population. By contrast, there was almost no representation of Dalits. Consequently, analysis of mainstream media representation of Dalit issues reveals how often the caste basis of exclusion and violence is hidden in media reporting (Khan 2006; also, see Balasubramaniam 2011). In the regions under the present study, for example, sporadic reporting on Dalit issues occurs primarily through the local Tamil newspapers. Only the Mallibakkam shrimp farm struggle attracted the attention of both the English and Tamil print media. However, this media attention focused solely on the villagers' blockade of the highway in protest against the shrimp farm, without reporting on the subsequent police violence against the Dalit villagers. As for Dalit women's access to information, the current research revealed their lack of knowledge: few knew of the key laws that are intended to protect them and promote their rights.[17] Biased media representation and exclusion from access to information reinforce each other: they ensure that Dalit women are poorly equipped to pressurize the state to counteract social exclusion.

Socio-cultural Exclusion

Socio-cultural exclusion comprises Dalit women's being denied social recognition and dignity through their symbolic devaluation as 'inferior' or 'polluted'; spatial isolation; non-recognition of their social contribution through traditional services, paid and unpaid (household) labour; and denial of equal participation in socio-cultural life (Kabeer 2000; Louis undated; Nayak 1995). Research suggests that this form of exclusion is more acutely felt by Dalit women than by Dalit men because the women experience greater 'untouchability' and ill-treatment from dominant caste women and men, in that order (Shah *et al.* 2006). Exclusion is also apparent in certain cultural practices, such as dowry, which encourages the treatment of women as less valuable and transitory members of their natal households, while setting a price on their heads for their marital households. Through these processes, by which Dalit women construct their identity and which condition their freedoms in the social, economic, and political spheres, exclusion is normalized and structural inequalities perpetuated. Hoff and Pandey (2004, 2005), for example, conducted a series of experiments with 'low'- and 'high'-caste students, which showed Dalit students faring significantly worse in activities when their caste was revealed, and taking fewer gambles when assessors were allowed to exercise discretion in judging their activities. The experiments illustrated how Dalits have low expectations of how they will be treated by others, because society believes them to be inferior and excludes them. Anticipated ill-treatment affects their motivation and performance both absolutely and relative to 'higher' castes; it contributes to the perpetuation of group inequality and subordination.

Social exclusion also contains a spatial dimension. Space is used to express symbolic power. In conformity with 'untouchability' norms, Dalit residential areas are isolated on the fringes of villages. This segregation is reinforced through separate references to the Dalit *cheri*

(colony) as opposed to *ūr* (village).[18] It is the village that contains all
public services, such as schools and the meeting place where village
decisions are taken. Space, moreover, is not only caste segregated
but also gender segregated according to norms of female seclusion,
which dictate limited mobility in public spaces for women (IIPS and
Population Council 2009). In the case of Dalit women, higher levels
of engagement in productive labour necessarily enhance their freedom
of movement in public spaces. This freedom, however, remains closely
bound to their productive and family roles.

Dalits' access to both private and public spaces, moreover, occasions
exclusion and discrimination. The 11-state study of rural 'untouchability' practices revealed that Dalits in over one-quarter of the villages
were not allowed to enter police stations, while equal access to water
facilities was lacking in almost half of the villages. Much more prevalent,
however, were social sanctions against inter-dining and the practices of
denying Dalits entry into dominant caste houses or into public places of
worship, which were found in around two-thirds of the villages (Shah
et al. 2006). The general trend is that Dalits have had most success in
eradicating exclusionary practices related to the use of public spaces
and services. Nevertheless, exclusionary practices remain in situations
involving family and interpersonal relations between castes, as well as
common traditions such as temple worship and festivals (Kumaran
2002). Further, while a number of traditional 'untouchability' practices
have stopped as Dalits asserted their rights, or as socio-economic interdependence between Dalits and dominant castes weakened, new tools
of exclusion continue to emerge: for example, caste discrimination in
the women's savings and credit SHGs formed in the 1980s; or new
'untouchability' norms around drinking water in areas with increasing
water scarcity (Mangubhai and Irudayam 2003).

Legal, Policy, and Programme Responses

Given the magnitude and durability of social exclusion processes that
affect Dalit women's livelihoods, the question is whether the Indian
state is fulfilling its human rights obligations towards these citizens.
Here, the state is understood as 'shaped by two paradoxical elements,
the *image* of a dominant and coherent state that controls all rule-
making and the actual *practices* of its multiple parts that may promote

conflicting sets of rules with the official law' (Midgal 2004: 15–16, emphasis original). As will be seen next, formal institutional arrangements create new interfaces between Dalit women and the state, as well as new interests, entitlements, and bases for new identities. At the same time, the actions of state actors at these interfaces expose the serious contradictions between state institutional rules and state practices.

Constitutional Rights and their Interpretation

Indian rule of law is founded on four core notions that are seemingly ideal to ensure substantive equality among citizens: rights, development, governance, and justice (Baxi 2007: 13). The Constitution of Indian 1949 guarantees a democratic political framework in which all citizens have certain fundamental rights, including the right to non-discrimination on grounds of sex, caste, race, religion, or place of birth (Article 15). The practice of 'untouchability' against any person is prohibited (Article 17), while equality before the law, and equal protection of the law, are guaranteed (Article 14). Freedom to practice any occupation (Article 19[1][f]) and prohibition against forced labour (Article 23) also exist, alongside equal opportunity in employment, which enables the state to reserve posts in government services for SCs (Article 16 [4][a]).

In addition to these justiciable rights, and crucial for their interpretation, are non-justiciable Directive Principles of State Policy, which guide governance and law making. The Principles marry a vision of social and economic democracy, which is to be established through progressive state action, to civil and political rights, which are to be protected by the state (Visvanathan and Parmar 2005: 339). In other words, the Principles suggest a development model that emphasizes the redistribution of resources to ensure social justice for excluded citizens. A key provision is Article 46, which articulates the state's duty to promote, with special care, the educational and economic interests of SCs and to protect them from social injustice and all forms of exploitation. Matching this provision are principles of gender equality, which are expressed as the equal right to an adequate means of livelihood for women and men (Article 39[a]), coupled with the duty of citizens to renounce practices that are derogatory to the dignity of women (Article 51A[e]). Finally, a National Commission for Scheduled Castes, established under Article 338,[19] is charged with monitoring the constitutional and legal safeguards for SCs, inquiring into specific complaints regarding the deprivation of their rights, and advising on all issues concerning their welfare.

Complementing these constitutional provisions is judicial activism by the Supreme Court of India, which has translated several livelihood-related freedoms under the Directive Principles into justiciable rights. This has been based on widening citizen access to the justice system through public interest litigation (PIL): that is, with writ petitions that allege violation of the rights of an entitlement-deprived group and request remedies in the public interest. The Supreme Court has widely interpreted the right to life under Article 21 to include the right to live with dignity, requiring a means of livelihood[20] and access to adequate nutrition, clothing, and shelter.[21] Other judicial interpretations have included similar socio-economic rights, such as a healthy and sustainable environment,[22] education,[23] health,[24] and adequate food[25] (International Human Rights Internship Programme [IHRIP] and Asian Forum for Human Rights and Development [AFHRD] 2000; Kapur and Duvvury 2006). Social justice has also been given legal meaning as the right to social and economic justice.[26]

Moreover, in keeping with its effort to foster respect for international law and treaty obligations (Article 51), the Supreme Court has established recourse to international human rights law to enlarge the meaning and context of rights guaranteed under the Indian Constitution.[27] This applies especially where there are gaps in domestic laws,[28] and allows the Indian courts to incorporate and enforce international norms (Rana 2009). International human rights treaties ratified by India[29] thus oblige the state to respect Dalit women's rights in the way it behaves, to protect them from violation of their rights by others, and to provide an enabling environment to fulfil these women's rights. In particular, the CERD interprets discrimination based on 'descent', under Article 1(1) of the International Convention on the Elimination of All Forms of Racial Discrimination 1965 (ICERD), to include discrimination based on forms of social stratification such as caste.[30] In addition, the CERD (2002) emphasizes the need to implement measures to eliminate multiple discrimination against women from communities that are discriminated against by reason of their descent. Implementation would include appropriate social, economic, political, and legal arrangements to establish Dalit women's equal access to resources required for secure and sustainable livelihoods.

Protective, Preferential, and Developmental Measures

Three categories of measures by the Indian state—protective, preferential/promotional, and developmental (Teltumbde 2012)—flow from the constitutional provisions given earlier; they match many of its obligations under international human rights law. Protective measures include special laws enacted to protect Dalits from 'atrocities' or crimes committed on the basis of their caste identity, many of which are related to livelihood resources[31] (Scheduled Castes and Scheduled Tribes [Prevention of Atrocities] Act 1989). There are also special laws against social exclusion based on 'untouchability' (Protection of Civil Rights Act 1976). These are social laws to which the ordinary proof of *mens rea* (criminal intent) does not apply; it is sufficient to prove the act occurred against a Dalit (Ramasamy. 2005).[32] Special criminal procedures, crime prevention cells, separate courts, as well as mechanisms to prevent atrocities have concurrently been established to fulfil this state obligation.

Other special laws related to livelihoods include the Employment of Manual Scavengers and Construction of Dry Latrines (Prohibition) Act 1993, which outlaws manual scavenging; the Bonded Labour System (Abolition) Act 1976, which aims to eradicate bonded labour and thereby prevent the economic and physical exploitation of socially excluded communities; and the Right of Children to Free and Compulsory Education Act 2009, which obliges the state to ensure Dalit children's freedom from discrimination in pursuing their primary education. Specific legal protection of women's rights extends to gender equality in wages and recruitment (Equal Remuneration Act 1976); criminalization of the giving or taking of dowry (Dowry [Prohibition] Act 1961); and protection of women from violence in the family (Protection of Women from Domestic Violence Act 2005). In addition, a statutory National Commission for Women (NCW) holds powers similar to the Commission for Scheduled Castes.

Preferential measures, by contrast, seek to correct historical and cumulative discrimination and promote inclusive development. They consist of reservations of seats in national and state legislatures,

government-run educational institutions, and public sector employment for SCs and women, as well as three separate quotas for SCs,
women, and SC women in the panchayats. Developmental measures,
in the form of development and empowerment schemes, were implemented in the 1980s to tackle the exclusion of SCs and women and
to promote the redistribution of resources.[33] These schemes form
one prong in the broader development strategy implemented under
India's Five Year Plans (Appasamy *et al.* 1995). They include a host of
national and state government schemes that enhance education and
skills development in order to equip SCs for alternative employment;
welfare schemes to improve their access to housing and civic amenities;
separate budgeting for SC and women's development; and women's
empowerment through SHGs for livelihood development (Ministry of
Social Justice and Empowerment (MSJE) 2010; Ministry of Women
and Child Development (MWCD) 2010). Importantly, since 2007,
the Indian government has recognized the diversity of women. It has
formally adopted an intersectional analysis in order to identify marginalized and vulnerable women, and aim programmes at them. The
government has said that the implementation of protective laws should
be combined with distinct provisions for SC women in programme
planning, financial allocations, and distribution of reservations in education and employment. This indicates 'zero tolerance for discrimination
against SC/ST women' (Planning Commission 2008: 195–6).

Rights in Reality: The Large Accountability Gap

There is, however, a clear dichotomy between constitutional rights and
state measures, and their implementation. The implementation gap
exists at several levels: executive, law and order, and administrative. At
the level of executive action, the Supreme Court's judicial orders are
ignored. As Baxi noted, positive judicial outcomes 'are not perceived
[by the state] as opportunities to reshape power but rather as obstacles
in the exercise of real power' (Baxi 1993, quoted in Steiner and Alston
2007: 286). One example is the ongoing PIL filed by Safai Karmachari
Andolan against the Government of India in 2003: it demands time-
bound action to eradicate manual scavenging and to rehabilitate those
engaged in this occupation—mostly Dalit women—into other, more
dignified work. While a number of state governments have filed counter

affidavits, either denying the existence of this practice or committing themselves to eradicate it, manual scavenging continues, even in public sector undertakings. Another example is the government's categorical refusal to accept that caste is covered under 'descent' and, therefore, that the ICERD applies to Dalits (Government of India 2006: paras 16–17).

The second level of implementation gap relates to the state's regularization of legal standards within a social context structured by caste, class, and gender. Studies highlight the failure by the police and state government administration to exercise due diligence to protect Dalit women and ensure effective legal remedies when rights violations occur. Under-enforcement of the law is the norm rather than the exception (Irudayam *et al.* 2011). Violations of the rights of Dalit women, in particular, tend to be trivialized, if they are brought to light at all where victims face threats from the perpetrators or biased treatment from state officials (Centre for Human Rights and Global Justice [CHRGJ] and Human Rights Watch [HRW] 2007).[34] Consequently, government statistics reveal that fewer than 10 per cent of registered cases of violence against Dalits end in court convictions annually (National Crimes Records Bureau [NCRB] 2010). For Dalit women, conviction rates are as low as 0.1 per cent (Irudayam *et al.* 2011). Given this situation, in 2010, the National Commission for Scheduled Castes criticized the Tamil Nadu government on multiple counts, including the large number of pending cases, the long delays in police investigations and the low conviction rate for atrocities against Dalits, and the failure to retrieve lands appropriated from Dalits by dominant castes (Dorairaj 2010). Under-enforcement of the law by state actors, the majority of whom are dominant caste, thus institutionalizes a hierarchy of social groups based on the extent to which they enjoy formal rights and entitlements.

The operation of the reservations policy also attracts criticism for its paradoxical reinforcement of social exclusion, and because state bureaucracies fail to enforce it. The majority of reservation beneficiaries are Dalit men or dominant caste women, owing to the de facto exclusion of Dalit women. First, in the panchayats, they tend to be ghettoized into the small SC women's quota, despite the availability of SC or women's quotas they could be included in (Mangubhai *et al.* 2009). Second, in work and higher education, Dalit women often become excluded because of the existence of two separate quotas for them; that is, they are told to apply for the women's quota when they try to access SC quotas and they are directed towards the SC quota when they apply for women's quotas (Singh 2000, quoted in Grey 2005: 131). Additionally, quotas operate as a form of rationing: because of the existence of quotas, Dalit women cannot apply for non-reserved categories (Das 2006). Compounding this situation is the state's failure to fill many reserved seats, its failure to improve Dalit women's educational levels so that they can access reservations, and its failure to extend reservations to the growing private sector (Borooah 2010; Narula 2008). As a result, reservations benefit few rural Dalit women, particularly in education and employment. It is for these reasons that reservations, as a form of state-arranged entitlement, are insufficient 'by themselves' to transform structural inequalities.

Similarly, the incoherence of the Indian state's development policies plays a role in perpetuating the social exclusion of Dalit women. In particular, the state pays insufficient attention to the interrelations between different policies, such as those for women and those for SCs, despite the intersectional understanding of Dalit women's vulnerability mentioned in the Eleventh Five Year Plan. Consequently, targeted schemes continue to exist for SCs and women separately. Further, as with reservations, at the level of state bureaucracies, de facto exclusion of Dalit women takes two major paths, one of gender and the other of caste. Hence, on the one hand, between 1997 and 2004, there was a large shortfall of approximately Rs 7,143 crores in the funds allocated under the Special Component Plan (SCP) for Dalit development in Tamil Nadu (Social Watch Tamil Nadu 2004). On the other hand, most of the benefits of development programmes, and the bulk of state resources distributed as entitlements to Dalits, have gone to Dalit men (National Human Rights Commission [NHRC] 2004).

Additionally, the biased or poor implementation of government schemes also explains Dalit women's livelihood deprivations. The following three examples provide evidence of the state's failure both to redistribute resources and to provide for rural Dalit women's livelihood needs, either through SC-targeted or general development schemes. The execution of these measures, as with laws, is mired in corruption, clientelist politics, indifference, incompetence, inefficiencies, and outright failures (Posani and Aiyar 2009: 5) as much as by caste and gender biases. Hence, 50 years of land reforms in Tamil Nadu have merely institutionalized the socio-economic divide between middle caste–class landowners and landless Dalit agricultural labourers in rural areas (Jacob and Bandhu 2009). This is partly because 56 per cent of the government land that was redistributed up to February 2010 went to dominant castes, despite government guidelines that made land for SC agricultural labourers a priority (Revenue Department 2010; also, see Viswanathan 2004). The NHRC (2004: 85) concludes that behind failed land reforms is the absence of political will and bureaucratic commitment, excessive judicial interference, and the ability of dominant castes to exploit loopholes in the laws and appropriate Dalits' lands.

Another important measure that enables many rural Dalit women to acquire adequate food is the nationwide public distribution system (PDS), which sets up ration shops selling essential food commodities at subsidized, below-market rates fixed by the government. Patterns of discrimination and exclusion, however, have been shown often to obstruct free and equal access to ration shops, which are operated primarily by dominant castes (Thorat and Lee 2006). Social activists, moreover, argue that the heavily subsidized PDS should be judged in light of the Tamil Nadu government's running of all liquor shops in the state. Tamil Nadu State Marketing Corporation (TASMAC) liquor shops, today, generate a huge revenue of around Rs 14,000 crores per annum (Sivaraman 2011). A group of women in Kovilur village explained the link between these two government activities: 'We see in the newspapers the crores of rupees the government gets from the wine shops. We are given Rs 1 rice at the ration shop, but our men spend Rs 70 each day at the wine shops!' Women also attested to increased male alcoholism following the government's taking over and increasing the number of liquor shops near villages, leaving the women to bear the brunt of providing food for their households.

Finally, an important scheme for the livelihood of rural Dalit women is the Mahatma Gandhi National Rural Employment Guarantee Scheme (MGNREGS), which grants a legally enforceable right to work. The scheme is aimed at the poorest families without adequate labour. One member of every rural household is entitled to 100 days of unskilled manual work at the statutory minimum and gender-equal wage. Since 2008, when the scheme was implemented across all districts of Tamil Nadu, the link between class, caste, and gender has become evident from the concentration of Dalit women labourers: this can be gauged by cross-referencing the presence of 58 per cent SCs and 83 per cent women labourers under the scheme (Ministry of Rural Development [MRD] 2010).[35] Serious concerns, however, exist about its operation and objectives. A government-sponsored study across eight states, including Tamil Nadu, found large-scale corruption and irregularities in implementation, such as fraudulent job cards, improper maintenance of muster rolls, and inadequate monitoring mechanisms (Press Trust of India 2010). The scheme also has generated widely varying claims as to its gender-empowering effects on employment and financial autonomy (see Pankaj and Tankha 2010): some have found that piece-rate wages often result in women working longer than normal hours to obtain the full daily wage (Narasimha Reddy *et al.* 2010). Moreover, notwithstanding its value as a social protection scheme, landowners gain the most economic benefits via MGNREGS-created irrigation water sources or road linkages. The scheme perpetuates Dalit women as unskilled, manual labourers, while it increases their subsistence levels. Concurrently, it generates tangible material benefits mainly for dominant caste landowners in support of *their* economic development. In sum, power relations and relative livelihood deprivation levels among Dalit women vis-à-vis dominant castes remain unchanged.

The given discussion reveals a consistent pattern: despite the proliferation of state laws and policies and the development or welfare programmes, the Indian state often does not, or cannot, act consistently to counter social exclusion and discrimination against Dalit women. Off the record, a District Rural Development Agency (DRDA) official opined that there was little chance of Dalits' development reaching parity with dominant castes, even within the next 50 years. His reasons—that Dalits still lack awareness of government schemes, contacts to access these schemes, and money to gain the benefits from these schemes—highlight the ways in which socio-political power and corruption determine entitlements through state institutions. In other words, state actors are complicit in entrenching structural inequalities where access to formal entitlement arrangements becomes dependent on factors other than formal rules, and where public officials lack credibility to enforce measures fairly. Prime Minister Manmohan Singh (2006a) noted in this regard: 'Legislations alone are not sufficient... What is needed is the political will to eliminate atrocities and to enforce the law...the will to ensure that all sections of society feel that they are part of our polity and society and are equal partners in processes of growth and development.'

This deficit in political will attests to the strength of dominant caste and male informal institutions and caste patronage networks, which coexist with and influence formal state institutions. It also highlights the multiple, conflicting interests embedded in the state where its own law enforcement and administrative machinery are constructed by caste, class, and gender (Narula 2008). Dalit women, consequently, do not acquire livelihood resources on equal terms to dominant castes, or even Dalit men, because legal entitlements and state entitlement arrangements are subverted to align with hierarchical, informal institutional norms and practices. The institutional environment that Dalit women encounter in claiming resources can therefore be characterized as hostile and unpredictable, rather than enabling. This is compounded by the operation of different state agendas, such as revenue generation through state-controlled liquor shops and schemes for welfare and development. The outcome is to deny the women access to productive resources and entrench conditions of survival as opposed to development. This further weakens their ability to take action to secure entitlements and sets in place a cycle of continuing livelihood deprivation. The government's basic assumption that if one secures the economic resources to pull oneself out of poverty, inequality will decrease, is thus open to question.

The implementation deficit also stems from the inability of state measures to address intersectional identities, because state measures are geared to eliding intra-group differences. Hence, within an overall system of inadequate enforcement, Dalit women fall further through the gaps than Dalit men or dominant caste women, because measures are designed to respond to either caste or gender identity, not both. Without conscious efforts to address livelihood situations structured by intersecting caste and gender norms, land reforms result in land titles being primarily in men's names, and quotas for SCs or women result in excluding Dalit women. The lack of statistics disaggregated by gender and caste, outside of a few areas like education, health, and employment, serves further to obscure this reality. Dalit women have little space to claim livelihood resources through existing institutions; the 'glass ceiling' over the livelihood choices and opportunities available to them remains strong (Thorat 2002).

What the discussion serves to reinforce is the inadequacy of the 'trickle-down theory of human rights' (Narula 2008: 332). The idea that state actors can be relied on to neutrally implement laws to propel social change down to the grassroots has been exposed as, at best, an ideal. This is not to discount the centrality of the state in development and in the redistribution of livelihood resources. The previous section showed that the Indian state has a large role to play in fulfilling a number of its citizens' needs, from governance to welfare and social justice. In view of the institutional practices just discussed, however, it is clear that structural inequalities cannot be transformed by the state and laws alone. Instead, one's attention turns to people's collective action to secure their just entitlements and freedoms, and to how power relations might be transformed by state and non-state actors in the process.

State Discourses on Empowerment and Livelihoods

States are accountable not only for the enforcement of state measures but also for their responsiveness to citizen's needs (Posani and Aiyar 2009). Attention thus turns to what Fraser (1989: 144) terms the 'politics of needs interpretation'. This refers to discourses that concern strategies to fulfil Dalit women's needs, and the needs themselves; discourses that are promulgated by the state in development planning. The politics of needs interpretation includes the perspective according to which the state interprets and defines rural Dalit women's livelihood needs, and the ways in which it decides how to satisfy them. Equally important is how the state positions politically accepted needs within the wider strategy of economic development, as well as the political discourses through which certain needs are denied the status of legitimate political concerns. All these factors shape notions of Dalit women's livelihood needs, entitlements, and agency.

The example that follows interrogates the discourse of women's empowerment that entered into development planning with the Ninth Five Year Plan (1997–2002). It was supported by the creation of the Parliamentary Committee for the Empowerment of Women in 1997 and encapsulated in the National Policy for the Empowerment of Women in 2001. Whereas in the 1970s, there was no gender perspective in development planning (Lahiri-Dutt and Samanta 2002), today, the Indian state stresses the removal of multifaceted gender exclusions and discrimination. The state also seeks to address specific deprivations that arise from women's multiple locations in diverse castes, classes, and so on. This is complemented by an emphasis on women both as equal citizens and as 'agents of economic and social growth', part of which requires interventions to provide women with basic entitlements (Planning Commission 2008). The state's approach to 'gender equity' is to empower women economically, socially, and politically by creating an enabling environment in which they can freely exercise their rights, both within and outside the home, as equal partners with men (Planning Commission 2002). A core aspect of economic empowerment, set within the broader policy framework of 'inclusive growth', is overcoming the poor's limited access to formal credit and their high reliance on usurious informal credit sources. If women are able to get microcredit, they will become self-sufficient economically, and also become active participants in development (Planning Commission 2002, 2008).

In implementing this development agenda in Tamil Nadu, the state government envisages economic empowerment as women having greater access to financial resources, which will make them financially self-reliant and reduce their livelihood vulnerability. Complementing this is social empowerment through which women achieve equal status with men, increase their status in formal institutions, and overcome socio-cultural and religious barriers. Both forms of empowerment involve capacity building on health, education, legal rights, and leadership and communication skills (Government of Tamil Nadu 2003: 97). To this end, poor women are encouraged by non-governmental organizations (NGOs) to form SHGs under the Mahalir Thittam scheme.[36] The SHGs comprise 12–20 women, aged 18–60 years—the most economically active providers—who are living below the poverty line and residing in the same area. They voluntarily engage in self-managed savings to satisfy their consumption needs and also, obtain microcredit to enable them to engage in economic activities. Skills training programmes also help with economic activities. The majority of SHGs are formed on a caste–class basis, with few mixed-caste groups. According to a district Mahalir Thittam official, this is an outcome of most NGOs' preferring to work with existing social relationships. The government's professed goal is to build an 'SHG movement' that covers all poor women, with 50 per cent of funds allocated to SC women's economic activities. These SHGs are characterized by regular savings, periodic compulsory meetings, training sessions on group governance, and financial management and structural linkages to the state (Rural Development and Panchayati Raj Department [RDPRD] 2010; Tamil Nadu Corporation for the Development of Women [TNCDW] 2011).

An analysis of this scheme's discourses on needs and strategies reveals that the scheme prioritizes those economic needs that are connected to the key role of women in family maintenance. Economic empowerment, in effect, is seen as instrumental to achieving social and political empowerment. Mayoux (2000) identifies three paradigms on women's empowerment and microcredit.[37] The financial self-stability paradigm emphasizes women's economic development and access to the market as leading to individual economic, social, and political empowerment. The poverty alleviation paradigm sees interventions, including microcredit, as increasing household income and community development, so as to enable women to address gender inequalities. In the feminist empowerment paradigm, microcredit is an entry point to stimulate gender awareness and mobilize women, enabling them to challenge gender inequalities. Mahalir Thittam would seem to combine the first two paradigms with an increasing emphasis on the first neoliberal, market-driven development paradigm (Jakimow and Kilby 2006). In other words, the state assumes that promoting individual women's institutionalized agency and power in the economic sphere will be enough by itself to lead them to take action for their social and political empowerment. This has been contested, however (for example, Jakimow and Kilby 2006 and Sharma 2011).[38] It does not follow automatically that if women contribute more to household expenditure and decision making, intra-household relations will be changed. What underlies the state's assumption is the idea that women are responsible for their own development and that of their families, and that social change implies individuals' moving up hierarchies of power rather than collectively transforming those hierarchies (Wilson 2008).

A further assumption is that women are underemployed and, therefore, their time and labour is freely available for SHG activities (Kalpana 2008; Lahiri-Dutt and Samanta 2002). This disregards the burden imposed by the sexual division of household labour, as well as caste–class divisions that see higher numbers of Dalit women engage in casual labour. Besides, the emphasis on enhancing women's decision-making

power within the family through improving their economic contribution to the family effectively absolves men of assuming greater responsibility for their families. At the same time, it re-emphasizes women's
reproductive role and duties within the family (Kannabiran 2005).
Certain gender norms are therefore effectively instilled in Mahalir
Thittam, not the least the notion that women are self-sacrificing and
maternal by nature. Agency is consequently constructed around these
limiting female roles; the state establishes a correspondingly narrow
range of legitimate sangam activities.

The state's discourse on empowerment is arguably inadequate in four
other ways. First, it effectively relegates the social and political needs of
Dalit women to second place. The state pays less attention to issues such
as securing entitlements to productive resources, creating positive identities that overcome exclusion, changing the unequal gender division
of labour, and women's vulnerability to violence. Economic issues are
treated as though they were entirely distinct from socio-cultural issues;
class alone is seen as the basis for social change, and the complexities
of empowerment are ignored. This is common to a number of women-
related government schemes (Subramaniam 2006). These complexities
encompass the interdependency of different categories of needs based
on multiple, interlocking exclusions, which require diverse interventions in order to transform structural inequalities. Agarwal (2003) suggests that microcredit often exacerbates inequalities in resources, such
as land, where the emphasis is placed on access to credit and not on
control over what the credit is used for, which often lies in male hands.
Women are often deemed only to need microcredit schemes and not
access to and control over resources. Either way, unequal entitlements
to livelihood resources are sustained. Equally importantly, the state's
empowerment discourse occludes issues of state accountability and
state responsibility. The state has a responsibility to provide an enabling
institutional environment in which Dalit women can secure entitlements and freedoms (Kannabiran 2005), and to address these women's
livelihood needs within macroeconomic policies (Sharma 2011).

Second, this discourse of women's needs is inadequate to capture the
full dimensions of gender inequalities as they intersect with other axes
of inequality, such as caste. Hence, a focus on economic empowerment
does not acknowledge power relations among different women, or take
into account their different economic vulnerabilities and exclusions.

For example, Dalit women's lower ownership of assets, education, lesser market access, social identities, and poorer access to information combine to increase the risks of their engaging in new economic activities. As two district Mahalir Thittam officials pointed out, and Dalit women in Kovilur village confirmed, their enterprises are less likely to be successful because many dominant castes refuse to purchase their goods and services when they learn their caste identity. Similarly, they are less likely to be able to lease land from dominant caste landowners to engage in more familiar, land-related activities. Mixed-caste groups, moreover, tend not to develop strategies to address the key exclusions Dalit women face, because their interests divide on caste–class lines and Dalit women are subtly discriminated against (Murthy 2004). Additionally, uniform strategies implemented by government actors fail to address biases within institutions. Caste discrimination by banks means that Dalit women are deemed less creditworthy. They are therefore less likely to secure bank loans, and more likely to come under pressure to repay. Microcredit, moreover, inevitably excludes the poorest of the poor, hence many Dalit women (Chakravarti 2008; Lindberg *et al.* 2011; Srivastava 2005).

The third issue is the problematic idea of 'self' in SHGs as an organizational model. This idea is moulded around a bureaucratic image of women as scheme beneficiaries who need to be taught activities. The de facto goal becomes to achieve programme targets, not to ensure an empowering process that supports women's voice and sustainable socio-economic change. The SHG strategy is, therefore, one of directed empowerment in which women merely participate (Jakimow and Kilby 2006). It does not view women as actors who are able to reflect on their situation and take decisions to act (Lahiri-Dutt and Samanta 2002). Accordingly, they have no significant say in devising suitable economic activities or determining the pace of their development. The result is that few Dalit women have used loans to gain more profitable self-employment. Hence, SHGs resemble a survival rather than a development strategy. Only now, 15 years after SHGs started, are officials conducting a survey of the livelihood resources and opportunities for women in their working areas. The state's top-down strategies attempt to create new economic opportunities, but also seek to exercise greater control over women's lives. In the process, the state reinforces cultural norms vis-à-vis women.

Fourth, although the government professes an expectation that the SHGs will become strong, civil society institutions, the government's 'self'-help is inherently apolitical. Some argue that the government's empowerment discourse and SHG strategy act more as a disciplinary power that produces efficient economic actors working within the rules of the market (Lairap-Fonderson 2002). Their political agency consists only of entering the limited spaces for engagement with formal institutions regarding credit and microenterprises. Group solidarity is forged more for individual gains. This distances the women from citizenship and public–political action (Kannabiran 2005). Hence, according to one district Mahalir Thittam official, the term 'political' does not and should not feature in any government training materials. Only five pages in the current training manuals refer to women's rights. Many NGOs implementing the scheme, moreover, concentrate on its economic aspects alone.

The government's SHG model for social change-oriented collective action has several dangers. In particular, government-affiliated women's SHGs are less likely to engage in contestational politics with the government. Nor are SHGs likely to significantly open spaces through which women can make claims to the resources they need and expand their entitlements on the basis of equality with others (Jakimow and Kilby 2006). The SHGs are also creating new challenges for development interveners, such as NGOs and social movements. One challenge stems from the increasing dependency of women on the government for loans. The SHG membership is commonly viewed as granting greater access to government schemes. This raises expectations on development interveners to deliver equivalent benefits, and tends to negate the creation of collective political identities. Another challenge is a shift from collective, community-based demands to more individualistic, family-oriented demands. The women's empowerment discourse, therefore, effectively disguises the creation of new patronage relations between women and the state. It also hides the greater integration of women into the market economy, without capacitating them to seize economic opportunities on a par with others. All this supports the argument that economic-based collectives, as opposed to socio-political claims-based collectives, are less likely to challenge Dalit women's social exclusion and subordination (Thorp *et al.* 2005).

***

Dr B.R. Ambedkar, chief architect of the Indian Constitution and himself a Dalit, declared in 1949 that upon independence, Indians would
enter into a life of contradictions. The lack of substantive democracy
would ultimately place political democracy in peril. By this, he was
referring to a politics marked by equality, which instituted 'one woman,
one vote' and 'one vote, one value', and a social and economic life
which, by contrast, remained driven by inequality denying the principle
of 'one woman, one value' (Ambedkar 1949). It is this fundamental
contradiction that remains unaddressed by the Indian state 60 years
later. Instead, tensions exist between the state's principles and policies,
which support Dalit women's struggle for entitlements and equality,
and their mal-implementation in practice.

   This chapter has mapped out the multiple economic, political, and
socio-cultural exclusions that produce chronic insecurity of life and
livelihood for Dalit women today. While their social exclusion may
be culturally legitimized to maintain dominant caste–class and male
power, this chapter has shown that the practices of state actors significantly contribute to and reinforce the durability of structural inequalities. The assorted state institutions and actors that collectively compose
'the state' are often influenced by informal institutions that uphold
social norms in direct opposition to the plethora of rights-based laws,
policies, and schemes. This strengthens the argument offered for examining interlinked power relations at multiple levels in relation to Dalit
women's agency. The outcome is, at best, the state's fulfilment of its
minimum obligations to ensure Dalit women's socio-economic rights,
namely, promoting their survival through various schemes. However, it
does not guarantee their protection, nor promote their development
on a par with dominant castes. Another outcome is the state's failure
to tailor its measures to address Dalit women's intersectional identities
and the specific needs arising from these, despite its ostensible commitment to do so. This situation is compounded by the state's discourse on
women's empowerment. Dalit women's needs and agency are defined
in certain narrow (economic) ways that place the entire burden of
development and social change on their heads. The false assumption
that SHG economic activities are inherently socially and politically
empowering displaces forms of political mobilization that focus on
rights and entitlements.

In sum, the context is one of tension between competing entitlement systems, namely, between state institutional rules and social institutional norms. It is the rule of law versus the rule of patriarchal caste (Irudayam *et al.* 2011; Narula 2008). Competing notions of entitlement and agency, and of progress and development, clash and are transformed by one another. Underlying this tension is a struggle to establish the principle of equality on the one hand, while reinforcing a hierarchy of entitlements based on immutable characteristics, such as caste and gender, on the other hand. Moreover, informal institutional norms that establish hierarchical access to government schemes are complemented by formal institutional practices, such as corruption, that distort state rules on entitlement. Constraints on Dalit women's ability to acquire livelihood entitlements through existing formal institutions are intrinsically linked to factors of caste, class (which determines the ability to pay bribes), and gender. This highlights how economic growth alone is insufficient to ensure the redistribution of livelihood resources. Adequate, independent legal and political institutions must be built. It is this larger context that sets the field within which collective action processes among rural Dalit women occur. At the same time, as Chapters 3–5 will show, within the current institutional constraints, Dalit women incorporate state discourses and schemes into their collective action strategies.

The following section of the book—which comprises three case studies, each dealt with in a separate chapter—takes up the theme of Dalit women's collective action, set within the stated, broad context. The chapters reveal the myriad ways in which Dalit women deal with insecurity of life and livelihood as they engage with the state, and with social institutions of power, in staking claims to resources. Each case study highlights different facets of social, economic, and political exclusionary processes that the women overcome to differing degrees by exercising their agency.

Notes

1. The poverty line in 2005–2006 was set at Rs 356.30 per capita per month for rural India.
2. NCEUS estimates that if one pools those categorized as extreme poor (less than 75 per cent of poverty line) through to vulnerable (double the

poverty line), then 88 per cent of SCs/STs would fall into this broad category of deprived people. This forms the highest percentage of any social group (NCEUS 2007; Sengupta *et al.* 2008).

3. In 2005–2006, 59 per cent of sweepers in central government services were SCs, as opposed to an average of 15 per cent in the higher Group A–D services (Ministry of Personnel, Public Grievances and Pensions [MPPGP] 2006).

4. The SC women's work participation rate in 2001 was 29 per cent compared with 26 per cent for dominant caste women at the all-India level, and 40 per cent and 32 per cent respectively in Tamil Nadu (Government of India 2001).

5. In 2000–2001, only 10 per cent operational landholdings among SCs at the all-India level were owned by SC women; this rose to 17 per cent in the case of Tamil Nadu (Department of Agriculture and Cooperation 2001). Women were likely to own land only if they headed households or were an only child (Government of Tamil Nadu 2003).

6. Only 38 per cent of SCs compared with 61 per cent of dominant castes operated landholdings in 2004–2005, the majority of which were marginal landholdings of fewer than 2.5 hectares without irrigation (NSSO 2005).

7. The 2001 *National Census* (Government of India 2001) indicated 21 per cent of SC women as cultivators compared with 45 per cent of dominant caste women; in Tamil Nadu, the percentages were 9 per cent and 19 per cent (general women) respectively.

8. In 2004–2005, 95 per cent of SCs/STs were in the unorganized sector (Sengupta *et al.* 2008).

9. In 2001, 57 per cent of SC women compared with 29 per cent of dominant caste women across India were agricultural labourers; in Tamil Nadu, the comparison stood at 69 per cent and 45 per cent respectively (Government of India 2001).

10. An estimated 1.3 million Dalits, predominantly women, continue to engage in this degrading work despite its prohibition by law (Centre for Human Rights and Global Justice [CHRGJ] and Human Rights Watch [HRW] 2007).

11. This contests other research (for example, Kapur *et al.* 2010), which claims that these three trends in occupational mobility, migration, and lessening caste interdependence are leading to social transformation.

12. In 2004–2005, 78 per cent of SCs belonged to households without a single educated female member compared with 63 per cent of non-SCs/STs (NSSO 2005).

13. In 2005–2006, the dropout rate in Tamil Nadu among SC girls between Standards 1–10 was 74 per cent as opposed to 68 per cent for SC boys and

64 per cent for girls in general (Ministry of Human Resource Development [MHRD] 2006). This trend was confirmed by research in 2006–2007, which showed that other backward castes (OBCs) were more likely than SCs to have completed 10 or more years of schooling (International Institute for Population Sciences [IIPS] and Population Council 2009).

14. Vasavi (2003) points to the increasing ghettoization of schooling in India. Dalit and 'backward' caste children are concentrated in government schools with poorer quality education, while 'middle' and 'upper'-caste children attend private schools out of the economic reach of most Dalits.

15. The Constitution of India 1949 contains provisions reserving seats for SCs and SC women in the panchayats (Article 243D) and municipalities (Article 243T), and reserving seats for SCs in the Lok Sabha (Article 330) and state legislative assemblies (Article 332).

16. Suresh (2005: 26) points to the symbolic issues behind violence against Dalits in recent years: *mānam* (honour), *mariyāthai* (respect), *pangu* (share of resources and power), and *urimai* (rights).

17. Women were surveyed on their knowledge of the Scheduled Castes and Scheduled Tribes (Prevention of Atrocities) Act 1989, Protection of Civil Rights (PCR) Act 1955, Protection of Women from Domestic Violence Act 2005, Right to Information (RTI) Act 2005, National Rural Employment Guarantee Act 2005, and fundamental rights provisions of the Constitution of India 1949.

18. In this regard, Srinivas (1987: 21) designates caste and not the village in India as social reality, in that the village is only the dwelling place of diverse and unequal castes.

19. Originally, a National Commission for Scheduled Castes and Scheduled Tribes, this commission was later bifurcated under the 89th Constitutional (Amendment) Act 2003.

20. *Olga Tellis* vs *Bombay Municipal Corporation*, AIR (1986) SC, 180.

21. *Francis Coralie Mullin* vs *The Administrator, Union Territory of Delhi and Others*, (1981) 2 SCR, 516.

22. *M.C. Mehta* vs *Union of India*, (1987) 1 SCC, 395; *Consumer Education and Research* vs *Union of India*, (1995) 3 SCC, 42.

23. *Unni Krishnan J.P. and Others* vs *State of Andhra Pradesh*, (1993) SCC (1), 645. The right to free and compulsory primary education for children aged 6–14 years has since become a constitutional right under Article 21A.

24. *Francis Coralie Mullin* vs *The Administrator, Union Territory of Delhi and Others*, (1981) 2 SCR, 516.

25. *People's Union for Civil Liberties* vs *Union of India and others*, (1997) 3 SCC, 433.

26. *C.E.S.C. Ltd* vs *S.C. Bose*, (1992) 1 SCC, 441.

27. *Vishakha* vs *State of Rajasthan*, (1997) 6 SCC, 241.
28. *Apparel Export Promotion Council* vs *A.K. Chopra*, (1999) 1 SCC, 759.
29. These include the International Covenant on Economic, Social and Cultural Rights 1966 (ICESCR); International Covenant on Civil and Political Rights 1966; International Convention on the Elimination of All Forms of Racial Discrimination 1965 (ICERD); Convention on the Elimination of Discrimination against Women 1979 (CEDAW); Convention on the Rights of the Child 1989.
30. The CESCR (2009) has also clarified that the prohibited ground of discrimination based on birth under the ICESCR includes descent, especially on the basis of caste.
31. Livelihood-related crimes committed by dominant castes include: wrongfully occupying or cultivating any land owned by or allotted to an SC, or getting such land transferred (Section 3[1][iv]); wrongfully dispossessing an SC from her/his land or premises or interfering with the enjoyment of her/his rights over any land, premises, or water (Section 3[1][v]); compelling or enticing an SC to do 'begar' or other similar forms of forced or bonded labour (Section 3[1][vi]); and corrupting or fouling a water source ordinarily used by SCs (Section 3[1][xiii]).
32. *State of Karnataka* vs *Appa Balu Ingale and Others*, AIR (1993) SC, 1146.
33. Specific planning for SCs was introduced from the First Five Year Plan after independence under a section, 'Welfare for Backward Classes', that later became 'Welfare and Development of Scheduled Castes and Scheduled Tribes'. Meanwhile, women remained the target of welfare policies until the Sixth Five Year Plan, 1980–1985, when specific planning on 'Women and Development' was introduced.
34. Irudayam *et al.* (2011) found that in 40.5 per cent of all cases of violence against Dalit women, the women did not seek legal redress. They were heavily influenced by socio-cultural norms, family or societal pressures, or fear of how a dominant caste perpetrator might retaliate.
35. This is partly because male labour wages often exceed the MGNREGS wages in Tamil Nadu, which leads Dalit men to relinquish this work to women in the household.
36. The SHGs were first formed in Tamil Nadu in 1989 in several districts. They spread to rural areas of all districts from 1997, and to urban areas, from 2000 to 2001.
37. Similar to these three paradigms, Batliwala (1994) identifies three approaches to empowerment, namely, economic empowerment focusing on women's economic security, integrated development supporting poverty alleviation and reducing gender discrimination, and consciousness raising to tackle subordination.

38. Jakimow and Kilby (2006) note that equating women's self-worth with financial contribution justifies the lower value placed on their unpaid household work. As one district Mahalir Thittam official pointed out, SHGs have not changed men's attitudes towards women in any significant degree.

3

ASSERTING THE RIGHT TO ADEQUATE HOUSING
Kovilur Village

After the sangam *came, we are now able to speak in public. We were able to speak in front of the court. If people like you came to our village before, we would have to call an educated person to understand what was being said. But now we can understand more and more...We know we were not treated properly before and so we need our rights.*

Meena (died 2010)

This chapter examines a successful struggle by Dalit women in the village of Kovilur to secure housing land entitlements. Security of tenure—a foundation for the right to adequate housing—has long been a critical issue for Dalits: a majority 'are still prevented from owning land and are forced to live on the outskirts of villages, often on barren land' (Special Rapporteur on Adequate Housing 2005: 18), with the possibility of eviction ever present. The issue of housing plots for Dalits thus highlights both access and location as points of social exclusion and discrimination, given the caste-based segregation of Dalits into colonies on the outskirts of many Indian villages. The issue of securing entitlement in Dalit women's names brings into focus issues of equality, autonomy, and shifting power relations.

This chapter, first, narrates the process and outcomes of the housing and related entitlement struggles these women undertook, primarily between 1999 and 2007. It starts by situating the emergence of the

Dalit women's sangams within the socio-historical context of the village. Coterminous housing land and temple struggles are examined next, with specific attention paid to the interlinkages between these struggles in the disruption of caste, class, and gender power relations, and the shaping of the women's actions. Then, the chapter analyses several dynamics of power and agency present throughout the struggles, with emphasis on the catalytic impact of outside agencies. Three implications are drawn from the struggle and examined further. The first is how social exclusion both enables and inhibits spaces and strategies for collective action. The second is the necessary intertwining of struggles for redistribution (entitlements) and recognition (identity) in transforming power relations. The third is that successful securing of entitlements does not end the process of dislodging gender inequalities, which are embedded in social customs that determine control over resources.

Two notes will help the reader understand this chapter. The first is regarding the slightly altered use of the term 'Dalit'. Three major Dalit castes inhabit the village—Pallars, Paraiyars, and Arunthathiyars. However, given that the Pallars have aligned themselves with the other castes against the Paraiyars and Arunthathiyars, this chapter focuses on the joint actions of Paraiyar and Arunthathiyar women and refers solely to them as Dalit. This is done for ease of explanation, and in no way seeks to discount earlier histories of social mobility and struggle among Pallars to overcome caste-based exclusion. The second note is that, again for ease of explanation, 'forward' and 'backward' castes in this village are grouped together as 'dominant castes'. In reality, though, different caste combinations have shaped both Dalit women's livelihoods and how they engage in collective action. Moreover, dominant caste opposition should be understood as including Pallar opposition to the Dalit women's claims to housing land and temple rights.

The Context: Shifting Power Relations Shaping Subjectivities

Kovilur village in Sivagangai district lies 1.5 km off a main road, down a narrow road lined by large Chettiyar mansions dispersed between agricultural land and thorny bushes. The village is one of the largest in the panchayat, with a voting population of 477 adults, as per the village

administrative officer's records. There are approximately 200 households from 10 different castes in the village. Caste divisions inform how
the households are laid out. Forward caste Nāttukkottai Chettiyars own
the 80-odd houses adjacent to the tar road with the best outside connections. Dalits, comprising 47 Paraiyar and Arunthathiyar[1] families,
live together in the eastern part of the village. Both their residential
segregation and their positioning in relation to the 'main' village are
markers of their traditionally ascribed 'polluting' status[2] (Shah *et al.*
2006). Their residential area is divided into an older colony where
the majority live and the newer colony for which the Dalit women
obtained land title, with their Māriamman temple located between
the two areas. All the other Hindu castes (except the backward caste
Nādars, who are Christians), including Scheduled Caste (SC) Pallars,
live separately on the other side of the *ūrani* (pond), which provides
drinking water to all.

Residential segregation is matched by differences in livelihood
status. The majority of Chettiyars today are landlords or live outside
the village in the towns, where they operate businesses. Other castes,
such as the SC Pallars, most backward caste Chettinadu Vallaiyars, and
backward caste Agamudaiyars, primarily cultivate their lands in the
village. In contrast, while proud of how much they have developed,
Dalit women still have a vulnerable livelihood status. They spend six
months per year labouring in the rice paddy fields; the agricultural off-
season sees them engage in either brick kiln labour or Mahatma Gandhi
National Rural Employment Guarantee Scheme (MGNREGS) work,
and less commonly in other wage labour work in the area. Their daily
lives are characterized by a cycle of household work, daily wage labour,
and a return to look after their families in the evenings.

Shifting patterns of power relations, and their political and economic
context, have shaped Kovilur Dalit women's subjectivities and agency
over time, producing and transforming their knowledge and capabilities. Historically, the Nāttukkottai Chettiyars historically dominated
the village by controlling most of its lands and governance; by being
able to command services from others; and by claiming an associated
higher ritual status (cf. Breman 1974). Hierarchical relations of caste
interdependence were institutionalized through Dalits' performing
adimai vēlai[3] (slavery, bonded servitude) for Chettiyars in exchange for
'rights' to residence, food, and loans. This conformed to the established

pattern throughout south India at the time: 'untouchable' castes were held in a state of agrestic slavery to landowning 'higher' castes (Mencher and Saradamoni 1982: A150), with agricultural labour deemed defiling and indicative of low status (Breman 1974; Franco *et al.* 2000). These services, signifying both Dalit 'pollution' and dominant caste honour and power, were fundamental to maintaining the hierarchical social order (Dirks 1993). So, too, were caste interdictions and 'untouchability' practices[4] that symbolized and reinforced Dalit subordination, as did a discourse of inequality embedded in daily interactions. A group of Dalit men in the village summed up: 'We were treated like animals back then'.

Over the past 40 years, changing contexts, external intervention, and the collective agency of Dalits have all triggered changes in inter-caste relations. Dalits named three major gains in entitlement that ruptured social and economic caste interdependence, and challenged their exclusion. First, the advent of education for Dalits[5] developed their political consciousness and agency at the level of identity, along with their self-respect and sense of entitlement to equal treatment (Mendelsohn and Vicziany 1994). In the words of Roja (married woman, 45 years), 'We started raising our voices, saying we were equal and we too were human'. Second, 16 Dalit families petitioned the government for the first time to request allotment of the dominant caste land on which they resided for colony housing 'as of right'. This entitlement, notes Malliga (separated woman, 45 years), meant 'those conditions—compelling us to work for them—no longer applied'. Third, Dalits filed three legal cases against Chettiyars for various discriminatory practices and violence, precipitating the end of many 'untouchability' practices. Concurrently, the shift to a market economy via agricultural commercialization weakened Dalits' reliance on Chettiyar employers for subsistence and enabled them to sell their labour outside of the village (cf. Rudha 1984). Accompanying this trend, the Chettiyars' land stranglehold broke when many educated Chettiyar youth sold off lands to other non-Dalit castes in order to operate financial and trading ventures in the towns.

This historical background is significant for understanding Dalit women's collective action because it establishes certain frames of reference within which the women envisioned further change in their lives. These frames of reference are reflected in their perceptions and actions at the start of their struggle for housing land, and their expectations about development interventions, as seen later. A key point is the type of external intervention to which women were introduced for the first time. All three entitlement gains were linked to Chettiyar landlord Ramu, a 'patron' with whom Dalits had allied and who directed their collective action while providing protection against other Chettiyars. He was the most educated of the Chettiyars and, according to Dalits, interested in village welfare and sympathetic to the poor, several of whom worked for him. This was partly due to his affiliation to the Congress Party, which espoused Gandhian values promoting caste equality through eradicating 'untouchability' practices, as well as his economic interests as an employer in ensuring Dalits' loyalty. His interventions represented for Dalits an alternative patronage relationship, still hierarchically based, yet allowing them to move beyond survival to achieve some measure of economic independence and dignified living. His interventions were primarily with Dalit men, however, and addressed caste and class concerns much more than gender. He did little to develop Dalit women's sense of entitlement to further housing plots or to promote their agency.

Another point is that the above-mentioned socio-economic changes did not alter relative livelihood entitlement positions and entitlement norms. Dominant castes still retained control over many goods and services. Dalit women, who were landless and who had limited education and skills, remained locked into wage labour occupations.[6] As the women had no savings to fall back upon, and access to formal credit was foreclosed by lack of property ownership to offer as guarantee, another dependency relationship arose to replace that of adimai work. From the 1980s, many Dalit households relied on high-interest loans from mainly Chettiyar moneylenders and pawnbrokers. Additionally, the growing population made living arrangements both physically and socially difficult, with two to four Dalit families sharing one- or two-room *kudisai* (non-permanent) houses. This was compounded by the lack of electricity and adequate drinking water in the Dalit colony, while both were enjoyed in the main village.

Finally, these historical changes resulted in Dalit women's making housing needs a priority. This supports Rudolph and Rudolph's (1984: 282) assessment that the most disadvantaged often rank economic and physical security above increasing their productivity. Housing held symbolic significance as an important historical step taken towards greater liberty from exploitive economic relations. This accompanied an equally significant shift in consciousness towards the importance of property, and away from their previous narrower 'work for survival' outlook. This outlook was linked with non-permanent residential status. Housing became a vehicle for establishing a claim to village territory and the higher status of permanent residency. Its link with social status aside, Dalit women also wanted separate, secure housing in which to bring up children safely. These attitudes towards housing were all motivating factors behind women's collective action in the sangams.

Collective Agency and the Politics of Securing Entitlements

External Intervention: Developing Political Consciousness and Agency

The first development intervention to target Dalit women came with the arrival of local non-governmental organization (NGO), Vidiyal, in the village in 1999. Its purpose was to develop, among other things, the women's sense of entitlement and collective power though participation in the sangams. Vidiyal Mahalir Membāttu Sangam (Vidiyal Women's Development Association) is a grassroots NGO. It was established in 1994 at the initiative of a Dalit woman, Veronnika, to help women to realize livelihood-related rights and to develop their leadership qualities. The organization focuses on Dalit women in around 150 villages of three development blocks in Sivagangai district. Veronnika started by supporting Dalit women informally to seek solutions to livelihood problems. She later seized the opportunity presented by self-help group (SHG) organization under the state's Mahalir Thittam scheme to start formally organizing the women around livelihood issues. She chose to work in Kovilur village after observing that the Dalits' living conditions were among the worst in the area at the time.

Vidiyal adopts two strategies. One is to create women's sangams comprising Dalit and backward caste women. These enhance women's economic capacities through savings and loans activities. They also expose them to alternative livelihood opportunities. Organizing the women into apolitical, 'economic empowerment'-centred sangams creates socially accepted space for Vidiyal to engage in its main strategy. This is to capacitate Dalit sangam members politically, and to mobilize them to demand collectively that the government fulfil their basic livelihood needs and be accountable for any Dalit rights violations. This strategy relies primarily on negotiation with the government as opposed to outright confrontation through protests and demonstrations. However, they do not eschew the use of extra-institutional tactics should petitions and meetings with officials fail to achieve the necessary action.

Veronnika's rationale for working solely with Dalit women emphasizes that they have different room for manoeuvre within prevailing social norms, relations, and practices. Women have a greater capacity to organize collectively and challenge dominant caste–class interests because they are less entangled than their men in local patronage relations with dominant castes and in local politics. Equally, dominant caste or police reactions to collective action by Dalit men are more likely to be violent. Moreover, Dalit men often fail to prevent negative repercussions of their actions for their families. Veronnika's allusions to a form of women's power were thus reliant on subverting notions of female exclusion and the protection of women. Simultaneously, she drew upon, and thereby reproduced, gendered ideas of women's self-sacrificing, altruistic nature:

> If women go outside the village, they will not involve themselves in unnecessary things as each time they are thinking about their family and children. The same responsibility women have to their families is what they show in their public work…Women should sacrifice themselves for their sangams, stay firm, and not be swayed from their goals by men.

She thus highlights a fundamental contradiction in attempts to organize women that are unable to completely escape reiterating the gendered construction of women as they simultaneously challenge that construction. At a practical level, Dalit women were an obvious target group for livelihood interventions given the gendered nature of many livelihood activities and the link between resource ownership and women's physical safety.

Despite the pressing need for housing, prior to the sangams, women were unaware of their right to decent housing and what they were entitled to as a consequence of this right. They mentioned that they had had no idea to obtain more housing plots, let alone how to do so, in the face of poverty and the death of their 'patron', Ramu Chettiyar.

Previous patronage-based interventions, therefore, had failed to promote their sense of entitlement and collective power to access institutional entitlements, including state-sponsored schemes. In the initial stages, therefore, Veronnika brought the Dalit women together to articulate their specific needs in the village. She built towards motivational discussion on how women should be at the forefront of struggles to develop their livelihoods. Indira (married woman, 37 years) recalled: 'She explained that by joining together in the sangam we would be able to get electricity, water, roads, housing facilities…everything [we lacked at the time].' Chandra (married woman, 30 years) continued, 'She also said that if one person protests or goes to the government offices alone, nothing would happen as no one would give us respect, but if we went as the sangam and protested together, then officials would listen to us and our problems could be resolved more quickly'. Collective action under the banner of the sangam, therefore, was promoted as a strategy to overcome marginalization and voicelessness, opening an alternative discourse of collective Dalit female power. This effectively 're-valourised female identity' (Villarreal 1994: 227) and delinked it from gender norms that excluded women from public–political action.

As well as offering inspiration, the NGO mobilized women to act by imparting practical information about various government housing-related schemes. This marked the start of forging links with formal institutions and raised a real possibility in the women's minds that they might secure such entitlements. According to Chandra, 'Veronnika told us a government scheme existed that if a poor family had some land, the government would build housing for them. That's what motivated us to try to get some land…Before that, we lived as a crowded family in the one house for 12 years.' Moreover, women like Jeya (married woman, 47 years) realized, 'We had to fight for our rights. If we want to get government schemes, first we need a permanent place to live in.' Women thus came to perceive housing land entitlement as a base for acquiring other necessary entitlements from the government. This shows the knowledge–power nexus. Knowledge of what they are entitled to from the state makes people conscious of how they can act together to meet their livelihood needs. Many women were persuaded by this combination of motivational and practical discussions to negotiate permission from their husbands or to make the independent decision to join the sangams. They were also attracted by the prospect of gaining access to information, to low-interest loans, and to a separate gender space to share their concerns.

As Chapter 1 showed, the link between motivation and action is the development of political consciousness and the capacity to exercise power by acting collectively. Capacity building refers to activities which facilitate the sharing of experiences, knowledge, and strategies, enabling consciousness raising and creating networks among women (Subramaniam 2003: 192). Political consciousness raising is a process in which women re-evaluate themselves, their subjective experiences, their opportunities, and shared interests (Taylor and Whittier 1992, quoted in Subramaniam 2003: 192). Three levels of capacity building and political consciousness-raising activities marked the NGO's approach. At the first level, fortnightly meetings provided a space for women to voice their views on problems in the colony and to consider the means available to solve these problems. Anjali (married woman, 60 years) recalled that 'in meetings we discussed who needed what facilities...what petitions we should write.' The NGO staff guided many of these discussions, explaining about government schemes, how to write petitions, and which officials to target. This women's space also strengthened bonds of solidarity, though differences among the women remained. Prominent was the hierarchy among adult women within a family, structured by varying access to power in the form of control over the division of labour among women (Sangari 1996). This hierarchy enabled mothers-in-law to attend meetings, while daughters-in-law performed household work.

The second level was the occasional meetings of all village sangam leaders in the emerging district-level Dalit women's liberation movement. These were to promote exchanges of information between the women in different villages as well as between NGO staff and women, and to identify areas for further capacitation trainings. These meetings also enabled the planning of joint action on common issues such as demands for agricultural land for Dalit women or police action regarding cases of atrocities against Dalit women or girls.

The third level involved two types of ad hoc training sessions. One concentrated on helping sangam leaders to analyse their social situation and forms of discrimination and exclusion that required them to assert their rights, and to link this to sangam activities and resource claims. The second training, open to all sangam members, focused on

more practical aspects of monetary savings and livelihood opportunities, as well as building knowledge of government schemes and laws to
promote women's rights. Veronnika described the outcomes as to some
extent bridging the knowledge divide between the majority of illiterate
Dalit women and others, even if only a limited amount of information
was retained.

In the absence of these efforts to conscientize and capacitate women
to take collective action, economic empowerment through savings
and credit activities alone would not have led automatically to social–
political empowerment. Comparisons between these Dalit women's
sangams and the three other sangams in the village started by another
NGO prove this. The latter comprised women of all other castes and
operated solely to promote microcredit activities, enabling women to
manage their families even in the absence of financial support from
husbands. Other caste women, however, claimed to lack the knowledge
and capacity to intervene in village affairs, and evinced no sense of
agency to secure entitlements.

Despite the achievements, Dalit women revealed a number of
interconnected barriers to participation in sangam activities. Malar
(separated woman, 50 years) differentiated between the articulate
few who listened and responded in training sessions, and the majority
who stayed silent and comprehended only a little. She thus pointed to
enduring links between illiteracy and lack of self-confidence. Veronnika
also suggested that the women found it difficult to shift focus from
daily survival to examining wider issues such as experiences of gender subordination and abstract concepts such as rights. She said, 'The
women leaders can understand about rights if you give them training
and adequate responsibilities, but members often cannot grasp the concept.' Another problem was that sheer physical exertion of their work
sapped their energy. Malar, for example, admitted that she would doze
in meetings when she was too tired to concentrate after her burden of
work outside and inside the home.

These barriers are further reflected in the dynamics of leadership and
sangam decision making. Women's personal characteristics—their interest, ability to retain information from meetings and trainings, and confidence to articulate demands and lead any action—primarily determined
sangam leadership and, therefore, a hierarchical form of representative
voice. Indira, for example, increasingly recognized that 'if we sit in our

houses, government officials will not do anything for us. Because of this we are coming out and asking them directly for facilities.' Response to fear of authority figures also partly determined leadership. Leaders such as Chitra (married woman, 37 years), once she learnt who different officials were and how to speak with them, felt, 'Why should I be afraid of officials? They are humans just like us.' In Anjali's words, leaders were women who 'knew how to talk'. By contrast, sangam members perceived themselves as more passive participants who accompanied the leaders but did not speak in public or fully understand the rationale behind the collective decisions taken. The strong association of education with 'authentic' knowledge and authority to speak partly explains the members' lesser participation. Even in informal interviews, many women prefaced their comments along the lines of 'I am not educated so I can only share what I know from experience...you should speak with the leaders to know everything.' Another part of the explanation lies in the social construction of women's roles and behaviour, which emphasizes the silencing of their voices.

Decision-making processes reflected another set of dynamics between both sangam members and leaders, and the NGO Director, Veronnika. These dynamics were determined primarily by acquired patterns of interaction with outside agencies and differences of knowledge, experience, and social networks. The relationship between the women and Veronnika has to be viewed in the context of sangams being the first gender-targeted development intervention by an outside agency. As such, with no other point of reference aside from Ramu Chettiyar's involvement in their lives years ago, women arguably replicated with the NGO this earlier patronage relationship. The women relied to a certain degree on the NGO to set the agenda and direct what should be done. Veronnika's role was perceived as both a 'development broker' and 'patron'. That is, she was someone who could translate government schemes for the women and connect them with government officials, as well as confront or intercede with the other castes and government officials on their behalf in the process of securing entitlements. Andal's (married woman, 50 years) statement that Veronnika was like the goddess Māriamman[7] to them is telling. It is indicative of Veronnika's perceived role as both protector and provider. Most women emphasized that if Veronnika had not come and struggled alongside them, they would never have secured housing plots and other entitlements.

Consequently, this familiar model of a dependent, 'patron–client' relationship both empowered as well as constrained the women, because they took action but without independent decision making.

Constructing a Collective Identity

Political conscientization and capacitation both fed into the construction of a collective identity and interests 'as Dalit women' in the sangams, thereby motivating collective action. This identification process built upon existing dense, overlapping social networks formed by shared experiences of spatial and social exclusion alongside religious, caste, and kinship ties. These shared experiences downplayed any internal contradictions between women of the two Dalit castes. Residentially segregated together, these women daily interacted with one another both socially and during work—inside and outside the home—more so than with their men or other castes. Some went so far as to assert that marriages between their castes would be acceptable though none had yet occurred. A common identity was formed through natal or marital kinship ties within each caste and through relatively similar socioeconomic status. This common identity further generated solidarity. All these factors supported the women's identification as a collective, requiring strategies to address their common exclusion from livelihood resources. This would be less likely where sangam members have more disparate backgrounds (Murthy 2004). The sangams thus comprised two castes in which women privileged their collective identity over individual caste identity.

Conflict over symbolic resources (for example, temple rights) and a caste identity still inextricably bound to social exclusion further strengthened their collective identity. This identity was underpinned by subjective discontent over their livelihood situation. Social conflict between Dalits and dominant castes has been noted as a critical source through which identities are reshaped in relation to each other. It offers the strongest impetus for Dalits to become conscious of the low identity ascribed to them, and to motivate them to construct a new positive self-identity (Joe Arun 2007: 4). One basis for conflict is rights with respect to religious institutions and festivals. Such institutions and festivals are critical to exercising symbolic power and authority in local political systems in Tamil Nadu along with rights over resources (Mosse

2003b: 69). The impetus for collective identity formation in the present case was the conflict, from 1995, between Dalits and all other
castes in Kovilur village over rights to the Arulmigu Muthumāriamman
(Māriamman) temple. Dalits had founded this temple around 60 years
ago on Chettiyar land near their houses. A Dalit Paraiyar priest performed the worship rituals (pūjas) and temple tax (vari) was collected
among the Dalits for the annual temple festival. Dalits sought equality in religion by advancing an independent, new identity through an
autonomous temple for themselves. A group of Dalit men described
this temple as the 'turning point for our community after years of
neglect in society and religion'. This indicates the temple's intimate
association with issues of identity, status, honour, and dignity.

Kovilur dominant castes, however, found it necessary to challenge
the Dalits over temple rights once the Māriamman temple festival
became well known in the area and temple offerings increased in the
1990s. In doing so, they aimed to reassert and legitimize their caste
authority and status that had been diminished by the weakening of
caste interdependence in social and labour relations. The Chettiyars
thus persuaded the Dalits in 1995 to use collective village finances to
replace the original thatch structure with a more solid temple structure.
This joint financing as well as Chettiyar ownership of the temple land
then fuelled dominant caste arguments for greater rights over temple
management and the festival. Chettiyars also sought to introduce caste
hierarchical norms by demanding 'first honours' (muthal mariyādai)
in temple rituals, a means of rendering authoritative their share in the
temple and hence, temple rights (cf. Appadurai and Breckenridge 1976;
Ludden 1989). Further, according to Chitra, 'They started saying they
are periyavan [people of high status] while we are chinnavan [people of
low status], and so how could a Paraiyar remain as temple priest?...But
we all have the same rights to worship the goddess.' Competing discourses underlying the temple dispute thus were linked to relationally
defined identity and power positioning. Therein, Dalits' identity formation, based on equal religious rights, was seen to undermine dominant
caste norms and power.

Tensions over the temple festival simmered after 1998 and culmi-
nated in open caste conflict in 2001, despite the district government
intervening several times to reach a compromise. With no solution in
sight, the temple was locked and no festival was held. Meanwhile, the

Chettiyars attempted to block Dalit women's access to the village ūrani and the Chettiyar owner of the temple land erected a signboard forbidding access to his land. All interactions between the two sides then stopped. Dalits did not enter the main village and dominant castes did not enter the colony. Dalits who worked for the dominant castes or sharecropped their lands shifted instead to daily wage labour outside the village. However, caste tensions, petitions, and dominant castes' fights with the Dalits continued around the time when the temple festival would normally take place. A police presence in the village was then required to maintain the peace. These tensions continued until 2007, when the Chennai High Court handed down its judgement in favour of the Dalits on a case filed by dominant castes claiming rights over the temple management.

Against this background of ongoing caste tensions, Dalit Paraiyar and Arunthathiyar women allied together in opposition to the other castes. This opposition included the Dalit Pallars, who practised 'untouchability' towards them. In doing so, the Pallars showed how their social mobility has been dependent on asserting distance from, and rank over, other Dalit castes. Further, according to the women, the Pallars adjusted their interests in order to maintain harmonious relations with the non-Dalit castes they lived alongside in the main village.[8] Beyond this alliance, the temple conflict further helped Paraiyar and Arunthathiyar women to construct a common identity and to develop interests that propelled their collective action.

Collective Action Strategies and Outcomes

Building Organizational Strength through Practical Interests   Strategically for the NGO, the organization of the women around less confrontational practical interests was the first step in developing their self-confidence. The next step was the more difficult struggle for housing land, which touched on social relations of power. Hence, the first issues the women's sangams took up related to basic amenities, such as street lighting and drinking water taps. The latter highlights the gender specificity of certain livelihood concerns: Dalit men did not prioritize getting water on tap. They were not the ones walking to the village ūrani to collect 20–50 pots of water daily for household purposes. They did not have to fetch the water secretly when the temple dispute led to

Dalits being debarred access to this water source. These two issues introduced women to the politics of making claims on state institutions. Specifically, women petitioned the highest district official, the district collector, before meeting the relevant amenities board and other subdistrict officials. They experienced inordinate delays. They had to make many visits to government offices to press for action on their petitions. They had to cross-check partial information provided by lower government officials with higher officials. For example, the dominant caste panchayat president failed to disclose that Dalits were also intended beneficiaries of the new water tank, which was placed in their colony, but which provided water solely to the main village. Women also resorted to direct action, such as arranging for the delivery of street light posts and fixing the electricity line, when all else failed.

Meeting the Challenges of Petitioning for Housing Land Dalit women's claim to colony housing land introduced variations to the strategy used to obtain basic amenities. Chettiyars owned most of the vacant village land and caste-based spatial norms put limits on the colony location. The ongoing temple dispute meant that it was not possible to negotiate with the dominant castes over vacant land. Through the NGO, women learnt how to influence the government to act on their behalf. They would quietly identify a suitable plot of land and ascertain who owned it. Next, they would approach the district revenue officer and collector with a group petition for housing land. The district revenue officer acquired private lands for allocation as SC colony housing. The collector sanctioned land title. By bypassing lower government officials, the women overcame two disadvantages that flowed from their 'low' caste, class, and gender identities. They lacked the money to pay lower officials the expected bribes. Moreover, lower officials, being for the most part locals and intertwined in local caste relations, were more likely to be prejudiced against them.

Dalit women's lack of interaction with the dominant caste villagers and panchayat president, in comparison to their men, worked in their favour as they started to identify suitable housing land. They had already witnessed the men place undue faith in the panchayat president to help them in return for monetary payment. Instead of helping them, the president had advised two dominant caste landowners to take measures to counter any government attempt to acquire their uncultivated land. Dalit men's unwillingness to upset caste relations too much was also evident in their suggestion to build on flood-prone land that no one would contest. This land lay between the Dalits' graveyard and the *kanmāi* (irrigation tank), far away from the main road and all facilities. The men's actions confirm Hart's (1991) analysis that stronger patronage relations between men and local dominant actors and political authorities limit men's scope for political action to a greater extent than women's. This analysis is in line with Veronnika's rationale for organizing Dalit women separately.

The women hesitated when the NGO director's government contacts found suitable land near the roadside belonging to five Chettiyar brothers. Years of social exclusion had taken their toll. Women worried that they would never be allowed to live near the roadside traditionally reserved for dominant castes. Dalit men added their objection based on their desire to avoid another fight with the Chettiyars given the ongoing temple dispute. Veronnika, therefore, invested significant time in convincing the women to boldly ask the government for the land, saying that there was no harm in trying because the other castes would not know of their application until the government sanctioned the land acquisition. Before they could petition the government for specific land for colony housing, however, the women had to discover the addresses of the Chettiyar brothers who lived outside the village. They used the pretext of wanting to send out wedding invitations. Once they had the addresses, the women drafted petitions to the collector and district revenue officer in 2000.

Their encounter with the sub-collector who first received their petitions, however, revealed how social exclusion is embedded in the state as well as in society. This official, initially, reproduced relations of exclusion by advising the women to desist from applying for land belonging to 'these rich people'. He implied that the women were asking for physical reprisals and that the Chettiyars would just bribe officials to halt the land acquisition, such is the coercive and economic power this caste holds in the district. The women's counter revealed their understanding of the exclusionary politics at work. They emphasized the government's obligation to purchase the land no matter what the landowner's socio-economic status. At the same time, they 'released' the government from its obligation to protect them from any dominant caste retaliation over the land. Their arguments and persistence pushed through their petition.

Dalit women framed their petitions for housing land by manipulating their multiple identities in order to highlight those aspects they judged more likely to prompt a positive government response. Hence, women's requests for land in their names foregrounded their gender and class, rather than caste, identities. Their petitions used the women's sangams names, tied as they were to the government, and referred to their poverty and lack of livelihood security—'we are living like three families in one house'; 'we have no money to buy housing land and build ourselves another house', etc. Caste, however, found no place in their requests for 'land for living', nor any 'right to land'. As with the non-caste specific sangam names, this strategy aimed to prevent any caste bias from officials by instead evoking a discourse of government service to poor women sangam members. This was especially pertinent given the ongoing temple dispute centred on caste identity. In this dispute, the mostly dominant caste government officials supported the dominant castes over the Dalits because of bribes and caste affiliations.

The two years of official inaction in the face of constant petitioning shows the persistence socially excluded actors require in dealing with the state to secure entitlements. Women invariably described the process as follows: 'we walked so many times, worked so hard...we got too many troubles while getting this land...we did not do any demonstrations to get this land, create any problems, but officials would say each time they would give us the land, that's all.' Chitra described the hardships and patience required in the absence of socio-political influence:

> At any time we had to go and meet the government officials in different places. So late night we would come back home. Back then we had very little money, less money than now, and so we could not afford to eat outside during the day, only drink a coffee...We would be at the Collectorate by 8 a.m. and only in the afternoon would the officials actually see us.

Beyond the practical difficulties of scarce money and time, they also needed to maintain a low profile so as to not attract adverse attention to their actions. The women's apolitical savings and credit activities were low profile; they also had the advantage of physical isolation and lack of interactions with other caste villagers.

While Dalit women sought to downplay their caste identities in their petitions, a critical factor ending the paralysis in their housing land application was the allies women found among government officials. These allies were characterized both by caste affiliation and the absence of caste or political ties to the area. Sangam leaders like Chitra noted that only once they finally secured an appointment with the collector, a Dalit, to deliver their petition, did revenue officials visit Kovilur to view the proposed housing land. The women also credited the next district revenue officer, also a Dalit, with skilfully negotiating the land acquisition. He forestalled caste problems by stating the land purchase for 'government purposes' without providing further details. Meanwhile, the constraining influence of caste interrelations is apparent from two contrasting experiences women mentioned. One is the support for the women's land application by the backward caste village administrative officer without any social connections to the area. The other is the local Dalit woman panchayat vice-president, who was unwilling to take a position opposing the dominant castes and the president. Throughout this process, moreover, women gained access to information on the progress of their application thanks to the good relationships forged between the NGO director and Dalit officials. This contributed to their perseverance and to government action.

Despite their vulnerability where livelihoods were concerned, and despite caste tensions surrounding the temple, the women kept on going with the housing land struggle. They were buoyed by other, similar successes. At the same time as they were petitioning for housing land, action by Dalit women in two nearby villages had secured such entitlements. To keep them motivated, Veronnika also constantly reminded the women of the amenities they had already acquired. She also helped them to get tangible economic benefits in the form of sangam loans. Their determination could be gauged from each woman contributing around Rs 3,000 towards the struggle. Asked why they did not obtain money from their husbands, Andal replied, 'sangam is separate and family is separate'. By distinguishing between the women's public and private roles, she was referring to their attempt to construct an independent role outside of the dominant discourse that tied them to the family sphere. This role was contested by Dalit men. Further, some leaders like Chitra found their resolve strengthened by the lack of male support: '[Men] were so disparaging towards us. I then had it in my heart to succeed, that we should somehow get this land.'

Dealing with Dalit Men and Gender Norms   Chitra's statement points to a disturbance of gender power relations when women entered the political domain. Both Dalit women and men had a collective interest in acquiring housing land title. The NGO also established strategic relationships with Dalit male community leaders. Despite this, initial male reactions to the sangams were negative. They belittled the women's activities by reference to their gender 'inferiority': 'you are only women and yet you think you are going to achieve so much'; 'let us see how you are going to get the land!'; and so on. Additional cruel words from men for 'neglecting household duties, families, and children' when women returned home late after sangam work sought to remind them of their 'core' role in the family domain. Two sangam leaders, however, experienced more forcible reminders in the form of beatings and denial of food. Further, while women's travel as a group outside the village satisfied men of women's safety as well as 'protection', this freedom of movement was conditional on core gender norms remaining undisturbed.

The ways in which women dealt with these reactions expose the multiple factors determining intra-household bargaining over their political participation. These include support from other women and the NGO, and the adjustments made around gender norms to diffuse such opposition. Almost all women, for instance, accepted the double burden of engaging in productive labour for family maintenance as well as completing daily household duties, adjusting around rather than seeking to alter the gender division of labour. Women's position within their life cycle also determined their scope for sangam participation. As previously mentioned, women were helped to participate by the presence of daughters-in-law to undertake household duties. Gendered expectations that young mothers assume full-time care of their children also left these women least able to leave the village, while those with the fewest constraints had teenage or grown daughters to assume their household duties. Women's freedom thus directly correlated with an increasing work burden on daughters, thereby reiterating gender roles whereby girls help their mothers maintain family well-being (Kambhampati and Rajan 2007). Timings of sangam activities, consequently, remained fluid in order to cater to women's work and family schedules and allow sufficient time gaps between activities to lessen male opposition. This opposition decreased over time as men recognized the instrumentality of the government-affiliated sangams for gaining privileged access to state institutions, and therefore to resources.

Dalit men's opinions of the sangam work were mixed and contradictory. Though acknowledging that women brought benefits to the colony, they constantly qualified their support by claiming that the women could form sangams and act only with the men's permission and encouragement. Kathirvel (married man, 55 years) asserted, 'We can tell the women that they should remain in the house and look after the children. But we won't say this, as we understand that they are now in the sangam and need to meet sometimes.' Dalit men thus sought to reinforce gender relations of female dependence on male family heads within the new sangam institutional framework as a means of accepting these social changes. Other men disparaged the sangam's achievements as due more to the NGO director's relationship with government officials than to the efforts of the women, whom they labelled as merely following the NGO's instructions. If women were objects (and not subjects) of development intervention, men could reaffirm their dominant position within gender relations. Dalit women, by contrast, though often modest about their achievements and acknowledging Veronnika's prominent role in their struggles, nonetheless affirmed the importance of their agency. They pointed out that 'they had done all the walking', that without their actions nothing would have changed for their community.

Dalit men further sought to distinguish between issues which women and men could address. According to Chandran (married man, 60 years):

> If the women's sangams want to help others, they do so within the group only. The men will not allow the women to participate in common problems. For example, the men solved the temple problem and did not allow the women to get involved. The men said the women should do work within limits, and not try to cross those limits.

The struggles for basic amenities and housing land were deemed to lie within the realm of accepted sangam activities. They were linked to women's families as opposed to 'common problems' of the community. This attaching of women's public identities to familial roles constitutes

a subtle renegotiation and revision of rules governing the women's
conduct as individuals who did not usually engage in public life of the
community (Madhok 2007: 350). It shows how male power is dependent on the domestication of any perceived alteration to gendered roles
in order to maintain the distinction between public/male and private/
female spheres (Gedalof 1999; Haynes and Prakash 1991). What it
ignored was that women's collective action was a conscious expression of concerns and interests not only as women, wives, or mothers,
but also as members of the Dalit community (cf. Morgen 1988). By
contrast, women, as seen later through their contribution to the temple
struggle, developed views of their expanded role in the public domain
that were quite different to those men held.

**Dealing with Adverse Reactions from Dominant Castes and the
State**   Dominant castes learnt that the government had acquired 2.5
acres of *puncai*[9] land for SC colony housing only by reading about it in
the government gazette in 2002. Their reactions further enmeshed the
entitlement struggle within a web of power relations. One explanation
advanced for their opposition was their belief that this land allocation
would lend further credence to the Dalits' assertion of temple rights
and also enable them to acquire temple land title. The land allocation
would allow Dalit habitations effectively to encircle the Māriamman
temple. Most Dalit women, however, tended to associate the opposing actions of dominant castes with the temple dispute alone, rather
than connecting the two struggles. This was because the temple dispute
touched on so many fundamental questions of honour and identity,
and the inter-caste conflict was so intense. Combined with direct tactics, such as preventing Dalits' entry onto the temple land, dominant
castes also relied on their greater political connections, influence, and
economic power to try to stop the housing land title transfer. Political
leverage assumed the form of counter petitions to revenue officials, and
later to the chief minister of Tamil Nadu, meetings with whom were
aided by a Pallar man who was then a *tahsildar*. There were also, according to some Dalit women, bribes to officials.

Dominant castes' counterarguments against Dalit entitlement
reflect the connections between symbolic discourses and entitlements.
Despite the Chettiyar landowners' apparent acquiescence to the land

sale, other Chettiyars garnered support from other castes to oppose this move. They linked the dominant discourses of Dalits' 'pollution' and 'dirtiness' with preventing worship at their Aiyanar temple located behind the proposed new colony. They similarly informed the tahsildar that they would not be able to worship at their temple if the Dalits received the housing land, owing to Dalits being 'untouchable' (*thūttu*) and inauspicious to look at en route to their temple. In doing so, they appealed to the belief in social norms of impurity and karma, the idea that the Dalits' bad karma would transfer to them (Daniel 1983). The NGO director, however, happened to overhear these statements. Based on the strength of the Protection of Civil Rights Act 1955 penalizing practices of 'untouchability', she later used them to argue for criminal liability should officials accept the dominant castes' argument. Consequently, the tahsildar reassured the Dalit women during their next visit that the land acquisition would proceed.

Women responded with continued visits to the government offices in order to pursue and strengthen their case, relying on strength in numbers and continual reminders of officials' obligations to them. They switched to a more confrontational approach only when officials again started to suggest that the women settle for a less contentious plot of land in an attempt to avoid challenging power relations. Around 30 angry Dalit women entered the collector's office one day and refused to leave until they could press their demands with the collector. Women also had to contend with the government's commitment to only partial fulfilment of their right to housing, the district revenue officer granting land title but without conferring any entitlement to housing as such. By then, however, women felt emboldened to state that they would manage, by themselves, to build a hut once the land was sanctioned to them. After this official inspected the land himself, the land acquisition process was concluded, and 55 plots of land were sanctioned in 2003.

Formal versus Actual Entitlement   Dalit women actually received land title in their names only after another year, however, owing to continuing dominant caste opposition to the land acquisition. During this interval, the women interpreted the government's inaction as tacit support for the dominant castes and continued petitioning the collector on two counts required to translate formal into actual entitlement. The first was for officials to measure the land so that individual land plots

of 2.5 cents could be allotted, and second, for actual land title distribution. When they did not receive a reply to their petition, the women
resorted to clearing the land themselves. Veronnika encouraged them
by arguing, 'if both the Chettiyars and government were against us getting the land, how would we get the land by keeping quiet?' This direct
action was enough to pressurize revenue officials to measure plots for a
first set of women who immediately required land. *Taluk* officials then
sought to delay the handing over of land title deeds in order to extract
more money. In response, the women called on the village administrative officer's support to intercede on their behalf. Their actions point to
another subtle layer to entitlements analysis, between the granting of
formal entitlement and actual possession and enjoyment of an entitlement: it is the latter, and not the former, which constitutes the fulfilment of socio-economic rights.

In the absence of actual entitlement for the remaining women who
held only formal land title, Malliga's case exemplifies many women's
predicament after 2004: 'Even though we were given the land title they
did not come and measure the land, so eventually we started building this house [in the older colony]. Two years later, once this house
was half-built, they finally measured the land.' Continual petitioning
was again required, therefore, to make the government translate these
women's legal entitlement into actual land possession. Currently, 37
women have housing plots measured in the new colony, a second
land allocation being made in 2008 as a result of families multiply-
ing. Sangam members exhibited great pride in narrating how they got
plots for these women in the sangam's name, as individual applications
would have been less likely to produce positive results. The sangams
today, therefore, represent for women the collective power required to
succeed in claims on state entitlement arrangements. Around half the
women further indicated that they have a greater decision-making role
today on housing construction or renovations.

Obtaining Housing and Amenities in the New Colony   While housing landownership satisfies one requirement, the right to housing also
demands permanent houses and basic amenities of water, electricity, and roads (Committee on Economic, Social and Cultural Rights
[CESCR] 1991). Women undertook several more years of petitioning

for these under government welfare schemes, even bargaining for housing aid with panchayat election candidates. Only in 2007, by chance, did the women's petition to the collector as he inaugurated the new panchayat result in him immediately ordering the panchayat to install roads, street lights, and a water tank, along with several housing loans. Permanent housing with electricity in the new colony, however, is still pending today. The women's assessment of the reasons for this state of affairs reflects a combination of financial constraints, exclusion built into the government's housing subsidy scheme, and a non-supportive panchayat president.

Currently, the incumbent panchayat president has sanctioned only seven Dalit families the Rs 37,000 financial assistance under the Indira Awās Yojana scheme to enable rural families below the poverty line to construct or upgrade housing. Another three families have self-financed housing construction in the new colony. Dalit woman face two main hurdles. First, they are de facto excluded from this scheme due to the panchayat's stipulation of an initial Rs 20,000 down payment from potential subsidy beneficiaries. Second, the rising cost of housing materials creates a large shortfall even with the subsidy. Some women further attribute the president's unwillingness to help them to their failure to vote for him. Others cite common knowledge that this president represents Chettiyar interests and acts under their guidance in return for their electoral support. Still others assert that he is cheating them by drawing up false receipts for higher amounts on building materials. The president, on the other hand, points out how Dalit men choose to waste their money on alcohol instead of the subsidy down payment. Though this may be true, it ignores the fact that women need decent housing to keep them safe and to raise children. Over half the women cited housing as an important development in the past five years, though only half live currently in *pucca* (permanent) houses and only half in housing adequate for their family size.

Today, the sangam leaders' growing awareness of how to negotiate with political authority holders and utilize political spaces more effectively is clear from their discussions on petitioning for house electricity connections. Their dilemma is that though they wish to petition the collector directly about the government's one-bulb electricity scheme, they risk falling out of favour with the panchayat president who is likely to claim that they are giving him a bad name with higher officials. According to Indira, 'If we go elsewhere and then come back to [the president] on some other matter, then he may say that last time we went elsewhere to give petitions so this time also we should only go there and not come to him'. In other words, leaders have learnt to weigh the possibilities and risks in planning their actions, an indication of growing strategic agency.

Further Entitlement Actions and Sustainability   Another indicator of Dalit women's growing political consciousness is that they want other entitlements and freedoms. This has led to further action outside of the NGO's development agenda. The current village administrative officer observed that Kovilur Dalit women sangam members are more politically aware. They are willing to get involved in public affairs, for instance, by approaching him for information on government schemes. Two examples illustrate Dalit women's broadening engagement. They have tackled structural inequalities as workers and as Dalit community members, further countering any domestication of their collective action. In mid-2009, the sangam women, along with backward caste women, publicly protested against the lowering of MGNREGS wages. They extracted a commitment from the collector's office for decent wages in future. Earlier, in 2003, after acquiring the housing land, they asserted their political identity as 'Dalit sangams' through petitions to government officials requesting protection during the temple festival and resolution of the temple dispute. They succeeded in persuading officials to unlock the temple during the 2004 festival. Their second intervention occurred after caste fights broke out again and dominant castes filed a false police complaint against Dalit youth. Acting on Veronnika's advice, the women brought overt threats against Dalits to an end by filing a counter complaint naming the dominant caste youth who had been threatening and abusing them by caste name. Meanwhile, four women made court statements negating the dominant castes' assertion of temple ownership. This is more evidence of their breaking into hitherto male domains and substantiating their claim to an equal role in the temple struggle.

How far the women's ability to engage in autonomous action extends, however, is debatable. The limits to sangam members' participation and a degree of instability in the organizational structure of the sangam both constrain future action. Even if leaders undertake independent action in the name of the sangams, many members emphasized their continuing reliance on the NGO for information and strategy decisions before acting. Moreover, at the time of interviews, the two older sangams had become effectively dysfunctional because of a lack of accountability for sangam money pooled together for the housing land and subsidy applications. Sangam leader Chitra denies allegations of having misappropriated the money. She claims that everything was spent on the housing struggle, though illiteracy prevented her from keeping accounts. Chitra consequently feels that no one appreciates her efforts and expressed some resentment against other sangam women: 'Why should we go outside and they just go to work? If they want to get facilities, let them go outside and approach the officials.'

Compounding this situation, the women now believe the sangams' sole purpose is for savings and loans. Narrow family economic interest has taken priority over wider caste–class–gender goals. Potential contradictions in sangam purpose and NGO dependence thus arise where microcredit programmes are tied to political action through the same organizational structure and set of relationships among women (Kabeer 2005; Pattendon 2011). Veronnika, in response, feels that the sangams need to be revived by encouraging younger, more educated women in the newest sangam, which was set up in 2010. She wants to see a series of training sessions on collective action and how to secure further entitlements.

Discussion

This case study illustrates several dynamics of agency and power as they mutually shape each other, including the important role outside agencies play. By examining these dynamics and their outcomes for power relations pertaining to gender and development approaches, three key points emerge. First, social exclusion both inhibits and enables agency. Second, livelihood struggles involve interconnected issues of resources and recognition. Third, there is an analytical distinction between formal and actual entitlement, the latter including command over resources in reality. These points together highlight some of the complexities of Dalit women's lived experiences of social exclusion and livelihood entitlement struggles.

Agency, Power, and External Intervention

The results of Dalit women's collective action confirm their capacity to secure livelihood entitlements despite the interwoven constraints of institutional rules and multiple power relations. The workings of these power relations are obvious at a number of points in the women's struggle: from spatial exclusion norms driving their initial hesitation to request housing land by the road, to their negotiation of direct and indirect opposition from dominant castes, state actors, and Dalit men to their actions. All these counter the notion of women acting autonomously with free will in pursuit of their livelihood interests, uninfluenced by cross-cutting structures of power. Rather, the social construction of Dalit women's subjectivities links their agency to different levels of power exercised over and by them within a field structured by multiple, intersecting axes of difference (Sangari 1996).

It is not possible to disregard the important role external actors played in facilitating and supporting the agency of Dalit women, and their capacity to act. Mosse (1999) indicates that some external intervention may be necessary to challenge persisting dependencies and social subordination in a caste context. Dutt (2004) notes the increasing involvement of external agencies with poor rural Indian women in response to the women's difficulties in organizing autonomously. In the present case, alliances forged with Ramu Chettiyar and then the NGO, Vidiyal, have proved critical to Dalit women's obtaining livelihood entitlements and freedoms. It is pertinent to investigate the role and power of the intervener vis-à-vis interpreting Dalit women's needs, introducing alternative discourses and knowledge, and facilitating their agency.

In exploring these points, a useful contrast is provided by Vidiyal's engagement with Dalit women and Ramu Chettiyar's with Dalits (both women and men). Ramu Chettiyar assumed a benevolent patron's role within a historical context marked by patron–client relations. He used *his* socio-political power to help Dalits secure entitlements and freedoms. The cessation of adimai work highlights growing independent agency among those who interacted with Ramu Chettiyar. Dalit men, in particular, benefitted from education due to his intervention. By contrast, Vidiyal's focus on Dalit women reflects an understanding of the women as competent, if socially constrained, agents (Kabeer 1994). Veronnika enabled them to articulate their needs and take collective responsibility for getting those needs fulfilled. Political consciousness raising and capacity building provided women with access to new information and with alternative discourses. These discourses emphasized values such as equality and women's collective power and agency. The aim was to make the women conscious that they were disentitled and to give them a sense of entitlement to resources in their names. She also wanted to show them how to strategically secure entitlements. By motivating the women's transformation into political actors able to make claims on formal institutions, the NGO's work is in line with the 'empowerment approach' to development. This approach maximizes women's power to make their own choices, speak out for themselves, and to take control of their lives, in the process of which they reshape power relations (Wierenga 1994: 833).

In reality, however, historical patterns of interactions shaped by subordination influence the ways in which Dalit women understand external intervention. On the one hand, women regarded Veronnika as they would a patron. They consistently refer to how essential she was for their livelihood development and strategic decision making on collective action. Veronnika's challenge, therefore, was to transform the women's expectations that she would act on their behalf. On the other hand, the NGO catalysed the women to take ownership of the entitlement struggles, despite multiple barriers limiting their participation. Veronnika's role as an intermediary or 'broker' throughout this process was based on her social relations with both Dalit women and officials, and on her ability to bridge these two different 'worlds' and their knowledge systems (Olivier de Sardan 1995, quoted in Hilhorst 2000: 199). She could collect information and translate the process of accessing state entitlement arrangements into language understandable to the women. At the same time, she helped build the women's relationships with state actors and articulate their resource claims in ways that aligned with state discourses. These different, and at times contradictory, understandings of development interventions illustrate how the redefinition of relationships towards mutual solidarity and external facilitation needs time (Kabeer and Subrahmanian 1999). The interim period often demands brokerage roles in order to help remove institutional, structural, and personal barriers to Dalit women's participation.

We now return to the NGO's approach, which emphasizes empowerment based on transformative notions of women's agency. Gender and development approaches often incorporate an analytical distinction between practical and strategic gender interests. The former arise from women's role in the division of labour and are aimed at improving their conditions, while the latter challenge women's subordinate position within power relations (Molyneux 1985, 1998). This tends to lead towards a privileging of development approaches based on strategic interests as key to overcoming women's oppression, idealizing women's autonomy over the complexity of intersectional identities and social connectedness (Cornwall 2007). Dalit women's collective action on issues of housing and basic amenities, then, would seem to fall into the former category of practical gender interests. They did not actively and consciously analyse, and thereafter seek to destabilizes, gender relations. The effects of their actions, however, indicate shifting power relations that touch on strategic interests, though not all in progressive ways. These shifts are further examined later.

Dalit women's location within intersecting structures complicates the distinction between practical and strategic gender interests. It also makes it hard to examine gender interests apart from caste–class interests. First, the two types of gender interests cannot be viewed as completely dichotomous. Resources such as housing land located by the roadside or equal access to ūrani drinking water, for example, represented practical necessities. At the same time, they were also strategic to disturbing caste and gender power relations that excluded Dalit women from such spaces and resources. Second, waged labour by Dalit women enabled mobility and economic independence, but it also reaffirmed caste, class, and gender difference. It is, therefore, questionable to equate women's paid employment and financial autonomy with empowerment and agency (Cornwall 2007). Hence, the women negotiated around rather than confronted gender norms regarding the division of household labour, while using their relative mobility and autonomy to engage in collective action.[10]

Third, Dalit women gained strength in organization, as well as self-confidence, from dealing with more practical matters, such as separate amenities. This made them ready to tackle more problematic interests such as housing land, which touched on power relations. This suggests that any external interventions should consider the extent to which strategies that intertwine practical and strategic gender interests open up possibilities for the 'long-term' transformation of power relations (Clark *et al.* 2005; Kabeer 1994). Ascertaining this extent requires dialogue regarding women's continually evolving interests, their strengths and opportunities, taking account of their fluid socio-political contexts rather than basing them solely on analysis of their subordination (Paterson 2008).

Fourth, power relations embedded in mutually constitutive structures influence Dalit women's practical and strategic interests in ways that might, at times, contradict or complement each other (Wierenga 1994). The women considered a field of interests, some strongly tied to aspects of their identities other than gender. They chose to position themselves as working for their family and community development, and not as opponents challenging gender subordination. They showed that investing in women family members and their collective action brought results, which lessened male opposition. If they had articulated distinct gender interests instead, men would have seen them as a threat to caste and community identities. The course the women took enabled them to renegotiate their role within family and community networks. This process yielded new if divergent understandings and valuations of gender roles as women pushed at structural boundaries. Gender interests, therefore, cannot be detached from other interests generated by women's multiple identities, and other interests may become primary over gender.

Analysing Dalit women's agency, therefore, should not mean a narrow focus on transformative potential within a socially constituted self alone (Lovell 2003: 1). Nor should it mean giving automatic priority to strategic gender interests. Instead, one should understand the wider range of socio-structural factors and cross-cutting interests which shape women's ability to act and how they act. This allows for more nuanced strategies to promote effective collective action among Dalit women. These are strategies which create wider opportunities and spaces for women to manoeuvre and negotiate changes to multiple power relations. Patterns of both change and continuity, moreover, should be expected. This is clear from the subtle shifts in power relations consequent to Dalit women's actions, which can be broken down as 'power within' and power vis-à-vis their families/communities and dominant castes.

'Power Within' Meena's observation, quoted at the start of this chapter, on gaining new knowledge of 'how to speak in public' implies that the women gained the self-confidence both to speak and to operate in spaces typically 'reserved' for dominant castes and men. Woman after

woman echoed these as major personal changes. Two meanings lie behind Meena's words. One is that, despite being illiterate and female,
their voices count and do not require male mediation. The second, affirmed by Dalit male leaders, is women's expanded understanding of local socio-political issues and ways to address these issues through state
institutions. Women, thus, now perceive their knowledge and skills as
valuable potentials. They recognize how important it is to build this
power in contexts where caste and gender norms seek to control their
freedoms of knowledge and speech (cf. Mangubhai *et al.* 2009).

Sangam participation has other, expressive benefits: namely, recognition, identity re-evaluation, and enhanced personal and community
status. The respect and recognition they receive is similar in kind to
that enjoyed by Dalit women elected as representatives in local governance (Vijayalakshmi 2004). Both relate to their perceived enhanced
position, in this case as sangam members who have successfully secured
entitlements 'for their community'. Women cited as evidence the district collector's meeting them in their colony and even the researcher's
visits to the village. The suggested re-evaluation of women's roles, identities, and power then confirms the potential at the social interfaces
of entitlement struggles to generate structural discontinuities which
reshape women's subjectivities and promote their agency.

Power Relations vis-à-vis Family and Community   Just as the social
interfaces of collective action create structural discontinuities, they can
also reproduce structures, especially gender, and attendant power relations. Changes to family and intra-caste relations after women secured
housing landownership appeared minimal. Instead, they highlight
the 'percolation-cum-adaptation' of dominant caste-entwined gender norms and practices into the Dalit community (Rao 2003b: 280).
Many women sensed no increase in the respect men showed them.
They were not allowed to play a greater role in family or community
decision making. They continue to experience family life as before:
men beating them if they feel women have done anything wrong or
when they come home after drinking. Older women, in particular, still
reiterate cultural norms that insist on wifely fidelity, respect, and duties towards husbands. Moreover, women still contribute proportion-
ally larger amounts to household incomes.[11] This is noted as common

among Dalits where male domination is greater in the economic than sexual sphere (Kapadia 1995). That women are willing to concede these gender norms in order to retain their new freedoms reveals the interplay between dependence and autonomy with respect to family relations (Jackson 1999).

The focus of gender and development approaches on women's collective action to overcome gender subordination begs the question why the sangams failed to disrupt patterns of gender violence, divisions of labour, and alcoholism among men. The answer lies, partly, in which needs the women chose to make a priority. They chose those which were practically contestable and attainable (Khare 1998). Thus, the detrimental effects of regular alcohol consumption by the majority of men, both because of the drain on family income as well as the violence it causes, provoked strong reactions from women. This, however, neither translated into an expressed desire to close down the government wine shop located nearby, nor to periodically abandoning husbands to return to their natal families, as Kapadia (1995) found. Instead, women concluded that action on their part would provoke their husbands to beat them and send them out of their marital homes. Interpreting this as passive submission to gender inequalities, however, would ignore how women's choices enable them to inhabit their world (Mahmood 2001: 217). This is a world in which they may adapt their needs and preferences because they believe they lack better options (Agarwal 1997, 2003), or where the risks are otherwise too high (Kabeer 1994). Not only women's gender but also their caste and class position impacts on the types of claims that women will make on their husbands where they are tied to them in an economy of survival (Sangari 1996: 471). This is especially the case where they must confront dominant castes in order to secure entitlements. Hence, Dalit women expressed a sense of entitlement to a married life free from violence and male alcoholism even in the absence of any concrete expectation or practical remedy.

Further, notions of social connectedness and the complexity of relational ties mould Dalit women's agency and choices regarding gender interests (Cornwall 2007; Madhok 2007). Alternative discourses of gender equality or female power introduced by external intervention seek to displace a hegemonic gender discourse deeply implicated in the perpetuation of caste and community. Personal identity and sense of belonging are intimately bound to family and caste community in India.

Marriage makes a woman a full, respected member of her caste and thus a complete person (Dube 2003; Kapadia 1995). Women will not address gender interests for fear of negative repercussions and because cultural norms emphasize inviolable marriage bonds and wifely fidelity (Pant 2000). Nonetheless, women's frequent references to domestic violence, male alcoholism, and the double burden of labour highlight the fact that addressing questions of livelihood resources has made the women conscious of gender problems. It is, therefore, more likely that they will confront these problems eventually (cf. Dutt 2004).

Power Relations vis-à-vis Dominant Castes Finally, the family is not always where women are most oppressed. Dalit women's actions vis-à-vis livelihood entitlements and religious freedom show this. Their actions also affected caste power relations by further severing caste (inter)dependence in social and economic arenas. Dalit women expressed the view that separation, as opposed to integration, into village society allows them to minimize the power dominant castes exercise over their livelihoods. Meena expressed their sense of freedom from domination as: 'Nowadays the other castes would not dare to do anything as we would go to Sivagangai [to file a complaint with officials]!' Nonetheless, Dalits are still dependent on Chettiyars in three important ways: informal credit provision; Chettiyar ownership of former village common lands; and Chettiyar influence over the current Dalit panchayat president and hence, over allocation of panchayat development schemes. Caste discrimination also remains. This is evident from the caste tensions even today during the Māriamman temple festival and Dalits' concomitant exclusion from worship at the village Munniayyar temple. All this shows the fluidity and durability of hierarchical caste relations. It further challenges the idea that the solution to Dalit women's social exclusion is necessarily integration.

Exclusion and Intersectional Positioning as Enabling Agency

Caste, class, and gender structures converge to mould both the exclusion and agency of Dalit women such that certain aspects of exclusionary power relations enable agency. The social construction of gender varies across castes and classes in how it defines appropriate female behaviour and roles, and shapes experiences of exclusion and inclusion.

Consequently, Dalit women embody different principles of agency compared with Dalit men and dominant caste women (Moore 1994). They are defined in contrast to men as passive, self-sacrificing, and submissive. But they are also necessarily active in the public sphere to the extent that this supports (economically) their role in the private sphere. They are distinguished from dominant caste women as ritually 'polluted' and 'inferior', but also more socio-economically independent and mobile, and less isolated in the household (Franco *et al.* 2000; Kapadia 1995). Dalit women's relatively greater autonomy is linked to a 'non-brahminical cultural core' (Franco *et al.* 2000: 32–3). It is also linked to their caste–class status. In poorer households, economically active women are more important (Wilson 2004). Dalit women generally retain greater control over their income due to their key role in household provisioning (Kapadia 1997). This relative freedom to act, however, does not preclude Dalit women from also reproducing gender norms. They often concede decision making to their husbands in order to gain room to manoeuvre in family relations (Pant 2000).

Nonetheless, different aspects of their 'low' status and identity create opportunities for Dalit women to engage in collective action. For example, caste and gender divisions of labour underlie the collective nature of Dalit women's daily work in their households and in the agricultural fields, work that is perceived as an economic necessity rather than freedom to work (Lingam 1994; Subramaniam 2003). They also experience forms of discrimination from other caste women who either labour alongside them or command their labour. They are dependent on low-wage labour for dominant cast–class employers. All these factors create an informal organizational structure and solidarity, which facilitates their formal organization into Dalit women sangams (cf. Mies 1986). This solidarity is all the greater because they are excluded socially and economically; they have common experiences, needs, and interests.

Moreover, the enduring patron–client model of local politics and inter-caste interactions tends to constrain Dalit men much more than women. Women's interactions with men are strictly controlled, and women are excluded from the public domain. As in the past, dominant caste men gain information about Kovilur colony activities from their contacts among the Dalit men. As the housing land struggle shows, it was precisely the isolation of Dalit women that was central to their ability to form a collective identity. The fact that the women were excluded opened spaces for agency that did not rely on local political influence such as that of the panchayat president (cf. Kapadia 1997). It also partly explains why Dalit men expressed greater opposition to Dalit women forming the sangams than dominant castes with whom women had little interactions outside of labour. Segregation, which symbolized caste identity and power, also brought Dalit women closer together. In addition, physical isolation meant that women's quiet petitioning for the land did not attract the notice of the dominant castes until the government's announcement of the land acquisition.

The given discussion undermines any necessary equation of social exclusion with powerlessness and lack of agency. It also confirms the limitations of the exclusion–inclusion binary for conceptualizing fluid and complex power relations and intersecting identities (Gedalof 1999; Jackson 1999). Dalit women are located within a multiplicity of fluid power relations. An accurate analysis of their entitlement struggles will take account of these relations and how the Dalit women work with them. It will show how different situations attract different configurations of power equations which may bring to the forefront one or more axes of difference (McClintock 1995; Norris *et al.* 2010). In the case of Kovilur, both the temple and housing land struggles were primarily determined by caste power relations based on a history of caste/class-based exclusions. Gender relations were less at issue. Moreover, women responded to these power equations by choosing different discourses for different struggles. They highlighted different identities in order to secure different entitlements. Gender and class identities were to the forefront in their struggle for housing land, in order to prevent caste discrimination from officials. However, the successful temple struggle was built around caste identity; and it has promoted positive assertions of Dalit identity in other collective action. A strategy to secure multiple livelihood entitlements built on a single identity, therefore, would fail to appreciate how these identities interact and constitute each other. It would also fail to appreciate how empowerment in relation to one identity can leave women disempowered in relation to other identities (Ferguson 2004).

Redistribution, Recognition, and Religion

Further examination also falls on the interconnections between struggles over entitlements and struggles over identity. These struggles encompass material and symbolic values and effects. The meanings women attach to housing land already point beyond the materiality of survival or livelihood needs to symbolic issues of identity and dignity. Additionally, the women viewed the temple struggle, and the part they played in it, as vital steps in attaining a positive collective identity as Dalits. The effects were to mark caste as the master category. It explained their housing-related exclusion and motivated the housing land struggle. This suggests the importance, and sometimes overriding influence, of identity-related issues in determining Dalit women's livelihood priorities and interests. Issues of identity strengthened their resolve to secure entitlements. The reasoning behind this assertion is the mutually reinforcing nature of socio-cultural and political–economic exclusions. This causes entitlement deprivation to be a question of both resources and power exercised in multiple, overlapping arenas, including the cultural.[12]

The process of constituting a new collective identity is termed a political strategy of recognition. It encompasses actions directed against the social subordination caused by non-recognition or misrecognition of identity by other social groups (Fraser 2000). Such subordination establishes diminished needs and rights for Dalits vis-à-vis other castes. It reduces their agency to make claims on resources, and hinders them from seizing economic and political opportunities. At the same time, because dominant castes hold the power to both define and ascribe certain characteristics to the identities of excluded Dalit women, these women place great value on being treated with equal dignity (Taylor 1992). While the creation of a dignified collective identity can be considered as an end in itself, collective action is also instrumental in forging an oppositional consciousness, organization, and solidarity. Positive identification processes are tied to building a sense of entitlement. They delink Dalit and gender identities from norms of disentitlement. Positive identification and accompanying alternative discourses enable sangam participation based on equal dignity, respect, and entitlement. They form a crucial precondition for the effective assertion of rights to resources and for achieving material goals of equal protection and opportunities (Young 1997: 157).

Attention is thereby drawn to how Kovilur Dalits responded socially and politically to being thought inferior. They used symbolic resources to create an identity as far removed as possible from that of service and

dependency on dominant castes (Mosse 1999). Apart from the struggle
for housing land, the Māriamman temple struggle reveals how religion
can provide a strong basis for alternative, more positive articulations of
caste identity and status for Dalits. As mentioned previously, local politics in Tamil Nadu is intertwined with religious authority and symbolic
power with respect to religious institutions and festivals. The separation of religion and rituals from politics, therefore, 'is inappropriate at
the level of ideological (or cultural) analysis of Indian social thought'
(Dirks 1990: 60). Consequently, temples become important sites for
Dalits to contest their ascribed, degraded identities, and to destabilize
power relations. Collective action is an important factor in winning
entitlements, and collective action also creates a positive collective
identity, which itself contests socio-cultural exclusion. All this argues
for the recognition that economic change cannot be divorced from
socio-cultural change. Economic change is accompanied by change that
addresses power, prejudices, and discrimination based on reconstituting
and articulating alternative identities.

Political versus Moral–Cultural Economy, Entitlements, and Equality

Kovilur Dalit women's struggles introduce one last complication to
the study of entitlement acquisition processes. This is the relationship
between having protected access to resources and the power to make
a decision about resource use. Both affect actual resource shares, and
hence feelings of self-worth, social worth, and value. They must be
tackled in order to challenge enduring structural inequalities (Papanek
1990). Resources are controlled in many, distinct ways. Dalit men control housing land use and inheritance, but socio-cultural norms influence how women think about such male control. Dalit women talked
about the latter a great deal. It raises the question of intra-household
power relations. The household is viewed as a locus of competing interests, rights, obligations, and resources, where household members are
often involved in bargaining, negotiation, and possibly, even conflict
(Moore 1994: 87). Gender equality here means that Dalit women are
able to own and control property, just like men. However, securing
housing land entitlements in Dalit women's names, commonly defined
as a strategic gender need, arguably cannot be interpreted—as Moser
(1993) does—as leading only to gender equality. Their refusal to pass

that land to their daughters, then, should not be understood as merely negating that equality. Their motivations, desires, and goals (Madhok 2007; Mahmood 2001) also need to be examined to understand the reasons behind women's decisions on land control.

Initially, Dalit women wanted to fight for housing land, but did not suggest putting it in their own names. This lack of desire correlates to customary norms dictating that family property is acquired in men's names and passed on to sons, imputing different needs for women (or lack thereof concerning property) and for men (Papanek 1990). Hence, men held all the titles to the old colony housing land. Participation in the sangams, however, introduced the women to alternative discourses in which property ownership was linked to enhancing their security of life by providing a material base. This would accord them a higher position in the community and, therefore, ensure greater respect from husbands. This discourse shifted perceptions of women as asset-less dependents, to women as entitlement holders (Kabeer 1994).

Women's ability to adapt this discourse to their worldview, and in the process alter that worldview to incorporate the need for property (Hilhorst 2000), constitutes an important aspect of their agency. Indira's observations evidence this:

> Suppose my husband tells me to leave this house, where can I go? My father's house is given to my brother. That is the norm. So I will be standing alone. Because of this, Veronnika suggested that we should have the land title in our names. Beforehand, we women did not have knowledge to change such norms, but now we do and so we did like this.

Her statement vitally links housing land, domestic violence, and physical security. It also shows the strength of alternative discourses shaped around women's concerns about security. They then linked their collective efforts (without men) to secure the land with a sense of entitlement to put it in their own names. In their words, it became natural to put land title in their names because 'only we went to great difficulties to get this land', suggesting enhanced feelings of self-worth. These feelings were reinforced when, eventually, they received land title in their names.

Surprisingly, Dalit women's claim to the land title went uncontested by the men in their families. An explanation lies in the accord between women's decisions on housing land inheritance and patrilineal customary practices. That is, housing land title would pass to their sons, with women holding usufruct rights until sons inherited. When questioned why an understanding that land title was linked to their security did not translate into their wanting to pass this land onto their daughters to enjoy the same security, a typical dismissal of this suggestion went as follows:

Will you divide your property among your children equally?

Why should I give property to my daughters? In their in-laws' houses let them give them property. This land goes to my son.

But we have a law prescribing equal property for men and women?

No, I won't do like that. See, I have only one son. I will spend money for my daughters' marriages, but the property is for my son alone. (Chitra)

Provisioning for children's welfare, therefore, rests on understandings of fairness—dowry for daughters and property for sons—that obviate gender equality in inheritance. This adds another important point into the debate over inheritance laws and dowry, the latter widely practised despite its legal prohibition and noted as a key structural expression of women's subordination (Kabeer 1994).

That Dalit women did not perceive it necessary to transform gender inequalities with respect to property rights suggests either that they did not view them as inequalities or that they consented to these inequalities. Investigation into cultural norms of patrilineal property inheritance and material factors, however, provides a rationale for their choice to reproduce such norms. Given the lack of social security provisioning in India, informal systems operate wherein property passes to sons in order to create a relationship of obligation between parents and the oldest son who will look after his parents in their old age. Daughters, by contrast, receive dowry from their parents as a form of pre-mortem inheritance and thereafter rely on their marital family to provide for them. So long as women lack economic security and continue to depend on male family members, this practice ensures that the future livelihoods of women will be secure and so, arguably, represents their interests (Agarwal 1994a: 434–5). Agency and empowerment, therefore, cannot be reduced to evidence of women understanding their self-interests as gender equality in entitlements. External or material constraints may stop them from demanding such equality (Agarwal 1994a; Kabeer 1999, 2001). Development strategies that seek to achieve gender equality in property ownership, therefore, should not be confined to fighting to put property in women's names. They must necessarily incorporate a wider strategy to tackle cultural beliefs and practices and the underlying 'gendered scripts about affection, responsibility and dependence' (Basu 2000: 195) that naturalize such inequality.

***

This chapter looked at a successful struggle by Dalit women to secure housing land entitlements. The case study sheds light on Dalit women's collective agency and how power operates in their local context, providing spaces for agency despite and because of social exclusion. Specifically, it reveals differing yet interconnected aspects of their caste, class, and gender identities and positioning within multiple power relations. These shape their perceptions of livelihood needs, entitlements, and agency. They also are used by the women to shape strategies to secure entitlements. These women's intersectional identities mean that their lives cannot be reduced to simple equations. Social exclusion does not equal a lack of agency. Exclusion is not a problem to which inclusion is the simple solution. Moreover, Dalit women's agency cannot be equated with solely promoting gender equality. Instead, these women manoeuvre around exclusion and power relations. Some relations change; some stay the same. Consequently, the process of dislodging gender inequalities in property rights does not end with securing property in women's names. Furthermore, it is important to integrate collective identity struggles, and Dalit women's needs for dignity and status, into livelihood development strategies. The links between the struggles for housing land and for religious freedoms highlight this fact.

Development interventions by external agents emerge as catalytic to entitlement struggles. They introduce new discourses for women to incorporate into and reinterpret their understandings on entitlements and agency. They further develop the political consciousness and capacities of women to engage in collective action to secure livelihood entitlements. At the same time, external interventions promote new relationships of power and new structures for women to negotiate, which throws up issues of autonomy and accountability.

The NGO's development approaches, when compared to gender and development approaches, show how the latter cater to Dalit women's intersectional interests to a limited extent. This is particularly the case where excluded women's circumstances foreground caste over gender interests. These points are further illustrated in the next chapter by an ongoing struggle for agricultural land entitlement in a semi-feudal context. This involves the same NGO but a different socio-historical set of livelihood conditions.

Notes

1. While commonly referred to as Chakkiliyars in the village, most Dalit movement leaders consider this name to have negative connotations; hence, the more respectful name, 'Arunthathiyar', is used instead.

2. Traditionally, Dalit colonies in Tamil Nadu have been located towards the east and/or on lower or least desirable lands, segregated from the main section of village. This ensured that the wind or other elements did not flow from their colonies to 'pollute' the other castes living in the main village.

3. Pallars were permanent residents undertaking farm labour (*pannaiyāls*) and traditional services such as burying the dead. Nesavukkara Paraiyars, one of the three subgroups of Paraiyars who were migrant (as opposed to resident) villagers, were seasonal (non-permanent) farm labourers (*padiyāls*) for several landlords in addition to performing traditional services such as beating drums during festivals. Different rights accrued to them in comparison with permanent workers. Arunthathiyars, meanwhile, undertook all cleaning works in the village and for functions.

4. For example, Dalits should not enter dominant caste houses nor wear shoes on dominant caste streets; women were prohibited from covering their breasts in public; women had to draw water in a palm leaf basket while standing away from the ūrani; Dalits received water from coconut shells; they should not be educated; and so on.

5. Initially, access to education at the village primary school was restricted to the 'highest' castes—the Chettiyars and Vellālars—then later the Agamudaiyars, and then, the other 'lower-middle' castes. It was only around 20 years after the school started that Dalit children first gained access to education.

6. A similar position prevails today: as mentioned earlier, Dalit women spend six months per year labouring in the rice paddy fields; the agricultural off-season sees them engage in either brick kiln labour or MGNREGS work and, less commonly, in other wage labour work in the area. Female education levels, however, are improving. Survey results showed that mainly

young Dalit women aged below 30 years have accessed education beyond Standard 5 and can claim literacy, while many girls today complete at least Standard 10 if not all 12 years of schooling.

7. Māriamman is commonly known in Tamil Nadu as a village deity (*grāma-deivam*) who protects the village against any evil like diseases, accidents, and deaths.

8. Sudhakar Rao (2001) notes, and Kovilur Dalit women's words confirm, that whichever Dalit caste is closest to the dominant castes holding political and economic power in the village is deemed the 'highest' among the Dalits.

9. Puncai land is dry land that is not irrigated by a natural water tank.

10. Similar arguments have been propounded by Black feminists regarding Black women's employment (White 2003).

11. Data on male and female income contributions to the household do not take into account two points: one, the gender disparity in wages paid; and second is that most Dalit men contribute only around one-half to two-thirds of their income to their families at their discretion, retaining the rest for personal use.

12. Rege (2000) specifically rejects this dichotomization of the material and the cultural when it comes to explaining caste-based patriarchies, pointing to endogamy as structuring and reproducing the unequal distribution of resources.

4

ONGOING STRUGGLE FOR LAND ENTITLEMENT
Vettriyur Village

Women need to have property. Land in women's names gives them security, as their husbands cannot send them away. It also enables access to many government schemes, loans, etc., so we will be less dependent on men for everything...My parents gave me 1 acre of land and so I get more respect from my husband.

Santhanamary, Dalit woman activist

This chapter investigates an ongoing struggle by Dalit women to acquire legal title to agricultural land in Sivagangai district. Land entitlement, especially *nancai* (*kanmāi* [tank]-irrigated) land, correlates with wealth, power, and social status in rural India (Mosse 2003b: 152). Consequently, socio-economic inequalities have been structured along the lines of landownership, with coercive power or religious sanctions traditionally legitimizing land rights (Osmani 1988). As a result, 'low'-caste Dalits have been excluded from landownership[1] and relegated to supplying the bulk of labour power in agricultural production. Those Dalits with small and marginal landholdings, moreover, fight to hold onto their lands today. New economic policies under globalization emphasize a shift towards the consolidation of agricultural land, leasing of land for corporate farming and production, and a gearing down of land reforms as the government withdraws from intervention in the land market. All this, coupled with agricultural stagnation and young men shifting to urban areas in search of work, has serious implications for Dalits' access to land, with a knock-on effect for their livelihoods in rural areas (Teltumbde 1999). Nonetheless, for many Dalit women, agriculture, and therefore agricultural land, remains an important livelihood option given their lesser mobility for work outside their village locales and gendered role in the household.

Putting arable land in the hands of Dalit women who traditionally do not own property is seen as vital to ensuring their economic well-being, social status, and empowerment (Agarwal 1994a, 1994b). Female asset ownership also has knock-on effects for improving children's access to education and health care (Strauss and Beegle 1996). As such, landownership has the potential to transform gender inequalities in family life as well as caste inequalities in wider society. These implications for power relations make land a much contested issue in India. A village administrative officer in Sivagangai district pointed to land and sociopolitical domination as key flashpoints for conflicts in the area, while a number of studies (for example, Irudayam *et al.* 2006; McDougal 2007; Sakshi Human Rights Watch 2007) highlight land disputes as a primary cause of violence or socio-economic sanctions against Dalits.

This chapter focuses on the dynamics of interactions between formal and informal institutions, which produce competing notions of rights, entitlements, and obligations. It first places the Vettriyur women's struggle to secure land entitlements within a socio-political context where two parallel systems of governance operate. One is the governance of the Indian state; the other, the system of traditional governance called the *nādu*. In this context of interacting governance systems, the chapter examines three factors leading the women to actively claim land title: self-organization to cultivate the government land in question; non-governmental organization (NGO) intervention targeting Dalit women; and opposition from multiple state and non-state actors to their claim. This is a land struggle that started in the 1970s, that sparked Dalit women's collective action from 2005, and that continues today. The chapter then analyses the interacting influence of formal state and informal nādu institutions on Dalit women's agency. In particular, it looks at patronage relations and structural inequalities embedded in the informal institutions, which create distinct strategic pathways for the women to secure land entitlements. These pathways also enable them to delink further from informal institutions. This case also highlights the importance of external brokerage and of state institutions effectively enforcing formal rules. The chapter concludes with an analysis of organizational and collective action strategies in an adverse environment. This analysis sheds light on how tactics are chosen when people navigate multiple power relations in exercising agency.

The Context: Change and Continuity in Informal Nādu Institutions

Travelling to Vettriyur village, located 15 km away from Devakottai town, requires planning and patience. Only five government buses ply the route between the town and the nearest bus stop, by Vilapatti village, each day, with the last bus leaving the town at 6 p.m. If a person travels during the peak summer time or marketing days, the bus is packed and it becomes a meeting place to exchange information across villages. From the bus stop, a dirt road weaves past Vilapatti village to Vettriyur village, which is home to 19 Hindu Dalit (SC Pallar) families. Vettriyur consists of clusters of houses scattered between agricultural fields. It is surrounded by two other Dalit (Pallar) villages, Mannur and Aruppur, and Vilapatti village, where backward caste Agamudaiyar families live. These four villages reflect the caste demographics of the panchayat: Dalits form the largest population—around 75 per cent—followed by backward caste Agamudaiyars and Kallars, commonly called Mukkulathors.[2] In comparison with its neighbouring villages, Vettriyur is the least economically developed, with an average of 1 acre of nancai land (*vayalkādu* land) owned per family. Dalits in both Aruppur and Mannur villages own slightly larger tracts of land, while most Agamudaiyars in Vilapatti village operate larger landholdings of up to 20 acres. At the farthest end of the village, beyond their Munisvaram temple and adjacent to their small kanmāi, lies the *kollakādu* land (literally, rocky land, rain-irrigated dry land) that they have been struggling to acquire legally since the 1970s. Daily life, and indeed many conversations, revolve primarily around their families and their land for the Vettriyur women, the significance of the latter being laid out later.

A number of socio-historical features of the region bear on the Vettriyur Dalits' land struggle and the meanings Dalit women attach to arable land. These features are all connected to the nādu system of traditional governance. Vettriyur is one of 32½ villages comprising Muthu nādu,[3] a micro-region where socio-economic interactions revolved around production on a tract of cultivable land located by a reliable water source (Subbarayalu 1973, in Stein 1994: 92–5). Functioning as 'states within a state', Kallar or Maravar caste *ambalams* (chieftains), all men, had the power to adjudicate over all disputes within the nādu. They also had the power to maintain temple and common property revenue accounts, intervene in property transactions (Viswanathan 2003), and control irrigation water distribution from the main kanmāi (Mosse 2003b). They further reinforced their authority through the production of symbolic capital in religious rituals (Ludden 1989: 40) backed by coercive force.[4] Land and socio-political status were intimately connected in rural Tamil Nadu. Territory was linked with political identity, and castes were dependent on one another in agrarian relations which centred on a dominant landowning caste (Ludden 1989). Government officials, moreover, perpetuated these relations by 'adjusting' with the ambalams, especially in allowing them to retain control over nādu resources. Consequently, the nādu system continued to safeguard, according to local social activist Namasivaiyam, '*jāti ādhikkam* (caste domination), *jāti irukkam* (caste control), and *jāti dharma* (caste order)' within the broader state governance framework that later developed.

A history of change to and continuity of nādu institutions establishes the terrain on which Dalit women struggle for land entitlements today. Historically, Vettriyur Dalits were permanent farm labourers (*pannaiyāl*) attached to dominant caste farms in perpetual and hereditary bondage (Kumar 1992: 42). In exchange, they were assured subsistence and allowed to sharecrop some land. A combination of post-independence interventions by state and non-state actors, however, divested the Muthu nādu ambalam of much of his authority; it also unravelled caste interdependence. Inclusion in education led to Vettriyur Dalits wanting the independence to make a living, and in the 1960s, they successfully petitioned for nancai land title under the state's zamindari abolition law.[5] Later, external interventions by the social organization PALMERA and the then Communist Party of India fostered political consciousness based on caste–class identities. Dalits, consequently, established self-governance[6] and contested their social (caste–class) and economic subordination. Gender inequalities were ignored, however. Land title and village governance fell into male hands and women suffered from lesser access to education. Additionally, more men than women have lost their jobs in the agricultural modernization of the past 15 years[7] (Krishna 2007; Mies 1986). While caste inter-dependence diminished as men moved out into non-farm or urban-based occupations, the gender division of labour ensured that women did more unpaid work inside and outside the home (cf. Franco et al. 2000). All these changes ensured that Muthu nādu ceased to exist as an autonomous, integrated production and governance unit.

At the same time, power relations embedded in resilient and endur-ing nādu institutional rules or 'nādu discipline' (nāttu kattupādu) con-tinue to bear upon Vettriyur Dalits' livelihoods and the entitlements they receive. This is on account of three interconnecting factors. First, Kallars and Agamudaiyars circumvented land reform laws[8] to secure ownership of large tracts of arable land. These two castes' consequent control over the labour market in this agricultural region renders many marginal Dalit landowners economically dependent on them for supplementary labour work. Second, in contrast with Kallar villages, which have good transport links, Vettriyur village is isolated and there-fore, the women cannot access new livelihood opportunities easily. Dalit women, poorly educated,[9] immobile, and burdened by domestic work, are isolated in a rural area without any industry. They have little choice but to work in the agricultural sector. Land thus remains central to Dalit women's livelihood strategies, as there are few other ways of making a living.

Third, the intertwining of formal (state) and informal (nādu) sys-tems of governance preserves the socio-political power of the informal system. At the time of the interviews, one of the powerful Kallar nādu ambalams was also a Member of the Legislative Assembly (MLA). This position has been filled by Kallars for most of the period since independence. The formal local governance system also links together over 100 villages of Muthu nādu and neighbouring nādus, includ-ing the MLA's nādu, to form one panchayat union. This enables the ambalam to exercise considerable decision-making power over pan-chayat nominations. He also exercises power over voting preferences in all elections, development works, and inter-village disputes in that locality. Additionally, the hierarchy within state institutions allows the MLA considerable sway over local officials, most of whom belong to dominant castes. According to a Dalit woman from his nādu, without the MLA's permission nothing can be done in the villages.

Finally, landownership gains multiple social and economic meanings in a nādu context; it has material and symbolic value in power relations. In an agrarian economy, land provides secure livelihoods, as well as economic independence and freedom (Agarwal 2003). The higher social status accorded to landowners, moreover, endows them with dignity, recognition, and respect (Satya Babu Bose 2007). This also promotes children's welfare: good marriages for daughters are more likely; and propertied sons enjoy a higher status, too. The fluidity of these meanings, however, is clear. For example, Dalit male youths today exhibit more interest in non-farm occupations. This represents the delinking of caste from traditional occupations and from aspirations for higher-class status. Nonetheless, for most women, values of freedom, security, dignity, identity, and status make landownership their priority.

Collective Agency and the Politics of Securing Entitlements

Motivating Action: Entitlement, Opposition, and Patronage Politics

In contrast to Kovilur village (Chapter 3), Vettriyur Dalit women's sense of entitlement to the kollakādu land emerged before they were mobilized into sangams by the local NGO, Vidiyal. Around 40 years ago, when Dalits established their homes and started cultivating their own lands, they encountered flooding during the monsoon caused by the overflowing Vilapatti kanmāi used to irrigate neighbouring Vilapatti fields. The Vilapatti Agamudaiyars' better socio-political connections enabled them to block government action on the Dalit men's petitions for a water sluice (sarukkai) to stop this overflow automatically. Instead, in the mid-1970s, officials offered the Dalits the kollakādu land on which to relocate their houses, thereby choosing to reproduce caste exclusion of Dalits. Conflicting interests, however, prevented the relocation. Uma (married woman, 49 years) explains it thus: 'At the time our idea was that since we had come to this village and built our houses on our land, we should remain here. It is difficult to start again and we would need money to build new houses.' Dalit men's in-fighting over the number of land allotments also contributed to the decision. Instead, the eventual solution came from Dalit women, who persuaded the then sympathetic village administrative officer to build a water sluice. The outcome was that, even though they did not move to the kollakādu land, the women believed they had a moral claim on it because the government had allotted it to them in the 1970s.

Over the following 25 years, there were many examples of the contradictory roles that state actors can play in altering relations of exclusion. In 1977, the deputy tahsildar responded positively to the Dalits' petition to change the kollakādu land classification from *mēchal poramboke* (government grazing) land to cultivable land allotted to their families. His written reply stated that the land reclassification was in process. Despite Dalit men's periodic petitions thereafter, institutional barriers contributed to government inaction. An example of such a barrier was the collector's letter in English, which minimally educated Dalits could not read and act upon. Then, in 2000, through the socio-political influence of the Vilapatti Agamudaiyars, forest officials came to measure the kollakādu land for potential annexation to the adjoining forest lands. The Agamudaiyars' ostensible aim was to prevent Dalits from cultivating the land and thereby potentially drawing water from Vilapatti kanmāi that was meant for their fields. The Dalits, however, responded to this threat by persuading the forest officials to drop their plans. They then divided this land bordering Vettriyur and Aruppur villages, with Vettriyur Dalits claiming 40 acres of the total 106 acres for cultivation. When they pursued legal title to the land, they expected to be treated fairly by officials because these officials had treated Vilapatti and Aruppur villagers fairly. Those villagers had received title for their government poramboke (common) lands after proving that they had been cultivating them for years.

Meanwhile, the complex configuration of power relations in an agrarian, nādu context showed itself in the direct and indirect opposition by Agamudaiyars from Vilapatti village as well as in the opposition of Dalits from Mannur village. When the Vettriyur Dalits found out what lay behind the opposition, they were spurred on in their struggle. According to the sangam leaders, Agamudaiyars' opposition arose because they did not want to lose their (Dalit) agricultural labour force and thereby further loosen patron–client ties. In their words, 'The [Kallars and Agamudaiyars] never allow the Dalits to stand up in this area. If any Dalit is progressive in nature, they will even murder them.' Vettriyur was already viewed as a fairly independent Dalit village due to its historical ties with the Communist Party, which Vettriyur Dalits assert made the neighbouring nādu ambalam/MLA determined to suppress their rights. The Agamudaiyars also used the land issue to encourage division among the Dalits in this Dalit-majority panchayat. They did so by supporting two Mannur Dalit families who staked a claim to the kollakādu land based on their ownership of land within Vettriyur village and their payment of tax for the Vettriyur temple festival. After Vettriyur Dalits counter-reasoned that claims to village land were customarily based on residence, the dynamics of caste patronage became clear. Mannur Dalits drew upon their clientelist relationship with Kallar and Agamudaiyar castes, which came about because the Mannur Dalits worked on the MLA's lands, when they turned to Vilapatti Agamudaiyars for help.

A joint harassment campaign by Vilapatti Agamudaiyars and Mannur Dalits followed from 2005. This involved threatening and physically attempting to stop Vettriyur Dalits from cultivating the land, along with making complaints to the police, revenue officials, and nādu ambalam/MLA. They alleged that cultivation of the government poramboke land by Vettriyur Dalits prevented its use for cattle grazing and also diverted water from Vilapatti kanmāi. Police and revenue officials responded by issuing warnings to Vettriyur Dalits to desist from cultivation there. Dalit men, led by village elder Rengam (married man, 60 years), countered with petitions to higher government officials pleading that they had been entitled to cultivate the land for several years. Patronage relations between the MLA and their opponents became apparent when the MLA proposed an unacceptable solution, namely, to apportion Mannur Dalit villagers some land. Ponni (married woman, 50 years) further noted, 'If Vilapatti [Agamudaiyars] have any problem, immediately the MLA will ask them about it, but he will not inquire into any problem in our village.' The current Agamudaiyar panchayat president confirmed her point: 'the MLA is like a relative to us; we just tell him our problems, no need to write out petitions'. The effect, therefore, was to create an impasse over the land, with Dalits continuing to defy state actors out of a conviction of the legitimacy of their claim in ensuring a decent livelihood.

External Intervention: Constructing Collective Identity and Agency

The emergence of Dalit women's sangams and their collective action needs to be located amidst the intertwined power relations that obtained between Agamudaiyars and other Dalits, and between state and nādu institutional actors. It was in this tense environment, where women already had a sense of entitlement to the land, that local NGO Vidiyal began organizing the sangams. What the women lacked, and the sangams provided, was space to forge a collective identity as Dalit women who were capable of exercising agency to intervene in political processes. An analysis of how they and others interpreted their actions highlights the contrast between the spaces and tactics Dalit men and women were able to employ, given their different structural locations.

Vidiyal first entered Vettriyur village in 2005. Its Director, Veronnika, already knew about the kollakādu land struggle through work connections in the area and was aware of the structural implications of Dalits' asserting land rights in the nādu region. The NGO staff explained that the sangams were designed to gain basic livelihood entitlements for women, as well as to provide them with savings and loans. In that very first meeting, the Dalit women asked for guidance and support regarding their disputed land claim. Conflict, therefore, brought the women together around the common interest of securing land entitlement. Some women, like Valli (married woman, 48 years), were thus galvanized to contribute more to village life: 'Women and men were doing many things for the village. If anything happened here, however, people would call my husband to help but no one would call me. So I also wanted to join the sangam to do something for our village.' At the same time, as she contrasted their livelihood status before and after cultivating the kollakādu land, Asha (married woman, 40 years) acknowledged that their motivation to engage in the land struggle was so powerful because they were so dependent on that land for their livelihood.

With land title fixed as the sangams' main goal, the women had to be motivated to act together to fight Dalit men's active exclusion of women from previous petitioning efforts. Priya (married woman, 45 years) recalls, '[Dalit men] would tell us that as we did not know anything, we should not come with them to meet officials...So before 2005, we did not even know where Sivagangai (district headquarters) was, let alone how to meet officials to give petitions.' The NGO's strategy, as in Kovilur village, was based on introducing an alternative discourse of women's collective power outside the family domain. As Devi (married woman, 55 years) put it: '[The NGO staff] explained how we women only stayed in our homes and did not talk to officials, but now we had to stand and talk now, to come forward and bravely fight for the land...that our children should not remain as we were. So only we moved out of our homes.' Women's growing realisation after several meetings that they did not need to remain as they were, highlights the NGO's key role in providing a space for women to anal-yse their situation and become discontented. Discursive consciousness became political consciousness: 'we can solve problems only by com-ing together to help each other' (Uma). Women like Nalini (married woman, 35 years) came to recognize: 'By being part of the sangam, we get awareness. We get to know about our society, coming outside (our homes) and being as a group, and are part of the sangam for things to happen.'

Part of the success of the NGO's discourse was that it touched on a central concern of women, namely, protection or security (*pādukāpu*). This meant security of livelihood as well as the physical and social pro-tection that collective action afforded. For Devi, 'Sangam is not only for economic development, but for our security and livelihood. One woman alone cannot achieve our struggles, but if we come together as a group we can do so. We also get courage when we all go together to petition the government.' Valli added, 'We have security in the sangams because if anything happens to me, then other women will come and support me.' This also gave them greater courage to continue cultivat-ing the kollakādu land despite opposition, and to question officials who visited their village. Further strengthening this feeling was their par-ticipation in the district-level Dalit women's movement promoted by Vidiyal. This movement provided them with wider solidarity links and with more information. Priorities of livelihood and physical security thus underlay many women's decisions to come together as one, and later two, sangams.

Aside from their status as a separate village, as in Kovilur, the Vettriyur sangams drew upon existing networks of caste, kinship, and labour relations in forging a collective identity. Their collective identity also incorporated the fact that most women described themselves as the primary breadwinners of their families. They generally undertook more days of paid and unpaid (cultivation) work than men and spent their entire income on family maintenance. By contrast, almost all men retained between a third and all of their incomes for private use, including their income from paddy sales, and were not accountable to

their wives for how they spend their money. Devi voiced a frequently
heard assertion:

> If men are not giving us money, what can we do? We pay for the large
> expense of maintaining our families and seeing our children educated...
> they won't give a single *paisa* to us for our children or the household...
> If we ask for money or for men to take care of our fields, they refuse,
> saying, 'you take care of the fields, earn and take care of yourself'. There
> is only a *thāli* [marriage thread] around our necks to show our relation-
> ship!

Dalit women saw themselves as different from men because women
had to look after their families. This, coupled with the promise of greater economic security through sangam participation and social accountability through group monitoring of savings and meeting attendance
(see Kabeer 1994), supported and reinforced their move to create a
separate identity outside community and village.

Dalit women were further encouraged to collectively organize
because they perceived themselves as relatively independent of men
due to their greater economic contribution to the family. This was true
even if men still exercised their prerogative in decision making involving larger assets or expenditures. The women, therefore, argued that
greater space exists for them to take on new roles and identities which
promote family welfare. Priya indicated shifting gender norms:

> Ten years ago what you said—that women's work is only in the village
> and not to go outside—might have been true, but now we look after
> our houses, work as coolies and go to the police stations. If we only do
> kitchen and labour work, what will be the future of our children? Will
> our men look after all this like us?

A similar conclusion can be drawn from the women framing their
autonomy in contrast to that of Vilapatti Agamudaiyar women. Devi
noted that because Vilapatti men primarily provide for their families,
'all the power is with men and they rule the household, unlike in our
village'. In other words, greater autonomy enabled Dalit women to
participate in the sangams without requiring their men's sanction or
guidance.

Capacity training further supported the NGO discourse of women's
collective power and agency by building upon their interests and
autonomy with knowledge of strategic action. Constraints on both

sides, however, affected both the scope of the training and its outcomes. Vidiyal had the money to give only a few sangam members limited training in forms of political action, government laws, and schemes. The women also had waged and household work to do, which limited the time they could spend in training. To work around these limitations, Vidiyal strengthened political consciousness among Vettriyur sangam members by organizing public protests along with other Dalit women to demand title to government poramboke lands Dalits have cultivated for years. Knowledge of how to frame petitions to officials, and of when and to whom to give them, however, remains minimal. Several women cited functional illiteracy[10] as hindering their full understanding and participation, despite opinions to the contrary by the three illiterate or barely literate sangam leaders. Leaders like Uma instead noted the empowering effects of attending the district-level Dalit women's movement meetings and additional training sessions to develop their socio-political awareness and knowledge of their rights and political strategies: 'Beforehand, we were always afraid of the police, in case they suddenly came and arrested us for any demonstration. Now after joining the movement, we know for what purpose the police will come and arrest us, and also how to talk to the police. We are also able to question the police.' Consequently, hierarchies at sangam meetings, in terms of who speaks, the weight given to opinions, and the decision making, emerge because of differences in knowledge acquired during training, personal characteristics (such as self-confidence), and age. Sangam leaders, as well as older women, tend to head such hierarchies.

These factors also produce significant divergence of views among the women, especially regarding the role of NGO Director, Veronnika. Most sangam members rely heavily on Veronnika to help them when they deal with the government and to tell them what to do in general. They are functionally illiterate and have minimal knowledge of strategies. In particular, as mentioned in the previous chapter, her development brokerage role enables her to ascertain feasible tactics and navigate women through the complicated bureaucratic process of changing land classification. Decision making, therefore, is often preceded by informal discussions between Veronnika and the sangam leaders, before women collectively discuss and decide upon the suggested actions. Mayil (married woman, 33 years) voiced the need for external guidance to avoid the humiliation of displaying ignorance in government offices.

More educated sangam members, however, preferred to stress their growing independence. Nalini (Standard 8 educated) indicated how Veronnika's role had changed over time: from writing their first petitions and accompanying them to the collector's office, she now, often, merely specifies the petition contents for Nalini and Aarthi (who is 24, and the only female college graduate) to write. She also confines herself to telling them which officials to meet.

Nalini's comment sets up a distinction between these sangams and those in Kovilur village. Some Vettriyur women exhibit stronger political consciousness and confidence to take action to get what they want. This can be explained by the presence of a few educated younger women and long-term conflict over entitlements. Another important reason is Vettriyur Dalits' greater socio-economic independence. They know how to put their subordination into words; this is a knowledge gained by years of political action as a labouring class–caste. In Kovilur, historical changes occurred through the presence of a dominant caste patron. In Vettriyur, however, previous external interventions had organized Dalit women and men to undertake political action to change their situation. This also explained why Vidiyal's interventions concentrated more on gender power than on caste, because a positive caste–class identity had already been crystallized.

Collective Action Strategies and Outcomes

The sangams took diverse actions in response to the networks of obstacles and facilitations encountered on the way to securing land entitlements. In particular, Dalit women had to counter multiple strategies that dominant caste nādu power holders deployed to preserve socio-structural inequalities. Concurrently, contestations of gender roles within the family and community reflect how 'private' institutions affect women's agency vis-à-vis public institutions. Within this complex institutional context, Dalit women vied to press their claim on formal state institutions. Contradictions in the state, however, emerge during the struggle.

Targeting the State and Looking for Allies Within   At the start of the agricultural season in 2006, information provided by the Agamudaiyars led to a large police contingent descending on Vettriyur village and preventing Dalits from ploughing the kollakādu land. This marked Dalit women's first engagement in collective action. They confronted both the police and Agamudaiyars, while most Dalit men left to avoid arrest. According to Priya, 'We argued that this was our village land and others should not enter inside...that Vilapatti people had no right to take away the tractor key. [Vilapatti men] replied that it was government poramboke land and they were entitled to a share since it bordered their kanmāi.' The police impounded a tractor and threatened to arrest the women if they caused any trouble. Amudha (married woman, 45 years) stated their response was born of necessity: 'We women said we were ready to come with the police, as without this land we could not survive'. This 'police torture', to use her words, catalysed women's participation in the land struggle. To avoid further confrontation, they shifted tactics to quietly ploughing and sowing the land with bullocks on nights when there was no full moon. In addition, they halted agricultural labour and leases on Vilapatti land and cut social ties with Mannur Dalits.

Collectivization thus empowered and enabled the women to overcome their fear of the police in order to defend directly their livelihood resource claim. In doing so, they (and Dalit men) relied on the gendered notion that the (mainly male) police would exercise restraint and not harm women, whereas they would not spare Dalit men. The women also used the fact that they would not be harmed to protest against the Agamudaiyars' lack of rights in this matter; they were safe so long as the police were present. Indirectly, this could be seen as a protest against the socio-political influence of Agamudaiyars from Vilapatti village over state actors. Their subsequent disengagement from socio-economic relations with their Dalit and Agamudaiyar opponents then constituted an important condition for their subsequent actions.

Meanwhile, interconnections between dominant castes and state institutions were further reinforced by the dominant castes obtaining control over local government, enabling them to exercise authority and influence over other state institutional actors. Nalini pointed to common knowledge that the Agamudaiyar landlord won the 2006 panchayat elections through a combination of caste and class power. According to the women, he manipulated many Dalits' fear and economic dependence on the MLA, Kallars, and Agamudaiyars to stop their votes going to the independent Dalit candidate. He also relied on the old nādu loyalty to their territory and sense of shared identity (Dirks 1993): Vilapatti and a large village belong to another nādu. For Mannur Dalit villagers, he traded a promise to help them obtain title to the disputed Vettriyur village land in exchange for their votes. Consequently, Vettriyur Dalit women saw the president exhibiting clear caste biases in panchayat development works and encouraging the Agamudaiyars to oppose their land claim.

According to the Dalit women, dominant castes and the nādu ambalam/MLA actively sought to ensure their exclusion from landownership. Through the Vilapatti Agamudaiyar attendant in the collector's office and bribes, the Agamudaiyars convinced forest officials that the Vettriyur Dalits were cultivating forest (*kāttu*) poramboke lands. That is, revenue lands assessed solely for forestry and for which land title cannot be granted under the ordinary course of the law. In December 2007, therefore, police and forest officials threatened to bulldoze all the Vettriyur Dalits' crops on the kollakādu land. The Dalits' immediate petition to the collector received no response. Their petition had highlighted their status as 'lower'-caste marginal farmers and requested the security of land title in the face of opposition from other villages and the police. Instead, on 25 January 2008, around 50 police officials, forest officials, and the village administrative officer descended on Vettriyur and Aruppur villages. They pasted eviction notices in English on their doors. The notices informed them that the Forest Department was evicting them in 15 days' time from the kollakādu land as it was forest land.

Muniyan (married man, 50 years) described the attempts by the police to cheat them. The police requested their signatures on forms written in English allegedly to enable them to acquire the land title. These forms would have instead relinquished their right to cultivate the land. It was only through the intervention of the only Dalit male graduate that the signing of these papers was stopped. Meanwhile, the nādu ambalam/MLA merely reiterated that Vettriyur Dalits should 'adjust' with Vilapatti and Mannur villagers' demands to settle the matter, and said that forest matters were outside his jurisdiction. Later, responding to the Dalit men's last petition, forest officials confirmed that they could not grant title to any forest poramboke land, though unofficially, they might allow land cultivation. Taken together, the actions of the police, ambalam/MLA, and forest officials demonstrate the partiality of state actors in devising ways to deny the Dalits land title. The attempt to get the Dalits' signatures fraudulently illustrates the way officials are able to take advantage of the Dalits' low education levels in Tamil-medium government schools. Moreover, both the relative powerlessness of Dalits and links between power and knowledge are apparent from the dominant caste strategy, which relied on the complexities of formal institutional rules on land administration to stymie the Dalits' claim.

Most Vettriyur women, however, maintain that it was their actions that have at least halted overt opposition to their cultivating the land since 2008, if not gaining them land title. While starting with direct protest in the absence of socio-political connections, Dalit women also combined several institutional strategies in manoeuvring around power relations. They attempted to bypass the political influence of the Agamudaiyars by petitioning against the police actions over the tractor incident to higher government officials, who they believed would be less entangled in local caste/political power relations. The three married Dalit women who were manhandled by an Agamudaiyar man while trying to stop the removal of the tractor key also filed a police complaint of sexual molestation. Gender norms of female honour and chastity normally would prevent unmarried women from making such a claim (cf. Irudayam *et al.* 2006), but these women obtained their husbands' permission to do so using the social protection of marriage. They argued to their husbands that this police case, along with the Dalits' payment of a fine, would push the police to return the hired tractor quickly. When this occurred, the women withdrew their complaint. After they received the eviction notices and consulted the NGO director, the women visited the government officials dealing with this case to lodge both their protests against the eviction and their petitions for land title.

Dalit women's petitions and appeals to government officials combined references to multiple axes of difference, primarily their caste and class. The wider Dalit women's liberation movement was the petitioner, relying on strength of numbers to add moral weight to their claim, and their petitions highlighted their 'depressed caste' status. Years of land cultivation, the 1977 deputy tahsildar's order, and their inability to sustain their livelihoods in this isolated village without cultivating the kollakādu land were offered as proof of entitlement.

The only other reference to gender appears in the request for land title in the women's names. Its importance can be assessed against the male bias in land reform programmes in India. Men are the typical beneficiaries due to stereotypes of women as dependents in a unitary household characterized by equitable distribution of resources and incomes (Agarwal 2003).

Additionally, women sought to fall in with state entitlement arrangements and institutional norms. Petitions were written linking their land claim with the 2 acre government land scheme for the landless poor, with the deputy tahsildar's 1977 order appearing to grant them legal title, and with formal institutional norms prescribing equal treatment for citizens. Uma thus told revenue officials, 'If you will not give us title, likewise you should not have given title [to poramboke land] to the [Vilapatti] Agamudaiyars'. In other words, women pitched their claim in two ways, namely, by referring to their identities and by forming connections with democratic norms and existing state entitlement schemes. In both senses, their demands can be interpreted as based on principles of equality, as humans entitled to a decent livelihood and equal to other castes.

The ability to pitch their claim in ways that appealed to state actors aside, progress occurred when Dalit women found allies among Dalits in government. A Dalit ally saved them when the dominant caste revenue divisional officer entered the village soon after the eviction order to inform the Dalit women that they had to remove their drying paddy from the kollakādu land or it would be burnt. Women countered his disregard for their poverty by waiting an entire day to secure an appointment with the collector, a Dalit, to lodge their protest. Sangam leaders recalled the collector publicly chastising the revenue divisional officer for his action, saying, 'Just like a house is important to us, for them it is their paddy. So how can you say that you will burn down their paddy, when at the cost of their lives they will try to save it?' The women then received the collector's assurance that they would soon hear 'good news' from him about the land.

Demonstrating publically under the banner of the Dalit women's liberation movement was another tactic that drew political attention to the Vettriyur land conflict and introduced women to another ally. This supports Sen's (1999) argument of the instrumental value of political freedoms, including the right to organize and freedom of the press. Besides highlighting the interconnected nature of civil–political and socio-economic rights, it also demonstrates how collective action on multiple fronts is required to realize rights. The local newspapers reported that around 800 Dalit women were undertaking a hunger strike to stress the fact that land was being denied to them despite numerous petitions to the government, and demanding land title 'as our right'. As a result, the district revenue officer (DRO), a Dalit, visited Vettriyur village to verify the land petition. He lent his support to their land claim after physically verifying the Dalit women's poor livelihood conditions, learning about their land struggle and the reasons for opposition from various quarters, and viewing the 1977 deputy tahsildar's order. This official then assured the Dalit women on two points: first, they could cultivate the land in peace hereafter; and second, the government would change the land classification in order to grant them title since they had been cultivating the land for years, and provide them with receipts (B memos) to evidence their cultivation. According to Veronnika, the government records must reflect this decision, though the Dalits never received any written proof of this.

Their allies among higher government officials also gave the Dalit women further guidance on how to approach relevant officials and establish their entitlement to the land. This proved of vital help to excluded Dalit women when they were trying to negotiate the complicated bureaucracy of land classification and distribution. At one point, for example, the DRO instructed Uma to collect 10 women together and personally petition the collector. Dalit men, however, insisted that they would handle this, but then took no action. According to Uma, 'due to this we lost another chance to get the land title'. The targets of their petitions, acting on the DRO's and Veronnika's advice, did not include forest officials. The women understood that only the DRO and the collector could solve this land issue, as their case rested on questioning how grazing poramboke land could be converted into non-cultivable forest poramboke land when Dalits had been cultivating the land all these years.

Allies in government are only of use so long as they continue to hold their posts. In a long struggle, officials may be transferred. This occurred with the collector and the DRO. In the latter's case, according to Priya, his transfer a month after his visit to Vettriyur village was partly due to pressure from the nādu ambalam/MLA and local Kallars. They saw that he was supporting the Dalits in a number of disputes. Fortunately, though, the outgoing DRO put in a good word for Veronnika with his successor, a non-Dalit. This paved the way for the Vettriyur women to approach the new man. The former officer also continued to provide advice. He insisted that the kollakādu land is not forest poramboke land and, prior to his transfer, wrote a recommendation that the land be granted to the women. His suggestion, therefore, was that the Dalits hold open demonstrations demanding the land title on this basis.

Time and political context, moreover, play an equally important role in defining the process and outcomes of Dalit women's collective action. As of 2011, in the absence of further strong allies among government officials, the women continue to petition the collector every few months alongside meeting all levels of revenue officials regarding the land. They rely on Veronnika's contacts with officials to set up the meetings and obtain guidelines as to how to proceed. Requests for the land remain couched in terms of entitlement. At the same time, they now also ask for written evidence that the DRO granted permission for them to cultivate the land, in order to protect their 'quasi' entitlement in the interim. Officials receive the petitions, but no one except the local village administrative officer has visited the village to ascertain the legitimacy of the women's claim. Ultimately, the land, if indeed it is forest poramboke land, falls under central government jurisdiction. Hence, the women need to pressurize the DRO and collector to forward an application to change land classification to the central government. The current political context, however, is not favourable. According to a former village administrative officer, 20 years ago, it would have been easier to get classifications changed, but today, such changes are unlikely without considerable political influence, exactly what socially excluded actors lack. His suggestion is that the Dalits just silently continue to cultivate the kollakādu land without expecting title, which is the official line now.

Security, of income and of the person, is an additional, important influence on Dalit women's strategies. Security underlies Asha's concession that while she wants women to do another large land protest, this risks inviting official harassment once more for cultivating the kollakādu land. Fear of the Agamudaiyars' negative reactions similarly explains Uma's reluctance to follow Veronnika's suggestion to deliver the individual petition required under the Right to Information Act

2005, requesting the district administration to provide information on the status of their land application. Women, therefore, perceived the safer option to be continued petitions arguing their entitlement on two bases: their rights as 'depressed castes', needing a secure way to make a living after cultivating the land for years; and their qualifying for the government's 2 acre land scheme.

Meanwhile, the ongoing struggle reflects the Vilapatti Agamudaiyars' significant power to control the situation in two mutually reinforcing ways. One is careful monitoring of the Dalit women's actions by encouraging patronage ties with some Dalit men. Asha mentioned that everyone knows that a few of their men, who continue to work for the Agamudaiyars and enjoy their patronage, provide information on all their decisions. Second is the Agamudaiyars' exploiting their strong socio-political connections with state actors. Women suspect that their political influence blocks the women's petitions as well as scrutiny of the kollakādu land files detailing the positive response of the DRO to the Dalits' petitions. Dominant caste power today rests on combining traditional forms of social control with influencing the state to come into line within formal institutional norms on entitlement.

Negotiating Gender Norms and Male Authority   Having described, in the previous section, how Dalit women exercised and enhanced their agency through the land entitlement struggle, this section now turns to the relationship between gender and sangam participation. Relative autonomy, coupled with the prospect of loans for the family, enabled most Dalit women to participate in the sangams without inviting much male opposition. Nonetheless, Muniyan summed up the gender norms men relied on to limit women's ability to function fully independently: 'First of all, they want their women to do all the work in the family. Secondly, if the women go outside to work, then only they earn money. Thirdly, they fear that their women will become spoilt/immoral by going outside like this for petitioning and talking with government officials and the police, most of whom are men.' Dalit men's construction of power within the family therefore depended on female seclusion and the gender division of labour. Gender norms also formed part of the counter-strategy of the dominant caste Agamudaiyar men: they asked the Dalit men how they could allow their women so much freedom, thereby seeking to provoke Dalit men into adopting dominant gender norms of controlling women's mobility as a means to control their chastity (and thus sexuality). The underlying text was that any failure to control the women lessened the men's status. This tactic, the NGO director noted, is the easiest way to stop active women from political action and to divide the Dalits.

The sangam women were determined to respond to male resentment and obstruction by negotiation and persuasion. They also worked within the restrictions imposed on them by the gender division of labour and their primary role in agricultural production. Even where restrictions on women's mobility outside the village became pronounced, the women just cut down on their travels or went as a group. Uma provides the clearest example of women's manoeuvring within gender relations to overcome male opposition. Her husband forced her to disassociate from the first sangam by beating her and burning all her clothes. He also appealed to norms dictating 'correct' female behaviour in order to denigrate the women by alluding to their immorality when they went out all day and came back home at night. Uma, in response, developed her own counter-strategies. For example, she would tell her husband she was going into town to go to the market, in order to join the other women in their collective action. She eventually obtained her husband's acquiescence to her sangam membership upon holding out the prospect of economic benefits to care for their six children.

While men might concede a separate space for women to attempt to acquire land title, they did not want to share a public space with them. Neither were they happy about the thought of women having an equal say in decision making. This suggests that altering public roles to allow more equitable interactions between women and men constitutes a greater disturbance to gender power relations. The men, having become central to the land struggle simply by refusing to allow women to participate in it, refused to listen to women's suggestions for joint community action. One example is the women's suggestions on the village administrative officer's proposal that the villagers pay for the land receipts necessary to prove cultivation, and hence their entitlement. The men's sole reasoning was that 'they are only women, talking but not knowing anything'. Such comments continued to break women's unity and confidence to act at times. Women thereby learned not to plan joint action with their men, aside from the supportive village elder, Rengam. Their determination also grew as they recognized how they were left to face troubles over the land because men were too busy either with work outside the village or with fighting among themselves over how to take the struggle forward. However, some women, like Uma, have taken the men's words as a challenge to achieve land title and thus gain social respect and recognition: 'We want this land issue to be solved, as only then will our Dalit women's movement become visible in the area. We want people to know about our movement. Only then will people respect our work.'

Further evidence of the challenge women's collective action poses to gender relations is the emerging dynamic between the women and the de facto village leader, Rengam. He initially suggested that 'if the women take up these struggles without the men, this will be a strength for our village'. He viewed women's political mobilization as instrumental to opening new spaces for negotiation with officials. Towards the end of 2009, however, his opinion changed as the sangams presented several petitions without him and, therefore, now appeared to threaten his traditional authority. This dynamic, however, moves beyond the binary of male–female power relations. Rengam's wife, Máriamma (50 years), fuelled this rift by disparaging the other women's independent efforts in order to support her husband. Rengam further alienated all the other villagers by voicing his perceived right to a share of the kollakādu land. It was due to him, he said, because he had paid the temple tax separately from his two adult sons, who had both received land shares. After others rejected his claim because his family already enjoyed two shares, he refused to share documents he alone holds regarding the land struggle. Women, therefore, balance several pragmatic and affective factors in debating their next move. On the one hand, there is their need for Rengam's support, particularly in providing documentary evidence of their land entitlement, and there is the respect they have for him as a village elder. On the other hand, there are now new political spaces offered by participation in the sangams and the Dalit women's movement, with implications for disturbing gender power relations.

Sustaining the Land Struggle Continued collective action in the face of multiple obstacles from state and non-state actors requires Dalit women to expend the very resources they enjoy so little of, namely, time and money. Asked what sustains them in their land struggle, Priya replied, 'What else we can do? Unless we have land it will be

very difficult for us to live. We keep going to government offices, losing money, and still the struggle continues.' Their conviction of the
legitimacy of their struggle is now linked to its presumed legality, based
on the former DRO's statement on changing the land classification to
grant them title. Nonetheless, Uma also expressed the women's frustra-
tion: 'In our generation, we have seen all district revenue officers visit
our land but they do not give us title. So too my children's generation
are seeing the same thing.' Sangam leaders also pointed to dishearten-
ing visits to government offices, only to return without any meeting
despite having waited the entire day. When Dalit men question why
these leaders are always travelling outside and do not behave like other
women, Devi replies that they cannot stay at home. They have to do
this for their future.

Devi's comment shows that participation in the sangam has
enhanced the women's personal power. They have a stronger sense
of selfhood and of a social role outside the family, which is noted as
instrumental for collective agency (Kabeer 1994). Her comment and
the following indicate that there have been substantial gains in self-
confidence, knowledge, and organized collective strength independent
of men, and that there is emerging discourse of women's equality.

Now as a group if we have any issues, we can take them to the women's
police stations. We can achieve anything and I am bold enough to go
out wherever I want, that's how much I have gained confidence in the
sangam. Now I am not dependent on men for anything. (Nalini)

Not only have we cultivated the habit of saving money, we have also
become so bold. Before we used to always say, 'we can't do this'. (Asha)

See, because of the men doing like this [bending before others], they
have become *mūda paiyen* [submissive, mute], so we women now have
to come forward [to take up the struggle]. (Priya)

Notably, Priya's comment also indicates how ideas about men are
changing, reflecting the fact that women are now conscious that they
can fulfil roles traditionally allotted to men.

This discourse becomes obvious when women discuss the future of
their children, particularly what daughters should enjoy:

My own children should also sit and talk equally, even girls. There is no
difference between girls and boys; there should be equality. I tell my

daughter she should not be like I was. I struggle a lot on the land, but in future our children should be settled well and respected. Those days of covering our breasts with our *saris* and being afraid all the time—they should not be like this. (Priya)

The discursive shift is matched by a developing governance role for the sangams outside male-dominated social institutions, which strengthens the women's collective identity. They now expect interpersonal problems to be brought to the sangams to be decided on. Evidence therefore exists that women are moving towards equal status and power with men at both the personal and the institutional level.

At the same time, Dalit women need continual encouragement to keep going with their struggle, particularly given how expensive it is to travel to government offices. After instituting the practice whereby women spend their own money and later collect this amount from all families, the sangam leaders have recently tried to add fines for those families that do not send one woman along when land petitions are handed in. Their aim is to make the women accountable for the effort they put in. Two women, however, now insist that they will pay only once they actually obtain the entitlement. The women's frustrations are further exacerbated by Dalit women from Aruppur village refusing to share the burden of this struggle. Priya therefore hinted that they have started to think about separating their land claim from Aruppur's, in order to stop Aruppur villagers 'free-riding' on their efforts. Finally, some women like Nalini alluded to emerging village disunity:

We are all the same community and all related—that is the problem! If it was other community people living here, then automatically our unity will come. If any outsider creates problems in our village, at that time we will all unite together against them. But if there are problems inside our village, then only we will be split and no one will unite.

Her point was illustrated during the *Dīpavali* festival celebrations in 2009, exposing the underlying caste tensions in the area. Reacting to an innocuous incident in which a Dalit man from Mannur village got out of a vehicle and accidentally hit the leg of an Agamudaiyar man from Vilapatti village in the process, some Agamudaiyar youths beat up a Dalit youth from Mannur village. Caste tensions then erupted into several violent fights between Dalit and Agamudaiyar youths. The violence ceased only after Dalits from Mannur, Aruppur, and Vettriyur villages, encouraged by Veronnika, reached a compromise with the Agamudaiyars. One positive outcome of this inter-caste conflict has been that Dalits from all these villages have come together and, therefore, there are now more open social interactions among them, which displace the land conflict tensions. Another is an increasing recognition that while Mannur Dalits may have initiated opposition to their land claim, the Vettriyur Dalits' key opponents are the Vilapatti Agamudaiyars, who are determined to maintain Dalits' economic dependency and social control over them.

The NGO support of Dalit women as they attempt to gain other entitlements also sustains their collective identity and agency. At the same time, as the following two examples show, the women are exposed through other entitlement struggles to further forms of exclusion. First, in 2008, the women successfully petitioned revenue officials for a separate ration shop nearby. Until then, women had to travel 5 km to collect their monthly rations. Securing this entitlement may have reduced their domestic burden, but it did not translate into freedom from caste discrimination. An angry Radha (married woman, 29 years) noted that the dominant caste ration shopkeeper never provides them with full rations. They receive less than other caste women, but do not protest for fear of losing what little rations they receive. Second, the women have petitioned government officials for potable water, a priority because their village borewell has yielded salty water for the past three years and tensions arise when they are forced to draw water from Mannur village. Vettriyur Dalits suspect, however, that the panchayat president fails to arrange for water supply from other water tanks due to the kollakādu land dispute. Petitions to the collector indicating how the panchayat disregards their requests are also disregarded. These examples thus reveal both agency broadening into different areas and the limits of collective action where state actors replicate or contribute to Dalit women's social exclusion.

Discussion

This case study, set in an arena of overlapping formal and informal institutions, provides an example of the link between Dalit women's collective action over productive resources and a broader struggle to transform patronage relations embedded in traditional institutions of power. It also questions how far the Indian state is able to penetrate local informal institutions by changing the wider context in which these institutions operate. The study thereby draws attention to the methods by which informal institutional actors reinforce unequal entitlement norms and influence state actors to maintain these norms, and how far they succeed in using these methods. This complex environment shapes the distinct pathways through which Dalit women secure livelihood entitlements. In particular, oppressive social contexts influence the types of organizational and entitlement strategies available to these women, given the important role that landownership plays in expressing and reproducing relations of power in rural India. These contexts and the layers of interactions therein shape the women's agency. They also shape the role external intervention plays in bridging the power/ knowledge divide. These two themes, situating the transformation of patronage relations and informal institutional power within collective action strategies to secure land entitlement, are elaborated next.

Struggles for Resources and the Power of Patronage

Midgal (2004: 11) noted that social interactions are better conceived as conflict-laden, with different social groups endorsing different sets of formal and informal rules on social behaviour. This can be extended to multiple rules on entitlement. Domination is then characterized by the ability to force others to adopt one's rules by direct or indirect means, or to produce certain outcomes in any conflict over entitlements. This idea particularly fits a nādu context where informal institutional rules such as clientelism still dominate to a great degree. Clientelism is often found in postcolonial contexts where formal institutions were imposed on traditional authority structures (Helmke and Levitsky 2004). Deconstructing clientelism within the Indian context reveals 'a pattern of [patronage] relationships in which members of hierarchically arranged groups possess mutually recognized, but not explicitly stipulated, rights and obligations involving mutual aid and preferential treatment' (Breman 1974: 18). These relationships centre on both economic–political and social–symbolic exchanges (Auyero 1999),[11] which traditionally formed the most visible caste markers of identity (Gorringe and Rafanell 2007). Dalits' history of economic dependency on dominant castes, for example, ensured their co-option

by institutionalized clientelism. This reproduced the social hierarchy
supporting unequal entitlements between patrons and clients.

Viewed from this perspective, the nādu system produced a highly
localized and powerful form of patronage because of the addition of
religious, administrative, political, and juridical links to socio-economic
relations of interdependence. The caste–class and gender divisions of
labour, highly unequal power relations, and physical isolation of nādu
regions effectively stifled any caste–class or gender consciousness
forming among Dalits or women. Vertical ties to the ambalams and
their direct patrons superseded horizontal relationships of solidarity.
Moreover, in keeping with patronage patterns in general, these relations
were particularistic and private, falling outside state law. This implicated both the nādu ambalams and dominant Kallar and Agamudaiyar
castes in the structural production of poverty among Dalits for their
own economic benefit. The strength of this system, in comparison to
other areas that had multiple patrons (unlike this area), is the lack of
competition among different patrons to weaken inter-caste power relations. Hence, patronage in the nādus retains characteristics of deference
and dependency (Hopkin 2006).

Patronage relations provided Dalits with security and their daily survival needs (Leonard *et al.* 2010), as well as with relationships founded
on mutual, if unequal exchanges. Loosening the grip of patronage,
therefore, has depended on two push factors. One was an economic
separatism: Dalits claimed land, the main means of production, and
curtailed their dependency on irrigation water from the main nādu
kanmāi. Dalits also negotiated new labour relationships outside the
area, and therefore became less dependent on dominant caste Kallars
and Agamudaiyars for survival. The significance lay in loosening social
control over the labour process and, therefore, undermining the economic rationale for nādu patronage relations. This process disrupted
local practices of entitlement founded on unequal power relations.

The second push factor is symbolic separatism—Uma commented
that other castes have been forced to recognize that 'Vettriyur is a
Dalit village, our village'. The villagers affirmed their positive identity
as Dalits free of servitude and claimed autonomous territory (land)
within nādu/dominant caste territory. Separatism was aided by various
external interventions that persuaded Dalits, and later Dalit women,
to believe they could influence their fate. Their resulting autonomous

identity and concurrent claim to equal status has been expressed in several ways. For example, Amudha pointed to the changing embodiment of caste relations (Gorringe and Rafanell 2007) where Dalits dress well and walk proudly, while Devi noted: 'We are educating our children and developing, so [the dominant castes] are becoming envious (*porāmai*). If they spoke anything bad to us previously we would keep silent, but now we talk back to them...we no longer obey them.' Nevertheless, Dalit men's behaviour, in particular, continues to reflect tensions between vertical ties of loyalty to patrons, based on economic dependency, and horizontal bonds of reciprocity to caste community, kin, and family (Rudolph and Rudolph 1984). This is apparent from the loose patronage ties Vilapatti dominant castes retain with a few Vettriyur men, by providing the Dalit men with work opportunities and employing them for certain traditional caste-based services. The work and the services are paid for in wages and/or alcohol in exchange for loyalty and information on Dalit activities. In sum, together these two factors of economic and symbolic separatism further confirm the falsity of any distinction in livelihood development strategies between economic exploitation and socio-cultural oppression.

Against this background, Dalit women's effort to secure land entitlements arguably involves an ongoing process of negotiation and struggle with dominant castes located in both societal and state arenas. On the one side, Dalits seek to loosen bonds of dependence and control, which are based on inequalities in resources, caste status, and power (Auyero 1999). On the other side, Kallars and Agamudaiyars try to maintain their caste privileges, which are tied to caste affiliation and loyalty to the nādu ambalam/MLA, who retains de facto political authority over the area. Patronage relations embedded in economic dependency and coercive force, therefore, have not completely lost their relevance in constituting Dalit entitlements and obligations in lieu of the individual citizenship rights allocated by the state.

As the state enters further into areas like the nādus with parallel systems of governance, however, it may further disrupt the legitimacy of patronage relations. This disruption would occur if the state takes over the roles patrons provide, such as controlling access to resources and solving village problems (cf. Auyero 1999). The state may establish a new set of impartial entitlement rules. Socially excluded Dalit women drew on state institutional arrangements and development policies and programmes for access to 'state' resources and physical security, as well as delinking from informal institutions characterized by inter-caste interdependence. While informal institutional rules privilege certain ascribed caste, class, and gender identities over others in access to resources, the Indian state officially subscribes to norms of non-discrimination and special protection and promotion of the interests of SC citizens (Articles 16 and 46, Indian Constitution 1949). Dalit women rely on these formal institutional rules and claims to state resources to counter indirectly their relative lack of power, giving them leverage over informal institutional rules (cf. Pattendon 2011). Hence, they aligned their demands to reflect not only government welfare schemes meant for poor communities like them but also to appeal for equal treatment when other villages secured title for poramboke lands.

In doing so, these women push at the boundaries of what is possible, potentially gaining access to resources through the state, bypassing informal institutions. They also contribute to the difficult and longer-term process of transforming informal institutions. Helmke and Levitsky (2004: 732) noted that this process requires two concurrent changes. Formal institutions must alter the costs and benefits of adhering to informal rules and ensure more effective enforcement of formal rules; and social values must also change. Underlying both is the need to shift the balance of power between Dalits and dominant castes, and at the state–society interface (Fox 2005). Both these changes are currently lacking in the present context, meaning that formal institutions have limited influence in transforming nādu institutional norms that diverge from those of the formal Indian state.

As the case study shows, collective identification and mobilization through the Dalit women's sangams does not automatically equate with effective representation of their interests in the state political system (Leonard *et al.* 2010). The reasons are threefold and mutually reinforcing. First, the nādu ambalam/MLA still retains the ability to limit the state's entry into the nādu region. Second, informal institutional power holders have penetrated state institutions to assume significant positions of authority. Third, power relations between Dalits and the MLA/ Kallars/Agamudaiyars still shape the decisions formal institutions take about how to distribute state resources to Dalits, which results in unequal entitlement distribution.

These unequal power relations are seen in many strategies by dominant castes, including the undermining of Dalits' use of formal institutions to secure entitlements and delegitimizing their claims through both direct and indirect opposition. An example of the latter is their supporting other Dalits' counterclaims and garnering the support of police and forest officials to this end by manipulating both nādu and state institutional rules. Other manifestations are the dominant castes capture of local formal institutions (panchayats), which grants them control over the state's distribution of development goods and services. This is supported by the MLA's failure to sign Dalit job applications in the area, limiting their work opportunities. At a wider district level, in recent years, Kallars and Agamudaiyars have successfully applied political pressure by protesting against the implementation of the Scheduled Castes/Scheduled Tribes (Prevention of Atrocities) Act 1989. Consequently, local social activists claim that police stations in the area do not easily register cases under this law and prefer to work towards compromises, disregarding the unequal negotiating power between Dalit and non-Dalit actors. Changes to informal nādu institutions, therefore, prove difficult and slow to occur.

As a counter to the above, Dalit women seek allies in higher government officials who are sufficiently removed from nādu politics. The main basis for alliance forming has been caste affiliation. This follows the pattern of formal politics in India today, which is increasingly structured through caste relations with the rise of caste and regional-based political parties (Subramaniam 2006). Hence, Rengam pointed to more positive responses to their land petitions from 'our person [that is, Dalit] in power'. Devi elaborated: 'If our children are in government positions, when we give petitions then our issues will be taken up…We need our own people to uplift ourselves, for our security and protection.' While this speaks to the continuing power of caste identity and affiliation, other allies, exemplified in Kovilur village, are non-Dalit officials without any caste-based ties to communities in the area. Both types of allies exemplify the politics Dalits must engage in to counter the 'patronage democracy' in which mainly local dominant caste politicians and officials mediate access to the welfare state (Corbidge *et al.* 2005: 70). Relying on caste identification has limited value, however. Officials are transferred regularly, and nādu power holders are able to influence the transfer of officials supportive of Dalit entitlements. This indicates the need for systemic reforms of local formal institutions that will ensure more effective, independent, and impartial state institutions. These would have potential to transform informal institutional rules and ensure greater adherence to formal state rules, including by state actors themselves.

Likewise, linking with the NGO can be regarded as another strategic alliance for Dalit women: the NGO enables the women to challenge traditional patronage relations as they claim land resources. Dalit women's view of the NGO director as a development broker stems from her relative power in social interactions with the Dalit women, who follow her advice and directions regarding collective action. Specifically, Veronnika's superior access to knowledge and socio-political networks provides the bridging capital that Dalit women require to link effectively with state institutions and strategically align their demands. This effectively opens up knowledge and political spaces for securing entitlements outside traditional patronage relations. These openings are vital if women are to overcome social exclusion, including exclusion from knowledge and power, in order to build their political agency.

Strategic Choices and Dilemmas in Adverse Environments

As in Kovilur village, both the presence of a facilitating NGO and its approach, which is based on building collective identity and interests as Dalit women, are critical in shaping the Vettriyur women's agency. These women were clearly aware of their suppression and exploitation at the hands of the dominant castes within the nādu system. They further realized the connection between this and current dominant caste opposition to their securing land entitlement. They only required a facilitating actor who could help translate these understandings into strategic action. In this regard, Rudolph and Rudolph (1984: 287–8) refer to the objective and subjective determinants of mobilization. Objective determinants are historical changes to nādu structures, agricultural change, conjunctures of the land claim leading to a general sense of entitlement, and caste, gender, and community bonds. It is these factors that the NGO translates into discursive consciousness in order to justify the women's organization for collective action at a particular time and place. Subjective determinants require building action strategies around the goals, values, and meanings women attached to land entitlement. Doing so sustains their motivation to struggle over a long period. Vertical patronage relations should also be replaced through the construction of horizontal relations and alliances with other Dalit women based on 'values of solidarity, self-reliance and collective action' (cf. Kabeer 2005: 183). Achieving this entails providing women-only spaces for discussions, capacity training, and a formal organizational framework in which to feel secure and confident to press their claims on state institutions (Mies 1986).

Underlying this mobilization process are a number of strategies brought into play from the organizational stage right up to collective action, each complicated by accompanying dilemmas and contradictions as women navigate multiple, complex power relations. The organizational structure of the women's sangams, combining economic development programmes of savings and credit with political mobilization, is arguably strategic in an environment that is historically hostile to Dalits' mobilization around their rights. The 'savings and credit' aspect is in line with the state government's promotion of 'politically manageable' women's sangams engaged primarily in individual self-help as opposed to collective development (Batliwala 2007). The sangams' potential for disrupting power relations thus is disguised. Dominant castes familiar with the state's sangam structures and discourse do not perceive them as challenges to their power and authority, while Dalit men appreciate the sangams channelling economic benefits to their families.

Dalit women acknowledged, however, the paradoxical impact of this form of group organization on intra-household power relations (Wilson 2008): they may achieve economic freedom and security by calling on sangam savings for emergency loans without relying on their husbands. However, some men use this as an excuse to neither support their families financially nor help repay sangam loans, thereby strengthening unequal gender relations. Women's use of the sangams outside the role the state intends them to play, moreover, sits uneasily with government officials. This is evident from the officials' attempts to persuade the women against disturbing power relations by claiming land title. Further, any attempt to place Dalit women's participation in the public sphere on an equal footing with Dalit men encounters gender-based resistance.

Locating Dalit women's agency within nādu power relations again draws attention to the juncture of struggles over resources and meanings conducted in multiple arenas—the family, nādu society, and the state. Successful strategies, therefore, can be broadened beyond those directed towards the as yet unrealized goal of secure land entitlement. Such broadening includes the construction of a new or transformed discourse around which entitlements are conceived, expressed, and contested (Hunt 1993: 240). In the present case, these are discourses of caste equality and gender equality. Caste equality is implied by their sense of entitlement to land in contrast to norms of caste-based exclusion. Gender equality of status and power comes from women recognizing 'their right to have rights' (Kabeer 2006a). The latter finds expression in the women's refusal to depend entirely on their husbands to secure the land entitlement. Instead, they chose to use the secure space that the sangams provided and their relative exclusion from patron–client relations compared to Dalit men (cf. Kapadia 1997) to assert their independent identity and exercise agency based on ideas of women's equal power to act. Women seek landownership for its own sake therefore, although most women value land less for themselves than for their children's development. Their consistent mention of enhanced freedoms of speech and movement through sangam participation are additional dimensions of equality. Another dimension is that they believe their sons and daughters should have equal access to education and professional work, and equal freedom of speech and actions.

Although they are incorporating ideas of gender equality into their demands and actions, this does not mean that Dalit women believe in absolute equality in all spheres. As Madhok (2007) found, their belief reflects a combination of old and new ideas through which new ideas adjust with the old. Hence, while the women may feel that women and men should have equal status and power, this does not apply to land title, which reflects other meanings and values attributed to ownership and control over this resource. Dalit women's demand for land title in their names met with little male opposition because landownership meant the women would have control over the land in terms of production alone. This land control did not necessarily mean that the women would have independent control over the product of their labour, contrary to Agarwal's (2003: 195) assertion. Men instead undertake all market interactions and control profits from the land. Women's exclusion from access to the market to sell their produce, therefore, diminishes their ability to exercise control over agricultural income.

At the same time, it strengthens bonds of interdependence with men forged in a common production process, which women value for the security this brings. Women's understanding of equality and power therefore assumes multiple, contradictory meanings that cannot be reduced to formal equality and autonomy. This understanding affects the strategic demands they make during the entitlement struggle.

The range of exclusions Dalit women face, especially from access to land title, and opposition from different quarters to their land claim produces a wide range of strategic discourses. These extend beyond gender equality and combine different legal and normative discourses. The meanings women attribute to land guide the way they frame their demands. Meanings derived from land acquisition play a central role in breaking caste-based socio-economic subservience to dominant castes. Land thereby becomes more important for the identity, status, and dignity of the community than for individual or even family identity, status, and dignity. Caste and class interests tend to play a greater role than gender interests. Their petitions for land entitlement thus relied on highlighting their 'low'-caste and class position, besides demanding equality of treatment from government officials and asserting the legality of their claim based on its acceptance by previous officials. Discussions with the women emphasized, in line with Rao's (2005) findings, how demands framed in these ways lessened resistance from Dalit men to their agency. Such demand-framing also arguably reflected the fact that women and men worked on the land interdependently. Male solidarity and interdependence became important considerations given the small village population and the opposition faced from neighbouring villages. The naming of the wider Dalit women's movement in their petitions, moreover, sought to demonstrate their larger collective strength beyond their village, a technique which emphasized the moral weight of their claim, backed by the legitimacy that wider support grants.

Only in their confrontations with the police over the tractor incident was gender identity brought to the forefront. The women manipulated gender norms—that the police would be less likely to arrest women than men, and would swiftly pursue cases alleging sexual molestation—to stand up to the police and push them to quickly resolve the problem. In doing so, they demonstrated their ability to manipulate strategically different aspects of their identity and position within diverse power relations. This includes aligning their demands with the

values of officials—legality and equal treatment of citizens—in order to
legitimize their claims. It also includes both exercising and conceding
power to different actors at different times and places. Hence, they
were prepared to fall in with gender norms when it came to labour
and 'female protection'. They did not demand equal decision-making
power and joint public action. In exchange, Dalit men acquiesced to
their separate public–political role. Moreover, they suggest that caste–
class interdependence and subordination can only be broken by gender
solidarity and interdependence. To cut both ties simultaneously would
effectively deny Dalit women the very security that drives their collective action.

In this conflict-driven environment, the women's negotiations with
state institutional actors combined a wide range of institutional and
non-institutional tactics, reflecting their complementarity. Neither set
of tactics would have worked by itself. Institutional tactics—petitions to
officials, police complaints—indicate Dalit women's engagement with
the state based on presumptions of equality and fairness in entitlement
distribution. However, as the previous section showed, they also reveal
to women the interlinkages between state and nādu institutional actors.
Institutional tactics also point to contradictions within the hierarchical
organizations of the state itself that generate both opposition to and
support for the women's claim. Non-institutional tactics—direct confrontations with the police, organized public protests, and 'avoidance'
tactics circumventing opposition—are partly a response to this situation for socially excluded actors. Thus, public protest, when combined
with press coverage, relied on public exposure and women's collective
power to pressurize higher officials to apply state entitlement rules to
approve their claim where lower officials and police created obstructions. Simultaneously, Dalits' deployed what Scott (1985) termed the
'weapons of the weak'. The covert cultivation of the land at night in
order to circumvent state opposition is an example of the everyday
practices of resistance that enable socially excluded actors to enjoy
resources. Here, the need for a livelihood lent legitimacy to their actions,
showing how women's encounters with the state compelled them to
act outside the bounds of strict legality. Women, however, unlike their
men, chose to bypass appeals to the MLA, in order to maximize their
independence from the caste-based nādu relations that led opposition
to their claim. Institutional and non-institutional strategies are, in this

sense, interdependent. They seek to alter the balance of power away from dominant caste nādu power holders towards socially excluded Dalit women, while simultaneously meeting the day-to-day livelihood needs that sustain their collective action.

The choice of which strategy to deploy also provides evidence for Dalit women continually balancing the 'depth of the challenge' against the 'breadth of appeal' to both sangam members and potential government allies (Downey and Rohlinger 2008). That is, women are constantly concerned with the extent to which their strategies will provoke adverse reactions from those opposing their land title claim, as well as with the time and financial constraints on their agency. At the same time, sangam leaders struggle to keep women motivated to continue petitioning government officials and to frame demands in ways that will ensure that officials support them and do not act further to take away their right of cultivation (cf. Tanner 1995: 688–9). The main strategic dilemma Dalit women currently face—namely, whether to continue quiet petitioning or just cultivate the land without drawing attention to themselves—exemplifies this constant balancing act. If women were ensured a livelihood and felt physically secure, the balancing act would be easier. Strategies for collective action should therefore make security a priority. Both security of livelihood and physical security recur throughout Dalit women's exercise of strategic agency; they indicate both the strength of collective power in the sangams and the continual vulnerability of Dalit women in exerting that power.

***

This chapter dealt with a livelihood entitlement many Dalit and women's activists deem crucial to equalizing power relations in social and family life. Interestingly, it is also an entitlement rarely focused upon by NGOs when they mobilize landless women to collective action (Agarwal 2003), indicating a large gap in current livelihood interventions. This case study examined the ongoing process of struggle by Dalit women to secure legal ownership of cultivable land in a region characterized by parallel traditional governance institutions. The study offers several insights into the interaction of formal and informal institutions. These institutions have different notions of rights, entitlements, and obligations. Informal institutional power holders are able to penetrate and influence state institutions. This means that such actors can continue to exercise material and symbolic power over Dalit women through formal institutions and perpetuate their exclusion from resources. Taken together, the actions of the nādu ambalam/MLA, police, and forest officials negate the notion of state neutrality. Dalit women's land struggle in the nādu region, therefore, becomes a struggle to transform patronage relations and caste interdependence between Dalits and dominant castes. It is simultaneously a struggle to ensure the impartial enforcement of the state's institutional rules on entitlement based on the principle of equality.

It is primarily external intervention that enables the women to navigate this difficult context. External intervention introduces alternative discourses of Dalit women's equality and collective power, and even builds their limited capacity to negotiate action. Women necessarily target state institutions to secure entitlement. They combine institutional and non-institutional tactics in an attempt to displace nādu institutional norms with more equitable state norms on entitlement. Women rely on caste affiliation of government allies to counter the influence of the dominant castes over state actors; they frame petitions primarily in terms of their caste and class identities. Again, as in the previous case study, gender interests assume lesser importance in the women's collective action on entitlements. This is because castes overwhelmingly determine how resources are distributed and how individuals find dignity and respect. It also shows how women pragmatically realize that male support is necessary for security, quite apart from bonds of female–male interdependence centred on family and land cultivation. The following chapter continues to sharpen the key themes brought to light in this and the preceding case study, this time through an unsuccessful livelihood entitlement struggle located in a different region and involving a different set of non-state and state actors.

Notes

1. Research reveals substantial transfers of landownership in Tamil Nadu from 'upper' castes to 'middle' and 'lower' castes, while access to land remains very poor for the Scheduled Castes (SCs). This is particularly true for landholdings in larger classes and for holdings with better quality irrigation (Athreya and Chandra 2000).

2. These two castes, along with the Maravar caste, are considered three clans of the Thevar martial community who have strong socio-political loyalties to one another despite practising endogamy.

3. Nādus came into existence in this area during the later Chola period (AD 900–1300 AD) as the basic unit of the agrarian society and political order in south India (Stein 1994). Fourteen nādus were originally located in what is now Sivagangai district, half of which still function today in some manner.

4. This linking of political authority with religion explains why violent responses to Dalits' assertion of religious freedoms have marked the history of this area. In 1979, in Unjanai village, Kallars murdered five Dalits, injured over 100, and looted their property in retaliation for the Dalits asserting their rights in the Aiyanar temple festival in Unjanai nādu. Caste conflicts again surfaced in 1992 after the Dalits of Muthu nādu asserted their temple rights and entered the main temple in Siruvāchi, and again in 1998, when Dalits asserted their rights to pull the temple car rope during the Kandadevi temple festival in Unjanai nādu. In none of these cases have the dominant caste accused ever been brought to justice.

5. The Madras Estates (Abolition and Conversion into Ryotwari) Act 1948 abolished the zamindari system formalized by the British colonial administration whereby landlords acted as legal intermediaries to collect taxes from peasant cultivators (ryots).

6. Vettriyur village governance today lies in Dalit men's hands. Reflecting how nādus functioned as agrarian settlements, two men are appointed annually to oversee irrigation water distribution, conduct auctions of common property resources, and resolve irrigation and other disputes in the village. Dalit women, therefore, proudly indicated that they no longer obey the Kallars.

7. Women's traditional roles in agriculture include planting and transplanting paddy seedlings, weeding, harvesting, and collecting the harvested paddy and 'waste' hay, while men plough, clear weeds from the bunds and gullies between fields, harvest, and transport the paddy harvest and hay back to the houses. The contribution of Indian women in farm production is estimated at between 55 per cent and 66 per cent of the total labour today (Food and Agricultural Organization [FAO] 2003).

8. Two primary laws in this regard were the Madras Estates (Abolition and Conversion into Ryotwari) Act 1948 and the Tamil Nadu Land Reforms (Reduction of Ceiling on Land) Act 1961, the latter enabling the state government to redistribute land owned in excess of a stipulated ceiling amount to the landless poor.

9. Mainly because of safety concerns for girls continuing education outside the area, most Dalit girls attain only 8–10 standard education before joining their mothers in the fields, while boys may complete Standard 12.

10. Of the 32 adult women in the village, as per the survey, 15 had no or minimal education up to Standard 5 in the nearby government primary school. They were often functionally illiterate. Taking sangam members alone, this was 10 out of 17 women.

11. Friedmann (1992: 17) distinguished this principle of reciprocal exchange governing client–patron relations as the moral economy, which falls outside the market economy.

5

UNEVEN POLITICAL ECONOMICS OF AN ENTITLEMENT STRUGGLE
Mallibakkam Village

See how one shrimp farm owner is spoiling a thousand people's lives here. He has one vote, and yet his vote counts more with the government than all our votes.

Kala (widow, 53 years)

The previous two chapters were about successful and ongoing struggles to secure entitlements in inland agricultural villages. The focus now shifts to an unsuccessful struggle by Dalit women to stop the operation of a shrimp farm in their coastal fishing and agricultural village. The unprecedented growth in commercial aquaculture along the Indian coastline in the past 25 years, much of it inadequately regulated, has pitched many local communities against shrimp farm entrepreneurs in a fight to preserve their livelihoods and a clean and healthy environment (Mangubhai 2004). In the present case, this was a struggle against legality in favour of 'legitimacy' (de Gaay Fortman 2011: 201), in which women argued for protection of their already precarious livelihoods from further erosion. At stake for Dalit women in Mallibakkam village were rights to work, health, and an adequate standard of living. Their struggle highlights contradictory state practices that entrench structural violence and reduce the effectiveness of collective action by socially excluded citizens.

The first part of this chapter describes how the Dalit women's sangams in the village were formed at the instigation of a local Dalit woman and non-governmental organization (NGO) staff member. It examines the political education the women received, and how they engaged in collective action on several livelihood and other issues. The organization of the women is examined in the light of government policies that promote commercial aquaculture. It was in this context that the women undertook action between 2003 and 2005 to oppose the construction of the shrimp farm near one of their residential colonies. The shrimp farm struggle is examined next, as is how livelihood entitlements and power relations were affected by the failure to stop the farm. The second part of the chapter analyses the role of state policies and practices in establishing new forms of exclusion of Dalit women. The analysis focuses on the state–citizen relations experienced by those excluded from resources and power, and the links between macro-level politics and micro-level collective action. A related theme is the effect of multiple discourses of entitlement on Dalit women's agency. The state and external development agencies introduced different discourses on entitlements, and they were (re)interpreted and incorporated by the women into their strategies.

The Context: Sangam Organization and Macroeconomic Policies

Mallibakkam village in Kanchipuram district is the largest of the villages researched. The around 3,000 residents represent 11 different castes, the majority—approximately 350 households—being Dalits.[1] Dalits reside in three colonies spread across the village, one of which comprises government colony housing land. All three colonies are situated in the lowlands alongside Buckingham Canal, a saltwater canal that connects the natural coastal backwaters to form a national shipping waterway. This is in keeping with segregationist caste norms. A small community of forward caste Reddiyar families owns most of the arable land and fruit orchards in the village, while another small community of backward caste Chettiyars operates shops and the only factory. Most Dalit villagers draw an economic dividing line between these two minority 'wealthy' castes and the majority 'labouring' castes. Dalit Paraiyars, along with most backward caste Sembadavars (known as *ullu-nāttu Meenavar*s or inland fishers) and Vanniyars, constitute the three communities that partly or wholly sustain their livelihood from fishing in the adjacent canal. Dalit women, however, increasingly have to supplement this fishing work with other labour work under Mahatma Gandhi National Rural Employment Guarantee Scheme [MGNREGS], agricultural labour, and labour in the nearby salt pans.

Dalit women claim that, of the villages in the area, theirs is the most neglected. They attribute the lack of development largely to the shrimp farm operating next to the canal, fewer than 100 metres (m) from one of their colonies. Tensions between the farm owner and the villagers are expressed in the farm's physical arrangements—electric fencing surrounding the six shrimp ponds and guard dogs—as well as in the lack of interaction between farm workers and the villagers. The backdrop to their struggle against this shrimp farm consists of two contradictory forces: Dalit women organizing to secure livelihood entitlements; and macroeconomic policies promoting commercial aquaculture.

External Intervention: Constructing Collective Identity and Agency

The Dalit women's sangams grew out of the first development intervention to focus on Dalits in Mallibakkam village in the early 1990s. This was the initiative of one of its own members, Kalvikkarasi, then working in a local Dalit NGO, RADA, established by her husband. Kalvikkarasi's motivation was both personal and professional. Her marriage to a Dalit Paraiyar man moved her to work for the Dalit community; and her prior work with another local NGO, which involved organizing women into self-help groups (SHGs) for savings purposes, now extended to a desire to work in her own village. RADA eschewed any role vis-à-vis the delivery of economic benefits or services. Instead, its main goal was to liberate, empower, and develop the livelihoods of Dalit bonded or adimai (agrestic slavery) labourers and those engaged in traditional caste-based occupations along the coastline of Kanchipuram district. In short, RADA aimed to mobilize Dalits to transform their caste and class status. Mallibakkam Dalits were targeted because their lives, back then, revolved around adimai work as *pannaiyāl* (permanent farm workers) for the main landowning and socio-politically powerful caste, the Reddiyars.[2]

The initial NGO activities, therefore, were characterized by political conscientization and capacitation, which led the first generation of semi-educated Dalit male youth to push for the collective withdrawal from adimai work. This was complemented by negotiations with the

Reddiyars for wages equal to those paid outside the village, and organized protests across the villages to eradicate a number of 'untouchability' practices. Ramu's (male youth, 25 years) statement, 'we got
the feeling of power that we could stand up to the other castes...',
reflects the ensuing change from Dalit subordination towards greater
independence and dignity. This was complemented by labour diversification, including a shift among women from subsistence fishing to
selling marine produce in the nearby markets.

The identification of caste and class as the roots of Dalits' problems
in this initial phase of organizing, however, meant that gender issues
received less attention. These included the unequal division of labour,
wages, and educational access. Kalvikkarasi, therefore, started discussions with the women about forming separate Dalit women's sangams.
The focus on women stemmed partly from RADA staff's experiences
of the difficulties in keeping men organized, given the large-scale problem of male alcoholism in the village (and the surrounding area). The
corollary was the premature demise of many men from alcoholism,
leaving behind widows. These women formed a disproportionately
large, socio-economically vulnerable subgroup of women-headed
households. Leela, widowed in her thirties, surmised: 'There are more
widows due to alcoholism in this entire area, more than twice those
who died during the [2004] tsunami!' Kalvikkarasi also observed other
outcomes of male alcoholism and village underdevelopment. There
was less solidarity and less respect for women here than in the neighbouring villages. Dalit women therefore were seen as more reliable to
engage with through the sangams. Equally important was the sangams'
potential to enable these women to decide what their most urgent
needs were and to participate in decision-making on village matters.
Until then, community governance was exclusively controlled by male
leaders of the 15 Dalit kinship groups in the village.

The organization of the women into sangams mirrored Vidiyal's
strategy (Chapters 3 and 4) of helping women to be more financial
secure through savings and loans activities; and at the same time,
helping the women to engage in collective action to secure livelihood
entitlements. Kalvikkarasi, however, insisted that these groups should
be independent of the government: 'I explained to the women that we
would not be able to effectively protest against the government if we
were affiliated to their sangam programme, despite the more regular
loans their sangams receive.' She further recognized the difficulties in

organizing the women. Women were confined to narrow roles within the family, forced by poverty into daily wage labour, and excluded from public–political life. It, therefore, took around two years of meetings and encouragement by Kalvikkarasi and some educated village youth before 30 Dalit women decided to form one sangam in each of the main colonies in 2001. According to one of the original members, Selvi (married woman, 35 years), these women were in employment and had husbands who agreed to their participation. They also were interested in taking up issues and had speaking skills. As others saw the benefits of sangam membership, this number slowly grew; today, there are eight sangams involving around 140 women.

Many women saw the sangams as an opportunity to improve their economic security and to learn about the world outside their village, including about government schemes. These improvements were often mentioned in the same breath as gender relations. Women viewed the sangams as instrumental in increasing male respect accorded to them. They wanted to counter a male discourse that created a gender hierarchy in contributions to the village and family. It claimed that women did not know anything and that only men 'really work' for the village. Rupa (married woman, 44 years) noted:

> I wanted to know how to speak well, and through the sangam meetings and trainings we would get information about the world, learn new things, ask questions, and give petitions. We wanted to do something for our village. Before, we women lived at a very low level, like slaves at home. Wherever we went, men would tease us that we only work in our homes and don't go outside, don't know anything, don't work in the village. How long could we live like this? That's why we started to take action in the village.

For more educated women like Deepa (widow, 33 years), who had grown up in Chennai city where gender norms are generally less restrictive, sangam participation held out the prospect of greater freedom in a village context. She also felt she had a duty to act as a guide to the majority illiterate, village-born women.

As in Kovilur and Vettriyur villages (Chapters 3 and 4), an important discourse that Kalvikkarasi introduced was the collective power of women to overcome structural and personal barriers. Collective identity as Dalit women was built by emphasizing solidarity based on their living conditions, as well as on the power they uniquely had as a group to obtain their livelihood needs. The effectiveness of this strategy is evident from the women's discussions on three sets of social relations. Jothi (widow, 47 years) highlighted the re-visioning of Dalit identity as a service caste for others by placing positive value on village service: 'The other caste people won't do anything for us or the village; we only have to do things for them. This has not changed...[So] we need unity among women because only by working together can we achieve the solution to many basic problems in our village.' Leela (widow, 37 years) and Sathya (widow, 42 years), by contrast, judged Dalit men as less likely to unite and persevere to solve basic problems such as village amenities. Sathya also referred to gender divisions in the representation of village interests: 'The male [Dalit] leaders are helping and support-ing only the men; only women help women'. Signifying the third set of relations were Kala and Jothi's suggestions that government officials and police are more likely to recognize women's 'right to speak' and respond to women's petitions. Women, therefore, could gain power by subverting gender norms relating to female exclusion from public–political life. Kala was adamant, however, that this did not entail men's exclusion from collective action; rather, their role was to provide the women with support from behind the scenes.

Again, as in the previous case studies, women's sangam participation was affected by their position in the life cycle as well as by their house-hold arrangements and the burden of household labour. What distin-guished this village was the large number of kinship groups among Dalit women: social ties among these women were formed mainly within the enclosed kinship marriage circles that are characteristic of south Indian marital alliances (Dube 2003; Kapadia 1995), though these circles were opening up through inter-kinship marriages. Another distinction was the proliferation of widows. They were stigmatized as inauspicious or immoral without husbands to keep them in check, which meant they had less social freedom than married women and less freedom to speak. Nonetheless, due to their large numbers and specific vulnerability, many widows joined the sangams and also took up leadership positions.

The NGO approached the challenge of constructing the collective identity and identifying the interests of the large number of sangam members through a series of meetings and training sessions. These meetings were aimed at developing their political consciousness. Women were encouraged to identify common needs and petition officials, and learnt about their entitlements under government schemes. Aside from separate sangam meetings on savings activities, Kalvikkarasi convened joint sangam meetings every three months at which women took collective decisions on which entitlements to pursue. Values of unity and equality underlay such meetings: Kalvikkarasi noted, 'We encouraged the women to share all that they were doing in order to help the groups to come up equally'. Women also attended meetings organized by other NGOs, to inspire them with the confidence to take up issues by hearing how other women solved their village problems. One important change women noted as a consequence was the expansion of their knowledge: from 'only living in a small circle within the village', Latha (unmarried girl, 21 years) said, 'we learnt how to speak before others...how to save money...how to take action and not just work and eat like before.'

Leadership and decision making, however, pivoted around Kalvikkarasi as the de facto head of the sangams, despite her attempts to build autonomous sangam leadership. Her role as development broker was perceived slightly differently from that of Veronnika in the other case studies. While Kalvikkarasi too had greater education and more knowledge of government schemes and of how to deal with officials, she was also a trusted village member who was not tied to any one Dalit kinship group.[3] Her identity as an independent villager generated greater expectations that she would speak on behalf of all the women and be their representative in their dealings with the state. Women expressed their relationship with her in the following terms: 'Blind people will always be at the back, while those with eyes will always be in the front'; 'Kalvikkarasi leads us—she is like a big officer while we are her guards!'; etc. They constructed a subsidiary yet active role for themselves: 'We may not speak up, but will resist boldly! We will sit boldly like this, even if the police come now'; 'We know about women's rights and how to organize if there is any problem'; and so on. What women failed to acknowledge was how Kalvikkarasi herself faced gender constraints: her husband occasionally reacted badly to her work and to her freedom of movement. Kalvikkarasi, in turn, was torn between her desire to build women's autonomous agency so as to ensure changes in her village, and having to take the lead where women were slow to act or constrained by their circumstances.

Despite these problems, sangam leaders were chosen. Each sangam elected three members for a three year term. This leadership was central to forging common interests and representation among such a large number of women. Leaders were chosen for their articulacy and their energy; there was a hierarchy with older, less educated, and often more silent women less likely to assume leadership than their younger, more educated, and more vocal counterparts. Leaders would discuss sangam and village issues with Kalvikkarasi once a month when Dalit male leaders held their separate village meetings. This served symbolically to impress on both women and men the new space being created for Dalit women's decision making on village issues. Because of limited financial resources, which allowed only a few to travel to government offices, leaders were responsible for meeting government officials with the petitions which were drafted by Kalvikkarasi and signed by sangam members. Through practical action, therefore, these women learnt how to secure entitlements. They gained the knowledge and confidence to meet officials, to speak and become active in their village.

Tackling Exclusions and Achieving Interests

The confidence and knowledge to which sangam leaders alluded were gained from the sangams' initial achievements on both conflictual (for example, temple entry and arrack sales) and non-conflictual (for example, water tanks and roads) issues. Importantly, these achievements touched on caste–class as well as gender relations. At the same time, interests perceived as firmly grounded in caste discrimination served to obscure gender inequalities. For example, women successfully petitioned government officials for the return of the government primary school. The Reddiyars had seen to its removal years ago in furtherance of their control over Dalits' labour. While this success symbolized another break from a past marked by caste-based exclusion from knowledge, it did nothing about the lower educational attainment of women.[4] A similar outcome resulted when a small group of Dalit women entered Silliamman[5] temple. This was an action with strong symbolic value in contesting religious exclusion and exposing 'untouchability' as a constructed, 'unnatural' discourse. However, though the Dalits gained equal access to the temple and its lands, it was the men who made the decisions about the management of the temple. The women were left to clean it. This reiterated gender norms distinguishing women's less important roles from that of men.[6]

Finally, unique to this case study, Dalit women also took up issues directly relating to their gender interests. They sought to tackle the problem of male alcoholism and arrack sales in 2002 by making a formal police complaint. Despite the ensuing police raid, however, the lucrative nature of the business eventually ensured its resumption. Thereafter, the women balanced the threat of men stopping the sangams with continuing protests against alcohol sales, and decided not to make another official complaint. Their alternative strategy was to pressurize several sangam women to stop their involvement in arrack production, and offer them financial aid to establish alternative small businesses. By contrast, family problems, such as egregious domestic violence, were often tackled by counselling and only rarely by sangam intervention. Pushpa (married woman, 28 years) suggested the reason: 'If we women get involved in family problems, the men of that family will surely say, "So you have started a big women's sangam and want to involve in our family problems?" Like this they will scold us and then our husbands also will create problems for us.' What men's reactions to these two issues reveal is how they enacted a public–private divide, where family and 'male business' (that is, alcohol consumption and sales) were private affairs exempt from public scrutiny.

Women's accounts of the above-mentioned developments in their village, however, highlight a multiplicity of views. Leela spoke for the sangam leaders: 'We have climbed all the steps and we know that only through us have these facilities come to our village…but we don't get the name [that is, recognition] for this.' She points to the challenge of communicating sangam activities to such a large group. Communication was hindered by the women's poor education, which meant they found it hard to retain information about all the activities the sangams were engaged in. Their lowly class status also meant that they did not have enough spare time in which to visit government offices. These issues recurred throughout the women's struggle against the shrimp farm, and explain the sometimes conflicting versions of events and meanings women attached to their actions.

Macroeconomics of Aquaculture and its Regulation

The Dalit women's struggle to stop the shrimp farm occurred in the context of macroeconomic policies pursued by the Indian state in the aftermath of the liberalizing economic reforms of 1991. The industrial farming of shrimp for export, which was introduced along the Indian coastline in the late 1980s, increased rapidly from the 1990s. It assumed considerable importance as a foreign currency earner,[7] particularly in the southern coastal states of Andhra Pradesh and Tamil Nadu (Asian Development Bank *et al.* 2005). In part, this was spurred by vast World Bank funds being poured into the Indian aquaculture sector in the 1990s, with the intention of starting a 'blue revolution'. The central government's policy to promote shrimp culture highlighted the benefits of bringing the vast saline tracts of the country's coastline under production: this would create employment opportunities for rural Indians living in brackish water areas and earn foreign exchange (Food and Agricultural Organization [FAO] 2002; Mangubhai 2004).

The regulation of commercial shrimp farming falls under the National Coastal Aquaculture Authority, established in 1997 after the Supreme Court verdict in *S. Jagannath* vs *Union of India and Others*.[8] The Supreme Court therein prohibited semi-intensive and intensive shrimp farming in the Coastal Regulation Zone (CRZ).[9] It also prohibited the conversion of agricultural or public lands into shrimp farms, in order to prevent serious environmental, social, and economic problems from afflicting rural communities. Further, the granting of operating permits was to be based on the precautionary principle: permits would be granted only if farms would not adversely affect the environment.[10] Notably, the scientific report on which this judgement was based recognized that employment opportunities for contiguous coastal populations had been considerably reduced by commercial aquaculture.

The activities of the National Coastal Aquaculture Authority, which was eventually legislated under the Coastal Aquaculture Authority Act 2005, include: inspecting aquaculture farms to record their environmental impact; registering all coastal aquaculture farms and ordering their closure if found to be causing pollution or destroying local livelihoods; and ensuring that agricultural lands and common lands are not converted into coastal aquaculture farms. Moreover, under its 2005 rules, the Authority specified a number of guidelines for regulating coastal aquaculture—for example, on-site selection, environmental impact assessments, wastewater management, and protecting the livelihoods of coastal communities. Additionally, the Water (Prevention and Control of Pollution) Act 1974 provides that any aquaculture farmer must obtain authorization from the Pollution Control Board to set up a disposal system for trade effluents, though most small farms do not set up such systems and effectively fall outside the Board's remit. There is no mandatory environmental impact assessment for smaller farms of less than 10 hectares. The Authority, moreover, has potentially conflicting environmental and economic goals. Its brief is to sustain an increase in aquaculture products, as well as to regulate their production (Coastal Aquaculture Authority 2006: 3).

Unfortunately, the Supreme Court judgement has not been implemented properly owing to the local political influence of shrimp farmers, who have subverted the law. The failure cannot be divorced from political and economic constraints under which the Coastal Aquaculture Authority currently operates. First, the Ministry of Agriculture, specifically the Department of Fisheries, exercises administrative control over the Authority despite the Authority's establishment under the Environmental (Protection) Act 1986. Second, the central government's Marine Products Exports Development Authority strongly pushes the expansion of coastal aquaculture and exports of aquatic products, particularly shrimp. Third, the large number of amendments to the CRZ notification has largely diluted its prohibitions on coastal land use. Proposed further amendments seek to shift the objective of the regulations from conservation to sustainable development. This would open up the coastal areas to 'economically significant activities' (Kasturi 2010). All this is relevant to the Mallibakkam shrimp farm struggle.

Collective Action and the Politics of Protecting Entitlements

Political and Legal Strategies against the Shrimp Farm

Initial Phase: Struggling as a Community   Unknown to the Mallibakkam Dalits, in June 2002, two Reddiyars sold off 10 acres of land alongside Buckingham Canal to a Christian businessman living in Chennai city. This sale pushed up land prices and included a pond used for irrigation purposes, thereby prompting neighbouring landowners to sell their lands to the same businessman. Dalits assert that all this land was originally government wasteland (*tharisu poramboke*), which was occupied by Reddiyars and converted into private land years ago, and which was partly being utilized for agriculture. The following year, the new landowner started to clear the land, at which point Dalits in the colony opposite learnt of the land transfer. Their queries were deflected by the assurance that the land would become a fruit orchard in which Dalits would find work. It was not until earth movers started to dig the ponds that they realized a shrimp farm was under construction. The site supervisor, however, dismissed Dalit women's accusations of deception. On the basis that the land sale was legal, he refused their demands to stop the construction.

Kalvikkarasi's subsequent ability to mobilize the Dalit women to take action against the shrimp farm rested on two arguments: the lack of employment opportunities in shrimp farming; and its negative impacts on the environment and on agriculture and fishing-based livelihoods. While some women already knew examples of such negative impacts, the others were emboldened to take action by their previous entitlement successes. The fact that an outsider was interfering in their village promoted solidarity. Dalits constantly mentioned the farm owner's much higher class position and greater political influence, as his name was connected with prominent Chennai-based politicians. He was able to influence and bribe state officials to support his application to operate the shrimp farm. Little was known of the farm owner beyond his identity as a non-Dalit. Hence, unlike the other case studies, women's perceptions of this struggle did not focus on their opponent's caste. Instead, the emphasis lay on his class and links to the state, though caste also underlay these aspects, as will be seen later.

The women's specific livelihood vulnerability also motivated them to engage in the shrimp farm struggle. This vulnerability arose from the caste- and gender-based division of fishing work, with its implications for class. Over half the Mallibakkam Dalit women traditionally fished by squatting in the low tidal waters of the canal to catch seasonal prawns (*irāl*) and crabs (*nandu*) by hand. In comparison, only around 30 Dalit men had learnt from their Sembadavar male neighbours and fishermen, the skills necessary to use catamarans (*kattumarram*) to catch fish with nets further along the canal. The only other fishing community in the canal consisted of Vanniyar men fishing further inside the canal waters using catamarans and different fishing techniques, while the prerogative to fish in the open seas belonged to other non-Dalit castes living by the seashore 1 km away. These divisions along lines of labour, equipment, and fishing location influenced economic profits: those men with nets and boats to access rich fishing grounds caught more fish. They also affected how long people spent in the water, and consequently, how exposed they were to water pollution. Additionally, Dalit women's vulnerability stemmed from their work as agricultural labourers and sharecroppers. Both kinds of work were expected to decline if the shrimp farm went ahead.

The following excerpt of a conversation with sangam leader, Kala, frames the situation in terms of competing rights. While often not expressed in the language of rights, rights lay behind many women's justification for interfering with the farm owner's right to use his private property.

> Once you come to my house, you can sit and go, but if you want to add any poison to my house, how can I allow that?...A person has the right to do whatever he wants with his own land, but not to spoil the common property of our village. He should not cross his boundary, as we only survive by eating from the canal. So he has no right to mix chemicals from his farm into the canal. He should not take our rights away; he should only take his rights.

Her statement appeals to two arguments. One is a perceived boundary around an individual's rights, crossing which constituted an unacceptable infringement of another's right. Second is that of individual versus collective rights, and especially the appropriation or privatization of the commons for 'development purposes', which is synonymous with the pursuit of economic growth policies in India (Visvanathan and Parmar 2005).

Even though they had their own, specific concerns, the women's first petition to the district collector in June 2003 was made on behalf of all Mallibakkam villagers. It was signed by Dalit women across the colonies in order to lend the weight of greater numbers. The women's appeal was based on the precautionary principle and rested a compelling moral case on their class identity—the need for state protection against the likely negative effects the farm would have on their agriculture-based livelihoods. They targeted the collector because he headed the District Aquaculture Committee, which inspects potential shrimp farm sites before forwarding licence applications for final decision to the Aquaculture Authority. Moreover, their previous experiences of petitioning had increased their understanding of how the state operated. Leela talked of their recognition that local officials, who are more enmeshed in power relations in the area, were less likely to respect them and act on their petitions than higher officials. On this issue, however, petitions to the collector and the Tamil Nadu Pollution Control Board met with no response. It took a collective protest outside the taluk office by Dalit women from several villages to galvanize the government to investigate the land status of the shrimp farm.

Faced with the officials' lack of response to their petitions and the continued construction of the shrimp farm, Dalit women and men adopted several extra-institutional tactics. They disrupted the construction of the pond and confronted the local manager overseeing the work on the farm. The possibility of direct negotiation with the farm owner was foreclosed by his eliciting the support of local police to threaten the villagers. Jothi's description of an incident when seven police vans descended on the Dalit colony implicates the police in the continuing disregard of Dalit women's claim. The police insisted that the women should submit petitions rather than resort to disrupting the construction of the farm. They further threatened to take action should Dalits persist, as 'there was nothing they could do to stop the farm and, moreover, they were too far away to be affected by the farm'. Dalit women's greater vulnerability was marked by a policeman employing vulgar, sexual language in his attempt to stop their protests.

While this shows how state officials' direct actions or failure to act both contribute to Dalit women's exclusion, institutionalized exclusion also contributes. The licensing process itself, with the district-level committee inspecting the proposed site to ascertain land and groundwater quality, presented the villagers with no opportunity to object, despite their livelihoods being at stake. The Aquaculture Authority, subsequently, issued the licence in March 2004 in contravention of its own mandate to prevent shrimp farming on agricultural or common lands. Endorsed by the state Department of Fisheries in June that year, the licence was then returned to the district collector for final approval.

The issuing of the licence focuses attention on a key state practice that determines the perpetuation of inequalities in entitlements, namely, corruption. Women allege that the farm owner bribed the land surveyor and tahsildar to ignore their argument that the land was originally government wasteland meant for landless poor. The officials instead reported the legal conversion to private lands years ago without mentioning its continuing use for agriculture. Further, according to Dalit women and local social activists, government officials received substantial bribes to grant the licence, and the police received substantial bribes to protect the farm owner. In a situation where state actors deemed legal a commercial operation that contravened the state's own formal rules, Dalit women had little choice but to continue to submit petitions to higher district and state government officials in the hope that the state's rules would be impartially enforced. Caste considerations further restricted their choice of political avenues of appeal. They chose not to engage with their local Member of the Legislative Assembly (MLA) owing to his Reddiyar caste identity and his kinship with the ex-MLA living in Mallibakkam village who had sold off his lands to the shrimp farm owner.

State corruption aside, the shrimp farm owner also allegedly bribed non-state actors. The allegations related to the Dalit male leaders, and especially Siva (married man, 41 years). Siva exercised de facto panchayat authority from 2001 to 2006 through his wife (who was the actual panchayat president), and thereafter was officially appointed as panchayat president. Women were split, primarily along kinship lines, as to whether Siva had received information on the proposed shrimp farm and nonetheless put his (wife's/president's) signature to the land transfer. The local village administrative officer affirmed that a no-objection certificate had to be obtained in order to run the shrimp farm, signed by, inter alia, the village leaders and the panchayat president. In addition to the allegations that Siva and other male Dalit leaders had received bribes to give the go-ahead to the farm, it was also alleged that Siva was unhappy with the size of the bribe he received, and retracted his support for the farm as a result. Deepening some women's anger towards Siva was also their knowledge of other shrimp farms that were stopped only where villagers learnt early on of the planned farm and stopped the land transfer or licence application. In his defence, Siva accused the police of spreading rumours of his bribe taking in order to discredit him.

The complex power relations surrounding male engagement in politics are evident from Siva's openly declining to criticize the government because of his position as de facto panchayat president. He also allegedly turned away a Dalit political party as a potential ally after local party members accused him of bribe taking. Siva's supporters, however,

promote an alternative version of events. They allege that the farm
owner's connections with the Dalit party leadership led to this party
ignoring the Dalits' struggle. At the same time, Kalvikkarasi recognized
that to involve political parties would have entailed giving prominence
to male leaders in decision making, which would have restricted the
sangam women's role. These nuanced political negotiations, coupled
with the probable culpability of the male leaders and Siva, strengthen
the argument that the women's exclusion from local politics means they
are relatively immune to being co-opted by corruption in comparison to
men (International Council on Human Rights Policy [ICHRP] 2010).

The granting of the licence produced a shift in tactics on both sides
of the conflict. This demonstrates the importance of the role that state
institutions play in shaping local power relations. When the farm owner
asked a priest to bless the land in July 2004, Dalits reacted with more
violent tactics. Women wielded their brooms and shoes alongside their
men and chased away the workers and the priest. The farm owner's
response was to resort to the law on the strength of his licence. He
filed a police complaint against 14 Dalit men, alleging rioting, wrongful
restraint, and assault. He also obtained an interim injunction to prevent
the Dalit villagers from disrupting the farm's construction. A High
Court petition requested a writ of mandamus to direct police officials
to provide adequate protection for the farm owner and his farm. For
their part, Dalits sought to disprove the petitioner's statement that his
company wanted to provide employment to local poor farmers. They
reiterated the case that the farm posed a threat to their livelihoods.

With the farm owner's entire land becoming off-limits, the shrimp
farm owner's formal legal entitlement to land came into direct conflict
with Dalits' informal entitlement to access the canal. These two conflicting entitlement systems were apparent in a reconciliation meeting
convened by members of several panchayats in response to the farm
owner's complaint against the Mallibakkam villagers. They decided to
petition the district government, using their authority to object to any
development within panchayat limits. The petition opposed the shrimp
farm on the grounds that it interfered with common access rights to the
land for grazing cattle. The lack of response to this petition, probably
due to the granting of the licence, points to conflicting priorities within
the state apparatus itself, and particularly the tensions and hierarchies
between local and higher levels of government.

The Dalits also sought the protection of law for their livelihood entitlements, introducing legal norms and standards into how they framed their demands. They filed a pro bono publico petition in the name of sangam member and fisherwoman, Natya (married, 61 years), before the Chennai High Court on the separate advice of Kalvikkarasi and the sympathetic superintendent of police. This petition requested a writ of mandamus to direct the district collector and State Pollution Control Board to halt construction of the shrimp farm. The argument was that the farm would cause water pollution and adversely affect the villagers' livelihoods, besides being situated on agricultural land in contravention of the *Jagannath* judgement. The court, however, decided not to go into the merits of the case. It instead directed the collector to make a final decision based on the Dalit women's original complaint and in accordance with the law. In the women's eyes, this allowed the economic power of the shrimp farm owner decisively to influence the collector's order in December 2004. The women's complaint was dismissed on the grounds that the Aquaculture Authority had approved the farm licence. The shrimp farm commenced operation in January 2005.

Contested Gender Positions and Men's Role in the Struggle   The preceding subsection described Dalit women's perceptions of their key role in the shrimp farm struggle. What follows reveals how men contested both that role and the women's new collective identity. Dalit men constantly disparaged the women's participation in the struggle, questioning what women could achieve by 'getting dressed up and giving petitions, moving about day and night' (Geetha, married woman, 44 years). They made statements like, 'You want to rule over men? You cannot do that!' (Sheela, married woman, 44 years). Sathya assessed the problem as one of male 'prestige' being threatened by women's collective power over a village issue. This prestige was maintained by imposing boundaries on the things women could do, via controls over their labour and sexuality, as in Kovilur and Vettriyur villages. These boundaries stood in tension with the women's instrumentality in accessing basic amenities and services.

The women's ability to negotiate male opposition was partly fuelled by the sense of power and security they gained by being associated with socially connected Kalvikkarasi. She spread knowledge to the women and encouraged them to speak out on village issues. They also had some initial successes in securing entitlements, which fuelled their desire 'to come up in life' (Sheela). Kalvikkarasi noted how women slowly stopped obeying their husbands without question and started to take decision on more household and personal matters for themselves. One woman recalled how her husband used to draw a line in the sand and stop her crossing this line to attend meetings, which she did anyway. She incurred beatings, which she took as just part of life, until he finally gave up. Other women adopted strategies of sharing with their husbands information they had obtained through sangam activities in order to show how sangam participation would benefit their families. To gain legitimacy for their actions, the women extended invitations to supportive Dalit male leaders and male youths to join them in presenting their petitions. The women's collective intervention was required in only a few instances; for example, where two men constantly made allegations of illicit relations against the women. When reasoning with the men, the women referred to family welfare and their irreplaceable role as mothers, thus reproducing gender norms. Structures of power thus persisted and were reinforced even while women tried to change male behaviour.

Moreover, conflicting narratives about the role of the men in enabling the shrimp farm owner to obtain the licence reveal another important facet of Dalit women's agency, namely, the importance of gender and kinship influences on women's actions as well as on representations of their actions. Kinship in the Indian context represents not merely affective relationships. It is also an important linking feature that structures hierarchical gender relationships within the family (Geetha 2007: 76). Hence, some Dalit women tended to boost the image of the men as having led the struggle, thereby diminishing the role of women in favour of representations that promote kinship and caste. In doing so, the power and the status of these women increased. This was particularly prominent in retellings of the role of Siva. His female kin emphasized his heroism in leading the struggle and dealing with the repercussions, such as the false police cases against him. The insecurity wrought by the shrimp farm also heightened notions of kinship and family as providers of stability and protection. Women talked up the role that male leaders played, in return for their protection. This was central to the kinship group's maintaining its social status and stability.

In the light of the above, women also voiced a number of conflicting viewpoints on whether their sangam participation has changed gender relations. While a few women agreed with Kalvikkarasi's assessment of growing female autonomy, others asserted that men continued to refuse to allow women to develop independently. Jothi gave the example of Siva taking over his wife's authority as panchayat president. As in Kovilur and Vettriyur villages, women here also highlighted the hierarchical distinction men sought to make between the female political domain (sangam matters, such as savings and basic needs) and the male political domain (village matters, such as temple management and larger village concerns). The former was trivialized. The gender divide in knowledge and education was seen as justifying women's inability to participate in village development. This perception informed many Dalit men's narratives of the shrimp farm struggle, which assigned women subordinate, 'follower' roles. At the same time, counter-trends appeared among younger, more educated men, who acknowledged that women were more united in solving village problems and had played a larger part in the struggle. These men, however, emphasized that women had an equal but not independent role in village affairs.

A final aspect of gender relations concerns Siva's oppositional stance towards Kalvikkarasi and the sangams, at the heart of which seems to be Siva's ambition to be *the* development broker-cum-political patron for the Dalits. According to Kalvikkarasi,

> He sees us women doing so much while he, as a man, cannot do as much. So he becomes jealous, saying we women are always rubbing our actions in his face…He says when women question his actions as president now, 'this is why the women's sangams should not exist, as Kalvikkarasi is making the women know and question everything'. The women's sangams did so much during the shrimp farm struggle, but Siva says *he* did everything!

Her last comment was substantiated in interviews with Siva and his female kin, who also claim all the sangam-led developments as his initiatives. Siva takes advantage of his formal position as panchayat president to reinforce his power as formal entitlement broker by directing panchayat development benefits towards his kin. This preferential brokerage, besides creating a new level of exclusion and division among Dalits in the village, undermines the functioning of the sangams. The corollary is to reaffirm male domination in the public sphere. Women

negotiated these gender dynamics throughout the shrimp farm struggle, from the first phase guided by Kalvikkarasi to a second phase with
widening support in civil society.

Widening Civil Society Support and State Repression   The second
phase of Dalit women's struggle to stop the shrimp farm is marked by
the tsunami that destroyed lives, property, and livelihoods in hundreds
of villages and towns along the south Indian coastline on 26 December 2004. Its aftermath saw systematic caste discrimination against and
exclusion of Dalits in the distribution of relief aid and rehabilitation
(Aldrich 2010; Gill 2007; Human Rights Watch 2005). Assessors of the
reach and impact of government relief programmes also paid insufficient attention to gender (Akerkar 2007; Burnad and Society for Rural
Education and Development [SRED] Team 2006). State entitlement
arrangements for relief and rehabilitation constructed victimhood nar-
rowly as 'fisherfolk', meaning sea-fishing castes, which excluded Dalits
despite their allied labour work or inland fishing. Additionally, agricultural land salinization and salt pan destruction along the coastline
affected the livelihoods of many Dalit labourers, including those in
Mallibakkam village, who were not considered in the initial damage
assessment (Burnad and SRED Team 2006). The task of helping those
who fell outside the state's definition of victims was relegated to a large
number of NGOs flooding the coastline following the tsunami.

As a result of NGO post-tsunami relief work, Dalit women were
given the opportunity to widen their support networks and to open
new pathways to protect their entitlements. At the same time, the
sudden influx of resources stirred up competition and divisions in and
between village communities, in part fuelled by the way NGOs distributed relief. The NGOs tended to establish their own women's groups
as the basis for selective distribution of relief materials. Dalit women's
accounts of this period centre on Kalvikkarasi's contacts with the Tamil
Nadu Dalit Women's Movement (TNDWM), which brought them
immediate relief and gave them loans to set up their own small businesses. The TNDWM also conducted training sessions on alternative
employment, women's rights, laws, and government schemes. These
activities testified to the economic and social power of the women's
movement, a power that transcended village boundaries and offered

the potential to equalize power relations with the shrimp farm owner. The women, therefore, appealed to TNDWM for help.

The TNDWM, a state-wide movement of Dalit women, was established by Dalit women activists in 1997 following extensive caste riots in southern Tamil Nadu. The activists believed that the women's and Dalit movements had failed to address the specific experiences and vulnerabilities of Dalit women, which relate to cross-cutting issues of caste, class, and gender. The main focus of the movement, according to one of its founding members, Fatima Burnad, is rights-based capacitation and leadership building among Dalit women. The goal is to support them collectively to take up issues in their communities and realize their rights. Simultaneously, she makes clear that the movement is not against Dalit men, but against patriarchy and caste oppression. The TNDWM coordinator, Magimai, distinguishes between eradicating caste and 'untouchability' as long-term goals of the movement, and helping Dalit women to become political leaders and secure livelihood entitlements in the short term. At the same time, she acknowledges that 'many Dalit men now follow *Manusmriti*',[11] meaning male tendencies to enforce the gender norms of dominant castes. The movement, therefore, takes up gender issues that tie in with caste issues, while foregrounding caste as the primary driver of power inequalities. The movement's members support one another's work, as well as help Dalit communities when they are asked to. They have assisted Dalit communities with issues they are unable to fight on their own, such as the shrimp farm.

The role that TNDWM members assumed in the shrimp farm struggle was to help in the next phase of strategizing on the shrimp farm. They made use of their wider social networks, provided some economic support, and fostered solidarity by bringing the villagers together with other Dalit women across the state. With the Dalit villagers, other affected fishing castes with whom Kalvikkarasi had initiated separate women's sangams, and Dalits from neighbouring villages, they mapped out potential strategies to have the farm licence revoked. Their strategies took account of what had been tried in the past. Under the guidance of the TNDWM, the women supplemented petitions to the collector by engaging with state-level officials. They contacted the agricultural minister because of his department's links to the Aquaculture Authority. Their petitions, however, shifted authorship to TNDWM in

an attempt to project a wider civil society base, which would legitimize
the Mallibakkam villager's concerns. Concurrently, with TNDWM support, around 2,000 people, primarily Dalit women, conducted a protest
outside the revenue divisional office in January 2005. They demanded
that government officials recognize their livelihood-related rights, and
they protested against corruption in the licensing process. Revenue
officials, consequently, promised to inquire into the matter.

Despite the change in strategies, the state still failed to treat Dalit
female citizens equally. No government official took any action. The
collector did not act, despite receiving instructions from the agricultural minister to inquire into the villagers' petitions. In addition, following
the revenue divisional officer's transfer soon after, the new office holder
indicated she could not reverse a decision made by her predecessor.
This inadequate state response drove Dalits to change strategies again.
They blocked the highway by their village. Their aim, by disrupting
transport services along this vital road link, was to force the government to listen to their demands for the cancellation of the shrimp farm
licence. The location of their protest was symbolic: 'We did so because
if the shrimp farm went ahead, we would die from all the chemicals.
And here if the vehicles hit us, we would also die.' The proximity of
the protest to their village boosted the numerical strength of protesters.
Dalit and other fishing caste women and men joined in; Chettiyars lent
their support and their Communist Party connections.

While the given discussion makes clear the state's role in perpetuating structural violence, what happened next shows the state engaging in
physical violence. Both kinds of violence attest to what women termed
arājagam (lawless practices) committed by state actors against them. In
response to the road block by around 1,500 villagers and Communist
Party cadre, around 300 police charged the crowd. They wielded *lathis*
(long batons) that caused multiple injuries. Police detained over 100
women, men, and children in two marriage halls for the entire day
before formal charges were laid against 21 Dalits. All were male, except
for the Dalit woman petitioner in the 2004 High Court case. Two Dalit
women's descriptions of the incident bear examination:

> The police chased us like dogs...they pulled our hair and saris, pushing
> all of us women into a vehicle like we were dogs...Those who raised our
> voices that day got good beatings. (Leela)

I was shouting in front of the women police after we were arrested that the police used '*vādi, pōdi*' against us, when even our husbands have not used such [disrespectful] language against us. The policemen have mothers, so why did they come to our village and torture us women like that?…They have not allowed us to live in our village, but if anyone did the same to their family, would they let this take place? (Sathya)

The women were so angry because this attack had made them lose trust in the police. They had expected that the police would uphold the law, despite prior experiences of police harassment. They also had believed that the police would respect women's bodily integrity and never attack them or treat them as less than human. Police actions thereby reinforce the interconnectedness of social inequalities. Dalit women had expected that their gender would protect them, but their low-caste status, combined with a lack of money to bribe police, effectively removed any protection.

This incident clearly shows the indivisibility of rights. State moves to restrict civil and political rights, such as the rights to freedom of assembly and speech, entrenched violations of socio-economic rights. These violations have to be viewed in the light of the prevailing political climate at the time. Civil rights were restricted by the state in the Tamil Nadu Essential Services Maintenance Act 2002. This Act was widely decried for making it illegal for state government employees in 'essential services' to go on strike or to refuse to work overtime (Viswanathan 2002). The police enforced the Act strictly, and applied it to anyone who halted essential services, such as road transport. The Mallibakkam villagers, by failing to seek police permission for their road protest, came to be viewed as transgressing the law.

The shrimp farm owner also used another tactic to undercut Dalits' liberty and security of life. He filed three police cases shortly thereafter against a total of 46 men and one woman, alleging offences that included poisoning the shrimp on the farm, destroying farm property, assault, and criminal intimidation.[12] While TNDWM provided legal aid in all the police cases, every one of which was eventually dismissed several years later for lack of evidence, open protests against the farm effectively halted. Women cited as reasons a lack of money as well as the superior political contacts and class position of the farm owner. In sum, their current strategic dilemma arises from fear of what government officials and police might next do should they continue to protest. This further affirms the indivisibility of rights.

Finally, national and international interventions have had very little impact on an issue that involves state practices bypassing state rules. This is apparent from TNDWM's actions since 2005. Mobilizing their contacts with regional NGO networks, international fact-finding missions made urgent appeals for action on the shrimp farm to the Government of India and to the UN Special Rapporteur on the Right to Food. The Dalit women were unaware of these appeals, although many were proud of foreigners having visited and inquired into their situation; it seemed to validate their suffering. Expectations that foreign intervention would alter their situation, however, have subsequently diminished. To date, the National Human Rights Commission has not replied to a 2007 petition filed on behalf of Mallibakkam villagers, which asked the Commission to intervene with the state government. This is despite a mandate to examine complaints alleging infringements of socio-economic rights.[13] Even if the Commission accepts the petition, it is unlikely to be able to hold the Tamil Nadu government to account: the Commission has an extensive backlog of cases and suffers from a lack of transparency (Asian NGOs Network on National Institutions [ANNNI] 2008). Meanwhile, the Aquaculture Authority's replies to TNDWM's right to information applications merely restate its opinion on the legality of the licence and the adequacy of environmental safeguards. Hence, the Mallibakkam shrimp farm licence was renewed in 2007.

Women's Perceptions of the Role of the State   When Dalit women assess their actions and the reactions of state actors, they talk of injustice and inequality in citizenship. While the general consensus among the women is that they fought their best against the shrimp farm, all highlighted the unevenness of the struggle when one individual's economic and political power determined state support. In the women's eyes, the outcomes were contrary to the rule of law and norms of justice. Kala's statement, 'we were only asking them to work according to the laws of the land, not their own laws', reveals an awareness of the biases resulting from non-implementation of the law. Women also remarked on their claims of not receiving a fair hearing as a consequence of their inability to pay bribes, unlike the farm owner. In other words, women not only pointed to inequalities in access to state institutions and thereby entitlements, but also critiqued state procedures and malpractices as contrary to law. They saw the resulting injustice as returning them to the poverty from which they had only recently escaped.

The balance in this struggle, according to Kalvikkarasi, might have shifted had higher government officials belonged to a Dalit caste. Her logic was that caste affiliation has the power to trump class power and relationships built through financial incentives. Without the equalizing power of caste identity, she stated, 'We cannot defeat money strength and political connections'. Newer district officials, moreover, claim their hands are tied by the decisions of their predecessors. They deny that they have a responsibility to monitor the conditions on which the licence was granted. Another possible lever in the struggle results from government officials tending to give respect and preference to those connected to political parties. Parties assume a brokerage role in securing entitlements for their local party members. However, an attempt by several sangam leaders to meet the new MLA in 2006 is evidence of the new inequalities this generates. They were angered by the MLA's dismissing their invitation to visit Mallibakkam. She would not hear their problems out of a lack of time to visit 'even her own people', meaning local party supporters. Political brokerage, arguably, conflicts with civil society strategies: a number of NGOs eschew party connections because parties are divisive and play a disempowering role in communities.

Effects on Entitlements and Power Relations

Finally, Dalit women's failure to shut down the shrimp farm has had many detrimental effects. Central is the violation of their right to an adequate standard of living, which is already lacking.[14] An adequate standard of living depends on there being water, food, and work of sufficient quality. The environment is polluted by frequent, unregulated discharges of untreated chemical-filled pond effluents into the canal.[15] Coupled with the extraction of groundwater to replenish the ponds, the pollution compromises the local drinking water supply.[16] It decreases land productivity on nearby agricultural lands and depletes marine life in the canal, thereby negatively affecting agriculture and fishing, both of which are fundamental to the livelihoods of Dalit

women.[17] This infringes their right to work[18] and increases food insecurity. Restricted mobility, the burden of household labour, and low
education limit women's opportunities for livelihood diversification[19]
in comparison to men. These serve to underscore their 'low' social position and increase their dependence on men. Gender norms, moreover,
intensify with male outmigration. This is because urban-based husbands try, from afar, to ensure that women are 'protected' by placing
greater constraints on their activities and interactions outside the home.
Related to this, water pollution is causing increasing health problems
that violate the women's right to the highest attainable standard of
health.[20] Healthcare costs are now prohibitive. Since work is less
available, Dalit women are increasingly reliant on high-interest loans
obtained primarily from dominant caste moneylenders. This fuels the
cycle of poverty, with negative implications for the women's ability to
engage in sangam activities.

Significantly, women's discourses have shifted from development,
as was seen in the early stages of sangam work, to survival. The shrimp
farm has taken its toll on their livelihoods. In Leela's words, 'If we get
any work opportunities, even if the wage is not good, we won't stay at
home now as we need some money each day to eat'. Livelihood insecurity thus forms a major obstacle to collective action today. Survival
imperatives displace some of the personal and collective gains that the
women made from participating in the sangam. Entitlement failure
limits women's freedom of expression, diminishes their sense of power,
and suppresses gender interests. Women said that they could no longer
protest against Dalit men selling arrack given the limited opportunities
to make a living. In sum, entitlement failure has ramifications beyond
the economic to the social and political arenas, which demonstrates,
again, how these arenas are intertwined as far as exclusion/inclusion
are concerned.

Discussion

This case study confirms that it would be a mistake to analyse only
those norms and standards that have been established in formal law and
policy. Such an analysis would be insufficient to explain how power
shapes entitlement processes and outcomes as it circulates among the
multiple agents that make up the Indian state. A more salient issue for

investigation is the interactions and power relations between state actors and Dalit women. This issue highlights the state's ability to perpetrate structural and physical violence in pursuit of an often-contradictory agenda of economic growth and social justice. These power relations determine the strategies Dalit women are able to employ and, in the present case, explain their inability to prevent new forms of exclusion. Another conditioning factor is their interactions with civil society actors. These interactions produce multiple discourses that further (re) shape Dalit women's perceptions of the entitlement process.

Citizen–State Relations, State Obligations, and Practices

A key point emerging from this case study is the disjunction between state laws and policies, and state practices, in a context of globalization and economic liberalization. This context is characterized by the rapid flow of capital, people, and goods across national boundaries. There are also fewer government regulations and restrictions; this relaxation is intended to encourage private investment and capital. Globalization creates complex interconnections between the local, the national, and the international. These interconnections structure the operation of entitlement systems and new forms of exclusion/inclusion. For example, the Working Group on Women's Empowerment (2006: 21) noted that while globalization generates economic opportunities in national and international markets, it does so primarily for those with higher education, resources, and access to capital. Globalization simultaneously intensifies existing inequalities and insecurities for many poor women. The interactions between formal and informal rules, and between state and non-state actors, reveal state practices that promote conflicting sets of rules on entitlement within the official law (Midgal 2004). In the current case, these practices disadvantageously position Dalit women in securing or protecting livelihood entitlements.

Accounts of the shrimp farm struggle indicate how various parts of the organizations, in particular the Aquaculture Authority and the Marine Products Exports Development Agency, have allied with shrimp farm entrepreneurs to promote shrimp exports above all else. Imperatives of international trade and macroeconomic interests have assumed priority over advancing the entitlement positions of local villagers. The practices of the Aquaculture Authority in particular, by granting the shrimp farm licence and renewing it, highlight two sets of contradictions, namely, between its practices and its own rules, and between its own rules and other legal rules. An example of the former is the contrastive experiences of Dalit women with the Guidelines for Regulating Coastal Aquaculture 2005. Paragraph 19.2 of the Guidelines require shrimp farm owners/managers to respect local community rights and needs, resolve any conflicts in amicable ways, and cooperate with community users of coastal resources in improving environmental conditions and community welfare.

The latter contradiction is reflected in the Aquaculture Authority's granting of the licence in contravention of the Supreme Court's *Jagannath* judgement, as well as in contravention of constitutional Directive Principles. These principles enjoin state actors to ensure the equal right to an adequate means of livelihood (Article 39[a]), distribution of ownership and control over material resources to best serve the common good (Article 39[b]), and special protection of the economic interests of Scheduled Caste (SC) citizens (Article 46). In contrast to the neoliberal notion that development under economic globalization is furthered by reducing state governance, the Aquaculture Authority's actions reveal the important role state actors play in intervening to ensure that macroeconomic policies are implemented (Das 2007). This includes restructuring the local rural economy for commercial fisheries production. The state has not been rolled back; rather, its redistributionist role has been curtailed. The state does not act to guarantee excluded actors their livelihoods. Instead, the caste–class divide has been widened by economic policies which have opened new trade opportunities in shrimp. It is only dominant castes–classes who are able to outlay the high capital costs to engage in commercial aquaculture (Mangubhai 2004). There is another link between these policies, international trade, and corruption by state actors (Robinson 1998),[21] which is explored later.

The key coalition between the dominant class shrimp farm owner and parts of the state suggests that the issue of class position is central. It also points to the role of the state in reproducing class inequalities. This makes a simplistic state–citizen binary problematic (Jeffrey and Lerche 2000). As Jeffrey and Lerche (2000: 858, 874–5) point out, based on their research in rural north India, the modes of class advantage shape the ways in which rural elites may co-opt and colonize the state, drawing state actors into local class-based conflicts. Dalit male elders like Muthu (married, 70+ years) in Mallibakkam village saw this class bias as 'the government only listening to the rich, never the poor'. Such elites buttress their position by establishing political connections with politicians and state officials, though their ability to establish a power base also depends on the wider political context (Jeffrey 2002). The comparisons Dalit women drew between themselves and the shrimp farm owner, therefore, often focused on differentials in political connections and class position. It was these differentials that determined access to state power and influence in the licensing process. In this case, the women's exclusion from political networks (itself a result of socio-economic exclusion) as well as their lack of funds contrasted with the shrimp farm owner, who had both connections and money. Muthu added to this their poor education and knowledge levels. He suggests that the Dalits lacked the cultural capital required to negotiate effectively with state actors (cf. Gupta 1995). Never mentioned by the Dalit villagers, but nonetheless pertinent to this situation, is the alignment of the shrimp farm with the state's macroeconomic policies.

However, while Jeffrey and Lerche (2000) explore class positions through caste groups, acknowledging the rough class–caste approximation, what they fail to make explicit is how different castes with roughly the same class position have different experiences as an outcome of state practices. This equally applies to women and men within castes. As a result of the shrimp farm owner's co-opting state officials to act in contravention of state law, Dalit women were particularly disadvantaged. Their livelihood insecurity, opportunities, and social position were all worse than those of Dalit men and other inland fishing castes of roughly comparable livelihood status. While Dalit men are able to outmigrate into new labour occupations, non-Dalit fishing castes have avoided work diversification. They have a greater ability than Dalit women to shift to fishing grounds away from the shrimp farm due to their possession of boats and nets. The current village administration officer's views on Dalit women's social position is telling about the distinctions drawn not only on the basis of class but also caste and gender. In asserting that the shrimp farm complied strictly with government rules, he dismissed the women's allegations of skin diseases caused by the farm chemicals by reference to how the women did not clean themselves after fishing in the canal. His words reinforce gender and caste representations of Dalit women as ignorant and dirty. The latter accusation is based on caste ideology, which posits the uncleanliness of Dalits as a symbol of their impurity.

By itself, however, this analysis paints an incomplete picture. What needs to be incorporated is an understanding of how Dalit women 'see the state' through their encounters with local state actors (Corbidge *et al.* 2005). How they see the state shapes their strategies to secure state entitlements. This focuses attention on the recurring discourse of state corruption (*ōzhal*). By definition, corruption is the abuse of public roles or resources for private benefit. It operates at the individual, institutional, or systemic level (Robinson 1998: 3). When Leela described the women's strategy of approaching the highest district official in order to secure entitlements, she was referring to the state at the local (district) level as a hierarchy. Higher officials should be more impartial, less corrupt, and command the power to direct lower officials to grant these entitlements. Gupta (1995), however, argues that this notion of corruption confined to the lower bureaucracy is inaccurate and instead points to corruption reaching to all levels of the state. Following the shrimp farm struggle, the Dalit women's view has changed. They now see corruption everywhere: from corruption at the local level to systemic corruption pervading all state institutions. There is, though, seemingly an incremental increase in the scale of corruption as one goes up the bureaucratic hierarchy. While paying bribes to lower officials was difficult, many Dalit women did so in order to obtain state welfare benefits like widows' pensions. But women pointed to their inability to match the bribes of hundreds of thousands of rupees paid to district and state officials.

Discourses of state corruption thereby foreground the dynamics of power and agency, and demonstrate the close links between corruption and social exclusion (Jeffrey 2002) via the complete distortion of entitlement systems. Corruption implies the organization and exercise of political power on a highly discretionary and personal basis. When law and state entitlement arrangements are corrupt, they cease to provide certainty; entitlement processes and outcomes are illegitimate. As a result, women's perceptions of the state change. They see it as a corrupt institution, which is unified in perpetuating their exclusion and entitlement deprivation. They talk of injustice and inequality in citizenship. In this situation, Dalit women's agency encounters a seemingly insurmountable block of economic and political power that NGOs, from the local to the international level, are unable to remove. The role of political parties, moreover, is ambivalent. Where their brokerage role is particularistic, they are likely to displace women's agency with patron–client type relations.

This understanding of the state and state practices explains, in part, the wide strategic repertoire Dalit women deployed during the shrimp farm struggle. The other part of the explanation includes: the women's perceptions of collective agency as shaped by their cultural–historical context (Tarrow 1994); adaptation in the face of opposition from the shrimp farm owner; and the diffusion of tactical knowledge through external interventions (King and Cornwall 2005). The initial stages of the women's struggle saw two concurrent tactics that originated from different sources. One was the socio-culturally defined tactic of direct obstruction, a key political resource given their socially excluded status. The second tactic was pursuing petitions through formal government channels, guided by Kalvikkarasi and the new knowledge she introduced to women. Their expectation was that the state would intervene to protect their basic livelihood entitlements, though this expectation changed as they witnessed police bias and harassment by the farm owner.

The state's role in granting the shrimp farm licence after receiving a bribe from the farm owner was central, as became apparent from his consequent counter-strategies. After he had secured legal entitlement to run the farm, he was able to resort to the law to protect that entitlement by penalizing Dalit opposition. The Dalits' attempt to use the same legal strategy, however, failed, primarily because the licence had been granted; this allowed the court to make a decision based on procedure as opposed to the substance of the petition. The Dalit women's claim, therefore, stood little chance. The corrupt district official who had approved the licence application in the first place was allowed the final decision-making power. The recourse to legal remedies to protect rights, therefore, cannot be viewed in isolation from those state practices and asymmetrical power relations which influence the outcomes of such remedies.

The determining effect of these factors is apparent in the latter stage of Dalit women's collective action strategies. Women understood that they made the shift from institutional and legal tactics to extra-institutional tactics (public demonstrations and the road block) because they had no choice. The new tactics were introduced by TNDWM into their strategic repertoire as the only option to force state officials to treat their claims more seriously, in the absence of economic and political power. The state's disproportionate use of force in reaction, however, was so unexpected an outcome that it reinforced the women's relative powerlessness, which constrained further collective action. This highlights the important links between structural violence and physical violence (Galtung 1969, 1990), and the way these can be mutually reinforcing. The state's repressive use of force against Dalit women compounds unequal power relations, an inequitable distribution of livelihood resources and opportunities, and a lack of voice; in other words, structural violence. Structural violence and policies that perpetuate this violence, in turn, increase Dalit women's vulnerability to physical violence and reduce access to remedies for physical violence. Distributive justice via securing or protecting Dalit women's livelihood entitlements, therefore, goes far beyond ensuring law and order.

The women's views on the corruption and violation of standards of conduct by state actors were complemented by their views on state obligations and accountability (*kannaku seyvuthal*). Gupta (1995: 389) highlights how the discourse of corruption, by singling out those actions that constitute an infringement of citizenship rights, thus acts to represent the citizens' rights to themselves. These are citizenship rights to development, to decent livelihoods, and to fair and transparent governance in support of these rights. Kala best captures women's perceptions on what the state *should* have done in response to their petitions:

> The main duty of the government is to help the people to develop... [the government] should be common to all. They don't have any right to do what they did in our village. Their duty was to stop the shrimp farm since it was destroying our agricultural land and livelihoods...They come to get our votes, but without giving us anything how can they do so? We eat *kanji* (rice soaked in water) once a day, while the shrimp farm owner's wife lives in a nice air-conditioned house. So why did the government support them over us?...We are in difficulties while these officials sit in their offices with their government salaries. But only if they get our vote can they sit in that chair. They know we are living in poverty and that's why we give petitions, but they don't think about

this at all. They get our petitions and then nicely sit and eat, while we are left hungry.

Kala is thus clearly aware of the gap between the state's obligations to its citizens and how those obligations are implemented. The obligations she defines parallel those codified under international human rights law. First, to respect people's rights by refraining from practices that directly infringe those rights, which she expresses as the government's 'lacking the right' to issue the farm licence. Second, to protect their socio-economic rights by stopping the shrimp farm owner from polluting the local environment and destroying their livelihoods in contravention of laws and aquaculture policy. Third, to fulfil their rights by measures to support their development (Committee on Economic, Social and Cultural Rights [CESCR] 1990; International Commission of Jurists [ICJ] 1998). Moreover, while her insistence on a 'government common to all' signifies principles of non-discrimination and equal treatment of all citizens, she goes beyond formal equality to insist on substantive equality. This means that the state has a duty to acknowledge the poverty of the women when compared with the shrimp farm owner's wealth, and accordingly pay special attention to fulfilling their rights (CESCR 2009). Her construction of state accountability and its legitimacy, therefore, rests on its fulfilment of the above obligations.

The basis for this accountability is an electoral democracy in which Dalit women exercise equal rights as citizens to vote. Without distinguishing between government bureaucrats and politicians, she correlates voting rights with duties incumbent on all state actors. Breach of duty is assessed as 'sitting and eating' (that is, corruption) while ignoring the women's petitions. The villagers had no opportunity to voice their concerns in the shrimp farm licensing process. The perception that the state is not accountable for its actions is related to the lack of participation and transparency in institutional arrangements. This confirms the centrality of participation, transparency, accountability, and non-discrimination principles as the basis of an anti-corruption agenda (ICHRP 2010). Additionally, if it is true that Siva and the village leaders signed the no-objection certificate on the shrimp farm, issues of gender arise: village leaders and panchayat presidents are invariably male. Hence, Dalit women's voices will often be excluded because there are no specific mechanisms to include them in such institutional processes.

This simultaneously weakens state accountability and deepens the women's perceptions of social inequalities in citizenship.

Shifting Discourses on Securing Entitlements

A second related theme is the way in which various entitlement discourses introduced by external agencies produce a multiplicity of meanings and expectations. Following Hilhorst (2000, 2001), women incorporate elements of externally introduced discourses and bodies of knowledge on entitlement strategies into their collective action. In the process, they reinterpret and redefine them. These understandings, however, are fluid and shift over time in response to different development interventions, each characterized by power processes regarding how 'new' meanings and knowledge are introduced (Long and van der Ploeg 1989). Moreover, development interventions take place within wider entitlement discourses circulated by the state through its laws, policies, and schemes. These state discourses also feed into the complex discursive process that frames Dalit women's collective action. These discourses determine the meanings that women attribute to their actions, and the attendant reshaping of power relations. As a consequence, the possibilities for Dalit women's agency become limited (Cornwall 2002).

Dalit women in Mallibakkam village have experienced two major external development interventions in the past two decades. First was the entry of the NGO RADA and Kalvikkarasi's organizing of the women into sangams. Second was the entry of multiple NGO actors in the aftermath of the 2004 tsunami, coupled with state relief interventions in the region. The first intervention succeeded in dislodging patronage relations with dominant caste Reddiyars as the primary way of securing livelihood entitlements. It did so by introducing a discourse of caste equality. This challenged the dominant discourse in which Dalits' 'pollution' and 'low-caste' status naturally bound them in relations of obligation to 'higher' castes. (This discourse of caste equality is evident today in Dalit women's joking remarks about sometimes 'accidentally' touching dominant caste women while standing in their separate queues in the temple or ration shop.) This was combined with a discourse of power derived from the strength of their labour force, which enabled them to negotiate entitlements to decent working conditions and freedom of employment.

Kalvikkarasi built on and expanded these discourses to include an element of gender in her creation of the separate Dalit women's sangams. Women thereby came to attribute a number of new meanings to the sangams' role in securing entitlements. These meanings were on three levels: the personal, the family, and the community/village. First, the sangams offered a way for women, especially widows, to gain financial independence for themselves and security for their families. Second, they were instrumental to village development, which was attributed uniquely to the women because of their caste, class, and gender positioning and power. By contrast, dominant caste–classes would not work for the village, nor help 'lower' castes. This can be understood in terms of the descending scale of duties (of 'lower' castes) and ascending scale of rights (of 'higher' castes) built into caste relations. Dalit men lacked the traits of unity and perseverance that were attributed to women, or would not work for 'women's interests' owing to their own interest in maintaining the gender hierarchy. In addition, state actors were more likely to respond to women than men. Third, the sangams were instrumental in bringing about changes in women, especially on the personal front. Women were exposed to wider knowledge; and they gained respect, especially from men, which enhanced their personal status and dignity. Taken together, all three meanings have particular significance for disrupting the male-constructed gender hierarchy of contributions to family and village welfare. In support of these meanings were discourses of women's separate power and role in public–political life, which spurred their collective agency.

At the same time, these new meanings existed in both complementary and contradictory relations to social norms. While kinship ties brought men and women together in a common drive for community development, these ties simultaneously worked against challenging male domination. Sangam and kinship interests and solidarity, therefore, at times came into conflict with one another, as seen in discussions on the role of male Dalit leaders in the shrimp farm struggle. Similarly, women interpreted discourses of women's power and public–political role not as opposing, but as complementary to their role and duties in the family. Hence, as with Kovilur and Vettriyur villages, women continued to perform gender roles in order to be able to claim new spaces for engaging in sangam action. The negotiation women undertook around these two sets of relations and the benefits they derived in return further argue in favour of the socially connected individual in analysing collective agency.

RADA and Kalvikkarasi promoted a fairly unified discourse of Dalit women organizing to alter caste, class, and gender relations in the process of securing livelihood entitlements. The second set of post-tsunami development interventions, however, introduced more diffuse and contradictory discourses. Natural hazards shake up existing entitlement systems, and this opens up access to new resources and the possibility of new entitlement arrangements. The impact of the tsunami on Dalit women's perceptions can be examined from two angles: that of the state and that of NGOs. Most Dalit women in Mallibakkam pointed to the highly visible presence of local government officials after the tsunami, which created greater expectations that they would receive official support to secure their entitlements. The government's emphasis on livelihood recovery programmes for sea-fishing castes, however, created three artificial distinctions. One was between those given formal recognition as tsunami-affected fishing castes and other (inland) fishing castes. Another was between government SHGs and autonomous women's groups. Government funds for rehabilitation were channelled through the government groups. The third was between those villages where people died and villages of survivors. As one Sembadavar woman from Mallibakkam noted, 'No one died in our village and so the government did nothing for us'. The effect was to create a hierarchy of suffering and entitlement to state-allocated resources. The line between the official failure after the tsunami, and the official failure during the shrimp farm struggle, became blurred. Both failures are examples of state injustice and inequality in the women's eyes.

On the other hand, the 'second tsunami' of international development aid (Nelson 2007) in the form of multiple NGO actors, along with resources and new ideas and discourses, also altered the local institutional environment. Citizens sought public goods and, by extension, the protection and services of the state (Kruks-Wisner 2011: 1143). Because injustice and inequality characterized the state's response to Dalit citizens, Mallibakkam Dalit women instead turned to NGOs to secure basic entitlements such as food and alternative work. The NGOs, thus, became a de facto fifth entitlement system during the post-disaster relief period. While several NGOs left after dispensing initial relief materials, and TNDWM engaged in the shrimp farm struggle, other

NGOs established women's SHGs for savings and credit activities. From eight sangams, the village today boasts around 30–40 groups, most comprising Dalit women. The plethora of sangams created after the tsunami arguably shifted the burden on to poor women to rebuild livelihoods, in addition to placing pressures on their time with meetings (Burnad and SRED Team 2006). The state government, moreover, effectively encouraged this process by promoting the greater financial reliability of women's savings and credit groups, which led banks not to lend to men's groups. The government's narrow discourse of economic empowerment also encouraged the process (see Chapter 2).

These processes put more strain on gender relations. Dalit male youths pointed out that no organization concentrates on men's development in the village any more. This is despite the responsibility men carry in the family and the fact that male livelihoods also were affected by the tsunami and the shrimp farm. Compounding this situation is the fact that the women's groups, including TNDWM, do not communicate effectively with men about what the groups do. Within Mallibakkam, Venkatesh (married man, 35 years) assessed the post-tsunami women's SHGs as having achieved little for developing their community. He saw them sidelining struggles to secure entitlements in favour of a state-sponsored discourse of economic empowerment. Further, many schemes introduced among women to promote small businesses have failed because their economic viability was inadequately assessed.

Another consequence of these processes is that women's understandings have shifted on both how to secure entitlements and which entitlements to secure. They also increasingly construct new, specific roles for civil society actors. There has been an increase in the competition to secure entitlements for families among different women's groups attached to different NGOs. Along with an increase in individualism, this has started to corrode the collective identity and interests built up during the shrimp farm struggle, even among the sangams initiated by Kalvikkarasi. Men also play a role in this process. Saritha's husband, for example, has withdrawn support for her sangam activities owing to his perception that her work is not producing any concrete benefits for their family. He refers to the absence of their names from applications for permanent housing that Saritha helped file with the government. He overlooks the fact that they are one of the few Dalit families to own permanent housing. The nature of entitlement priorities has also changed. The priorities are now to secure work, agricultural land for the roughly 90 per cent of Dalits without land, and permanent housing. These priorities are all indicative of livelihood insecurity and poverty. To quote Sathya, 'I am just thinking of when I can live in a cement house with electricity and a fan.'

These changes, however, are not matched by the women's knowing more about government schemes and the laws under which those entitlements could be secured. Instead, the women now expect the NGOs to deliver the changes. This signals the re-emergence of client–patron type relations in the village. According to Leela,

> Our women don't want to do anything now, but want their share of the sangam money. Only if they know that you are giving something, then we will not be able to see your head [for the people crowding around]. We come to know about some good schemes and try to apply, but our women still think, 'Why is she asking for money from us?'

Her last statement points to the fact that NGO patronage is thought to be a means of avoiding both the payments of bribes to access government schemes and the accompanying delays. Patronage is also the outcome when economic independence has been forgotten; immediate survival needs have taken its place once more.

This survival mode is symbolic of changes in the sangams and the wider community after the shrimp farm struggle. Male leaders like Muthu call attention to disunity and an 'each for themselves, stopping others from developing' mentality, which breaks down inter- and even intra-kinship ties. Several women reacted to initial interviews to the effect: 'Why talk about the past and the shrimp farm? If you have work for us, let's talk about that now.' Rumours abounded that Kalvikkarasi was receiving money from me in exchange for setting up meetings. Behind this trend is the expectation that outsiders will bring benefits to the village, which has reduced Dalit women's capacity to cope autonomously with the deterioration in their standard of living.

The women have been become more dependent on NGOs and on loans, and more reliant on panchayat President, Siva, to deliver benefits for their village. There has been a corresponding decrease in the stress they put on women's collective action. Women thus tended to highlight the post-tsunami NGO relief, rather than the women's own actions, as the most important development in the village. Their inability to secure entitlements was in part justified by invoking religious explanations of the *Kali yuga*. This is an age of moral degeneration, according to Hindu scriptures, linked to modernity as characterized by individualism and competition. Hence, women attribute their ineffectiveness to fate. Women judge the value of their entitlement struggles by the outcomes; and the outcomes affect their perceptions of how much power they have. Pushpa also pointed out that if only they had not protested against the shrimp farm, they would have received some money from the farm owner with which to build a grand temple. She feels that she has lost not only what she is entitled to but also her social status: redistribution and recognition are intertwined. The disempowerment many women feel today corresponds to their heightened expectations of NGOs. Thus, an angry Natya stated, '[TNDWM] kept telling us to be bold and strong, and that we could achieve anything together for our village. But if they wanted to do something for our village, they should have been in front.' State practices that cause livelihood deprivation are implicated in this discursive shift from collective agency and power to dependency on entitlement provisioning by NGOs.

Nonetheless, despite the negative outcome, some sangam leaders remain hopeful that women will continue organizing to take up issues, even in the absence of Kalvikkarasi. Leela voiced such a view: 'In the beginning Kalvikkarasi fed us food, but now we can eat on our own. So for us you cannot stop women's development.' More women pointed to their new knowledge of government schemes and of which officials to approach, which enables individual women to continue at least to secure entitlements for their families. Many would not deny that collective action has led to women's greater political conscientization and their laying claim to public–political spaces. Confirmation came from a block development official's comment on the women's increasing visibility in government offices. Other women, however, pointed to the continuing need for Kalvikkarasi's presence: no other woman has the equivalent social networks and knowledge to unite the women and drive their collective action. The problem now lies with their expectations for concrete benefits from the sangams. There is a disjunction between what the women believe themselves entitled to and what they believe they are likely to get.

***

This chapter underscores how the Indian state's implementation of macroeconomic policies creates an arena in which rural, poor Dalit women struggle to secure or protect livelihood entitlements. It is an arena marked by competing interests and priorities, not least between economic growth, private entrepreneurship, and sustainable liveli- hoods. These competing interests are reflected in the formal institu- tional environment: the non-implementation of established laws and administrative procedures denies local communities a say in issues that affect their livelihoods. In this context, Dalit women's claims become irreducibly political. Their claims are played out on a political terrain where economic power and political networks are key. Consequently, state practices supportive of structural and physical violence can deepen social inequalities and the uneven distribution of power and enjoyment of rights among citizens. This is clear from the inability of the Dalit women to protect their livelihood entitlements by stopping the shrimp farm from operating, despite many collective action strategies. Their exclusion thus became ingrained in new ways, with manifold negative implications for caste, class, and gender power relations.

The case study further highlights how discourses of state corruption become a central component in understanding structural violence. At the same time, it points to the potential in this discourse to empower Dalit women. It enables them to connect state practices with infringe- ments of their rights as citizens and correspondingly, to frame opposing discourses of state obligations and accountability. These latter discourses are shaped by the multiple interventions of civil society actors as well as by state practices, and require sustained political interventions. Without sustained political interventions, an empowering discourse of securing entitlements is displaced by one in which NGOs deliver entitlements, or by a narrow state discourse of women's economic empowerment. It is at this point that a more praxis-informed understanding of human rights-based approaches to development emerges. This is founded on the indivisibility of socio-economic and civil–political rights and is committed to context-based, power-attendant understandings of col- lective action to secure entitlements.

Notes

1. Three Dalit castes live in this village: Paraiyars (traditional drum beaters) form the overwhelming majority, while there is one family each of Puthirai

Vannars (*dhobis* or washer people for Dalits) and Valluvars (priests of life-cycle ceremonies for Dalits). All are referred to by the term 'Dalit' throughout this chapter.

2. Mallibakkam village caste dynamics are a slight anomaly in an area dominated by both Reddiyar landowners and Vanniyars. The Vanniyars have a strong demographic and political presence through their own caste-based political party, the Pattali Makkal Katchi. In Mallibakkam, however, the historical appropriation of lands by Reddiyars has cemented the Vanniyars' lower-class status and lesser political power in the village today.

3. Kalvikkarasi's family is the sole Valluvar caste family in the village, and Kalvikkarasi self-identifies as backward caste Christian. Note that the Government of India's current distinction between Dalit Hindus and Dalit Sikhs, classified as Scheduled Castes (SC), and Dalit Christians and Dalit Muslims, classified as backward classes, has potential impacts both on the latter's self-identification as Dalit and whether they are identified by others as Dalit.

4. Of the adult Dalit women surveyed, 78 per cent were illiterate, while only 10 per cent had gone beyond primary schooling (that is, beyond Standard 5). In comparison, 68 per cent of adult Dalit men were illiterate and 21 per cent had gone beyond primary schooling. No adult had completed their schooling (up to Standard 12).

5. This temple was built by the Chettiyars, hence their edict banning Dalits from entry into the temple.

6. Kapadia (1991) noted that while the ideology of female inferiority and 'impurity' is generally weak among Dalits (Pallars), the exception is in religious rituals where Dalit women are marginalized.

7. India is the largest producer in aquaculture after China and occupies fifth position in the world in shrimp production. Shrimp, 61 per cent of it farmed, contributed 54 per cent of the value of seafood exports in 2006–2007, and the majority of marine products by value exported to the European Union (Marine Products Export Development Authority [MPEDA] 2007).

8. *S. Jagannath* vs *Union of India and Others*, (1997) 2 SCC, 87.

9. The CRZ, which is intended to regulate land use along the coast, is defined as coastal stretches 500 m inland from the high tide line and the land between the high tide and low tide lines, vide Ministry of Environment and Forests (Department of Environment, Forests and Wildlife) Notification No. S.O.114(E), dated 19 February 1991. It also comprises land within 100 m of estuaries, creeks, and tidal-influenced water such as backwaters.

10. The precautionary principle or approach asserts that where threats of serious or irreversible damage are identified, a lack of full scientific certainty

should not be used as a reason to postpone cost-effective measures to prevent environmental degradation (United Nations [UN] Conference on Environment and Development 1992).

11. *Manusmriti*, or *Manavadharmashastra*, is the Hindu civil and criminal code that comprises religio-legal rules, a number of which relate to the caste or varna system as well as the position and conduct of women (Irudayam *et al.* 2006; Islam *et al.* 2001).

12. The filing of false criminal proceedings against Dalits was made a criminal offence under Section 3(viii) of the Scheduled Castes and Scheduled Tribes (Prevention of Atrocities) Act 1989, in recognition of the common use of this tactic to harass SCs and Scheduled Tribes (STs).

13. Section 12, Protection of Human Rights Act 1993; see also, Committee on Economic, Social and Cultural Rights (CESCR 1998b: para 3[g]).

14. See Article 11 of International Covenant on Economic, Social and Cultural Rights 1966 (ICESCR).

15. The environmental pollution arguably violates the Water (Prevention and Control of Pollution) Act 1974, the Environmental Protection Act 1986, and the Easement Act 1882, which allows the private right to use groundwater resources by viewing them as attachments to land.

16. The CESCR (2002) acknowledges that everyone is entitled to sufficient, safe (free of substances that could endanger health), and accessible water for personal and domestic uses.

17. Dalit women mentioned prawn sales of Rs 30–Rs 40 today, as compared to Rs 100–Rs 300 prior to the operation of the shrimp farm.

18. See Article 6, ICESCR.

19. Women's options are a number of low-wage labour works in their locality: primarily, MGNREGS labour (85 per cent of women surveyed), agricultural labour (45 per cent), and salt pan labour (44 per cent). Around 58 per cent continue to engage in fishing, though this is increasingly subsistence fishing.

20. See Article 12, ICESCR. Medical professionals and aquaculture experts who formed part of the international fact-finding mission in 2007 confirmed these medical problems as consistent with the effects of chemicals commonly applied in Indian aquaculture. The yellow-orange colour of water along the farm bunds and at the base of the ponds also constitutes evidence of pollution.

21. Jeffrey (2002) notes how liberalization of the Indian economy from 1991 does not appear to have reduced opportunities for rural elites to capture resources from the state by corrupt means.

CONCLUSION

Human Rights as Practice—Agency, Power, and Strategies

Our women now know how to confront government officials and demand their basic rights. But they won't say it is because 'this is my fundamental human right'. We have to simplify and adapt such concepts for the people. If you take the UDHR [Universal Declaration of Human Rights] or even constitutional rights, it is very difficult to communicate these concepts to the people as they are…[or] to translate what happens at the international level on human rights down to the people.

N. Fatima Burnad, Founder–President, Society for Rural
Education and Development (SRED)[1]

Bridging Two Divides

The end of fieldwork for this research brought me to Fatima Burnad. She is a well-known human rights activist, herself a Dalit, who has been working among Dalit, Adivasi, and landless women in Tamil Nadu for the past 20-odd years. Her comment, quoted earlier, highlights the need to translate international human rights law into language that resonates with people's lives and socio-cultural understandings (Merry 2005). This would give them practical tools to use in their struggles to realize rights. Yet, Burnad's comment goes to the heart of our discussion about a more fundamental and seemingly insurmountable divide: between rights in reality and rights in law. That is, on the one hand, between the grassroots experiences of Dalit women as they engage in collective action to secure entitlements and freedoms, and on the other hand, the gamut of international human rights laws and mechanisms which have been established in the past few decades to ensure equal protection, respect, and fulfilment of those rights.

A complementary divide also exists: between protections for economic, social, and cultural rights in law; and the absence of such protections in reality. On the one hand, there are the de jure laws, policies, and schemes of the Indian state as well as pronouncements on socio-economic rights by a judicially proactive Supreme Court; on the other hand, their de facto non- or mal-implementation. An assessment of human rights in India on legal and policy grounds would certainly support, if in a qualified manner, the Indian state's assertion that it is working to comply with its international obligations to put in place measures to ensure human rights. Such an analysis, however, would ignore the 'systemic crisis of accountability' that besets the Indian state today (Posani and Aiyar 2009: 5). This refers to the impunity with which dominant non-state actors or state actors operate above or in breach of those very laws, policies, and judgements made in the highest court in the land. It also encompasses wide-scale corruption.

This book is concerned centrally with these two divides—between international human rights law and its machinery and grassroots collective action to realize rights, and between de jure and de facto rights. My research investigated the ways in which Dalit women engage in collective action to secure livelihood entitlements in rural Tamil Nadu. It looked at how their actions shape or reshape power relations, and thus processes of social exclusion. The first half of the book situated rural Tamil Dalit women within the wider Indian context. This context is one where intersecting caste, class, and gender axes of difference structure power relations and processes of social exclusion. Concurrently, I built a conceptual understanding of collective agency as exercised under conditions of exclusion and subordination. In addition, I assessed the accountability gap between the arrangements the state puts in place to respect, protect, and fulfil rights, and what the state actually does.

The relationships between rights, entitlements, social exclusion, agency, and power were explored through four broad complementary or competing discourses, which generate a number of divergent practices. The first discourse underlies state laws and policies on women and

Dalit empowerment and rights; the second is a dominant socio-cultural discourse that emphasizes interlocking caste, class, and gender inequalities. These discourses shape Dalit women's perceptions of entitlements and freedoms; they invest livelihood resources with certain meanings and generate a sense of dis/entitlement. The other two discourses, which arrive through external interventions, are of development and human rights. Their introduction into Dalit women's lives means a process of adaptation of these discourses in relation to local understandings and social perceptions of entitlements and agency.

In the second half of this book, three ethnographic case studies illustrated the complex interactions between processes of social exclusion and agency. The case studies highlighted two types of entitlement struggles that are socially negotiated and politically constructed by these women with the support of external development brokers. The first type seeks to secure new entitlements, the other to protect existing inadequate entitlements from external threats. By examining the particularities of women's actions in diverse contexts, I illustrated how caste, class, and gender mutually construct each other and shape social relations of power and, therefore, the operation of interacting entitlement systems. Socio-historical contextualization also enables understanding of the changing social, economic, and political environment in which caste, class, and gender are constantly being reconfigured. Yet, they remain durable inequalities that condition the process and outcomes of Dalit women's entitlement struggles. These axes of difference are often treated in practice as though they were essentialized or fixed. This contrasts sharply with the intersectional approach used in this research, which views these axes as constructed and reproduced within an overarching structure of domination. This latter approach yields possibilities for studying the ways in which the axes may be transformed through Dalit women's collective agency.

The three case studies also form the basis for the discussion related to the question: what insights can Dalit women's experiences and actions provide for securing human rights-based entitlements and freedoms? In other words, how do these women's experiences inform ideas of human rights and the formulation of rights-based strategies to transform power relations and ensure that development takes place? This is particularly relevant given the key organizational role external development brokers play in each case study, which points to the need to articulate the functions and duties of rights-based development interveners.

Despite variations in entitlements, contexts, and power configurations, the following themes emerge from the case studies. In the following section, I enunciate key aspects comprising human rights as action-oriented practice. I put struggles for entitlements and freedoms in context, and focus on how the complex interplay of multiple axes of difference affect different people's power and the resources at their disposal. I take the latter point for further discussion in the next section, and seek to explain why Dalit women's collective action appears to have altered caste–class relations, while leaving gender relations relatively untouched. In the penultimate section, I focus on what the case studies suggest for more effective rights-based development intervention strategies. I highlight the indivisibility of rights and the need to factor issues of culture, status, and identity into entitlement struggles. The last section, then, presents some broad strategy- and policy-oriented recommendations for putting Dalit women's entitlement interests at the heart of development policy, planning, and practice.

Realizing Rights in Practice, Incorporating Intersectionality

The negotiations, bargaining, and contestations present in Dalit women's collective struggles to secure livelihood entitlements, which lead to both intended and unintended outcomes, are open-ended processes. Such struggles that contribute towards realizing human rights, like all social change, are: 'premised on the unpredictability of human agency and the diversity of circumstances under which such agency is exercised. While [a processual understanding] may identify certain key elements of structure and agency as having catalytic potential, it does not attempt to determine in advance how this potential will play out in practice' (Kabeer 2001: 28). In any given socio-historical context, a more dynamic perspective allows one to understand the factors that help socially excluded people to transform structural inequalities, and those factors that hinder them. These factors are constantly evolving as relations and behaviours change. They change when actors such as Dalit women exercise power, or when they concede to the power of others in the process of collective action. If one accepts that the process towards entitlement is non-linear, where power dynamics both shape and are shaped by collective agency, this holds certain implications for how human rights are conceived and rights-based development strategies implemented.

These implications are explored in this subsection under four main points. First, attention is drawn to the political economy of human rights and to the diversification of rights-based strategies. Such strategies are attuned to the local context and to Dalit women's perspectives, entitlement priorities, and collective action. Second, an analysis of collective action processes promotes an understanding of agency as exercised within power structures and the institutional barriers they create. Third, a more detailed picture is produced by examining how Dalit women's identities intersect and how these intersections position the women within power relations. It is from such positioning that their perceptions of power and spaces to manoeuvre are formed, altered by new discourses introduced through external interventions, and played out in entitlement struggles. Fourth, I look at the state's political accountability for creating an enabling institutional environment to realize socio-economic rights, and a wider scope of claim–duty relations.

The dynamic view of collective action and power relations that grounds this research necessitates a shift in the focus of the human rights enterprise in two fundamental ways. This shift would begin to bridge the divide between human rights in law and in practice as embodied in collective struggle, and reveal them as complementary. The first shift is away from the current political–economic divide implied by liberal rights theory. This privileges civil and political rights over economic, social, and cultural rights. Instead, one should examine the political economy of human rights. A political economy perspective acknowledges that patterns of allocation and distribution of livelihood resources are the result of socio-political forces and often engender structural violence as well as physical conflicts. Within the political economy of human rights, a focus on entitlements systems allows one to consider the process by which entitlements are acquired and protected through formal and informal institutions within a given socio-historical context. It exposes the structural inequalities within a society that determine resource distribution in ways which invariably result in entitlement deprivation for certain social groups (de Gaay Fortman 2011).

The pertinence of a political economy perspective is evident from Chapter 2 and the case studies. They highlight how social exclusion of Dalit women is interwoven into the economic, political, and socio-cultural spheres in ways that support structural violations of their rights by both state and non-state actors. Thus, in Kovilur and Vettriyur villages, Dalit women's lack of housing and agricultural land entitlements, respectively, was connected to their being denied an adequate means and standard of living, access to formal credit, physical security, or even a sense that they belonged to the village. These economic deprivations combined with limited socio-political networks. In negotiations over resources, therefore, Dalit women had little leverage to counter the political influence of dominant caste villagers or nādu leaders over formal state institutions. Mallibakkam Dalit women's struggle against the shrimp farm further demonstrates the nature of economic exclusion. Their deprivation was caused by landlessness and their being concentrated in low-wage labour, combined with a lack of socio-political power. Hence, the women were not able to protect an already vulnerable entitlements position against the actions of a wealthy and politically connected businessman and corrupt government officials. An examination of social institutions such as caste, society, and the family places Dalit women's collective action within complex, interacting institutional arenas through which power circulates.

The second shift is from human rights law, which prescribes judicial or quasi-judicial remedies for violations of rights, to the praxis of human rights. This is a move away from a decontextualized 'description and (universal) prescription' approach (Miller 2005, quoted in Yamin 2005: 1222). The shift acknowledges that excluded actors such as Dalit women are often constrained by unequal power relations and a lack of financial resources from accessing legal remedies. This is in addition to the challenge of ensuring that the state enforces its own laws and policies (see Chapter 2), or that, where there are conflicting laws and policies, the state resolves the conflict in favour of those enabling Dalit women to protect their entitlements (see Mallibakkam shrimp farm struggle). In situations marked by systemic entitlement failure, Dalit women often have little option but to pursue political strategies to secure livelihood entitlements. Human rights, as an ideological discursive practice and political tool, thus are understood as an area of political contestation (Devlin 1993: 993), in which recourse to formal law becomes only one of a range of potential strategies.

Collective action to secure rights-based entitlements and freedoms is therefore posited as a key analytical category, alongside law, for the study of human rights. This displaces the idea of the state as the sole actor to exercise power over Dalit women, as well as the sole or main agent of socio-political change and the realization of rights (Rajagopal 2003). Instead, my premise is that rights are defined through people's struggles, which are motivated by their sense of entitlement in their local context. In other words, it is Dalit women's collective action in a wider political arena, including and moving beyond formal state institutions, that generates discourses that are constitutive of human rights (Goodale and Merry 2007; Gready and Ensor 2005; Rajagopal 2003). Examples of such collective action are the three livelihood entitlement struggles detailed in this book. They show Dalit women engaging with state administrative bureaucracies, courts, or the politics of mass protest, deploying various combinations of institutional and non-institutional strategies, to attempt to ensure the state fulfilled its obligations to operationalize their livelihood-related rights.

Within these struggles, the meanings Dalit women attribute to rights found expression in their political demands, which combined rights with other discourses to secure needed livelihood resources. Dalit women in Vettriyur village, for instance, argued the legitimacy of their land entitlement based on three counts: first, a quasi-legal right flowing from government officials' assurances to change the land classification so as to grant them title; second, their right to equal treatment where nearby villages have been granted title for government lands; and third, a right to land title based on their years of cultivating the land to make a living. In Mallibakkam village, the women's petitions against the shrimp farm combined an environmental with a moral argument about protecting the livelihoods of the poor, alongside later references to a court judgement that upheld their livelihood-related rights. These political demands remained flexible, moreover, constantly adapting to the anticipated reactions of others. Hence, in light of the caste tensions around temple rights in Kovilur village, Dalit women chose not to highlight the fact that their caste identity entitled them to colony housing. In strongly adverse social environments like Vettriyur, discourses other than rights, such as reference to government land schemes, may even be preferable to diffuse dominant caste opposition and secure land title.[2] The realities of livelihood entitlement struggles thus expose the specific ways in which universal principles become concretely interpreted and deployed in local contexts and in relations between different actors having competing interests.

Viewing human rights through practices of collective action means viewing them in relation to structural power relations and the perceptions and priorities of actors. This is a contextualized and flexible approach. It recognizes that the Dalit women's perceptions of their needs, from which they develop a sense of entitlement, are constructed through power relations that have material and symbolic dimensions. Hence, given a history of agrestic servitude, Kovilur Dalit women connected housing land with belonging to the village, independence, security, and a decent standard of living. Meanwhile, agricultural land for Vettriyur Dalit women is of symbolic importance. It means freedom from caste interdependence, social status, and dignity, beyond what it means in material terms. Apart from the moral claim, the women became aware of what the state *should* grant to them as entitlements. In Kovilur, they learnt about the state's housing scheme; in Vettriyur, they recalled the state's previous offer of land title. By focusing on the interests that a right protects and not the legal formalization of interests as a right, a closer understanding develops of how culturally framed rights motivate struggles for entitlements and freedoms (Ensor 2005).

Dalit women's agency, likewise, is exercised within structures of power that shape their pathways to entitlement and institutional responses to their claims. External development interventions thus need to be grounded in an investigation of these power dynamics and the interactions between multiple institutions embodied by state and non-state actors, and Dalit women. These should be examined in relation to the wider economic and political environment. This includes the politics of resource allocations by the state, as well as state discourses about Dalit women's development needs and the means of fulfilment of those needs. The focus is on uncovering the ways in which the women are able to manoeuvre within multiple, complex power relations and the discursive, relational, and other factors that influence that ability.

A primary feature of this manoeuvrability is the women's reliance on state institutions to counterbalance competing informal institutions.

Vettriyur Dalit women, for instance, sought support from higher officials in order to counter the political influence that traditional nādu
institutional actors exercised over government officials. The Dalit
women's efforts to form alliances in government had limited results
due to the influence of dominant castes and the operation of caste–
class norms. These alliances were based on Dalit identity or were made
with officials from castes without local socio-political ties, and were
less based on gender per se. Other officials, moreover, often refused
to challenge entrenched exclusions and instead encouraged women
to alter their claims, as Kovilur women witnessed. Mallibakkam Dalit
women, by contrast, experienced the negative effects on formal institutional entitlements of deregulation, which curtails the redistributive
function of the state. They also saw the effect of the state pursuing
macroeconomic policies that prioritized exports in marine products.
Corrupt state actors, thus, proactively supported the shrimp farm operation despite indications of licence illegalities and the women seeking
both legal and political remedies. Additionally, in all three struggles,
women gained the support of Dalit men by reproducing gender norms
surrounding labour, sexuality, and inheritance (see the next section).
In other words, their actions are characterized by balancing multiple
relations and interests, which generate power to induce structural discontinuities as well as continuities.

This understanding of multiple power relations is strengthened
by an intersectional analysis of power and agency. Intersectionality
counters artificial ideas of homogeneity that are inscribed into the
notion of universal bearers of human rights (Baxi 1998). Instead, it
reveals how each axis of difference intersects with the others to create different positionings within power relations. These positionings
influence exclusion as well as the political and subjective constructions of identities and agency (Yuval-Davis 2006). For example,
Dalit women differentiated themselves from Dalit men in terms of
exclusions based on gender; from dominant caste women, based on
caste and class; and from dominant caste men, based on caste, class,
and gender. Moreover, in exercising agency, Dalit women balanced
complementary and conflicting interests centred on the intersections
of these three structures. Their diverse strategies primarily disrupted
caste–class power relations and much less so, those of gender. These
aspects are explored later.

An intersectional analysis, rather than one based solely on caste or gender, explains why those organizing Dalit women sought discursive shifts in the women's positioning within both caste and gender relations. Development brokers opened an alternative discourse of collective Dalit female power by recasting the women's caste identity in positive terms. The brokers used the medium of symbolic resources, namely, the struggle over temple rights in Kovilur village or entry into the temple in Mallibakkam village. Interconnected with this recasting was the revalorizing of the women's gender identity: the brokers introduced alternative discourses that women were necessary to succeed in public–political action. Interestingly, these alternative discourses did not emphasize a critique of existing hierarchies of caste and gender and the accompanying discourse of caste/gender disentitlement. Instead, they stressed the practical advantages the women had over Dalit men. Women were more likely to make their voices heard by government officials and were less at risk from caste–class retaliation from officials or dominant castes. In the case of Mallibakkam village, discourses also sought to distinguish between Dalit women's concern for the village and the dominant castes' greater concern for their individual family or caste development. The process of re-identification, however, created potential contradictions as established norms were reinterpreted in the light of new discourses. At the same time as caste and gender norms were disturbed by this process, they were also reproduced by the women: in Mallibakkam, they referred to Dalits (traditionally a service caste) as providing service to the village; and in Kovilur, they referred to the women's self-sacrificing, altruistic natures. These intersecting identities suggest that structural discontinuities are constructed within spaces marked by structural continuities. Women adapt new discourses into their lifeworlds and existing understandings as part of their political organization.

Viewing Dalit women's agency in this manner exposes the limits of agency understood as the abstract notion of the autonomous, rational individual acting in her or his own interests. This notion underlies human rights norms. Agency, instead, is conceptualized as a capacity for action by individuals as defined by their multiple identities and social relationships, and conditioned by structural constraints and opportunities. For Dalit women to act meant that they had to negotiate manifold caste, class, and gender structures, practices, and relations by which their entitlements position and interests are forged. They negotiated wage labour imperatives produced by poverty, as well as the additional work burden produced by the gender divisions in productive and reproductive labour. They were also influenced by historical conditions of hierarchical caste interdependence. Additionally, each woman's decision to act was shaped by changing fields of power within family, societal, and state institutions. This suggests that the Dalit women's resistance to domination and disentitlement, therefore, has to be understood in light of the scope for action they perceived they had. Their perceptions were based on their structural location within the complex weave of social relations of power.

The complexities of power and agency are also evident in women's reinterpretation of alternative caste and gender discourses, which express values of equality and collective power. These reinterpretations occur as women manoeuvre around a number of interconnected caste, class, and gender barriers to their participation. Such barriers include illiteracy, a lack of confidence to speak up, and engrained patterns of patronage and dependency, which arise from historical agrestic servitude conditions. They also include the sheer physical exhaustion of their double burden of work, the absence of much spare time, their positioning within the household, and their economic dependency on the men in their families. All these factors point to the limitations of the notion of transformative participation and 'power with', the idea of mutual decision making, and equal validation of the knowledge of all Dalit women sangam members. Because of the factors just discussed, there were hierarchies among the women when it came to who spoke, who was influential in decision making, and who undertook what action. At the same time, this did not preclude a sense of shared power and effective collective action. The implication is that more attention should be paid to local inequalities and social relations that shape participation. These need to be addressed in order to strengthen political action.

Moreover, Dalit women's identification and positioning within intersecting social axes reveal the explanatory limitations of social exclusion theory. This is especially true of the exclusion/inclusion binary and the automatic linking of exclusion with victimhood and lack of agency (Jackson 1999; Makkonen 2002). Exclusion can mean adverse inclusion, as well as exclusion per se. Adverse inclusion encompasses such things as caste-based confinement to labour work on a lesser wage than men. One may be included in a community or family, and have multiple duties or obligations within it, and yet, at the same time, experience exclusion in the form of lesser entitlements and freedoms. This paradox complicates neat divisions between exclusion and inclusion (Daly and Saraceno 2002; Jackson 1999). At the same time, my research shows that exclusion may simultaneously produce different spaces for manoeuvre in exercising agency. Networks of female solidarity existed in all three villages, even if these networks were submerged. The solidarity was formed by shared experiences of segregation, exclusion, and the caste and gender divisions of labour. These shared experiences supported the construction of their collective Dalit female identity and agency. Women were more politically excluded than men, more socially isolated, and less caught up in local politics based on patron–client relationships. The fact that women were less involved in interactions between castes meant that they enjoyed greater independence in organizing and taking action. This reduced the likelihood of their being co-opted by the corrupt practices of other actors, as seen in Mallibakkam.

Without sensitivity to these women's positioning within multiple power relations, therefore, including them and making them visible may result in constraining the women within power relations and reinforcing certain norms (Gedalof 1999; Lovell 2003). The clearest example is the common phenomenon of quotas in local government, which ensure political representation but not necessarily free and independent political participation by Dalit women. Such representation reinforces both caste and gender norms. In this regard, Mallibakkam women mentioned the previous proxy Dalit female panchayat president as evidence of unchanging gender relations. Moreover, the varied meanings women vest in resources and struggles to secure entitlements notably do not suggest that they want integration or inclusion in caste society per se, but rather independence and freedom within it. Kovilur women did not look for housing land within the main village, but away from it; nor do Mallibakkam women stake a claim to common water taps in dominant caste areas of the village for drinking water. These examples caution one against automatically assuming that the answer to social exclusion is inclusion as it is commonly understood. Instead, substantive equality in conditions and outcomes should be the goal, and the form of inclusion should be acceptable to Dalit women.

A final comment on human rights as practice relates to the rights–
claim relationship and accountability. As mentioned earlier, all the
women's livelihood struggles reveal barriers to entitlement. These barriers include the obstructions openly created by non-state actors, their
covert use of economic and political influence and patronage networks,
and state actors' corruption, delays, or refusal to disturb local power
equations. The difficulties that the women faced demonstrate that state
accountability has two main prongs, both of which require equal attention. One is legal accountability, which requires that violator, violations,
and remedy be identified. The second is political accountability. The
state must be accountable, in the first place, for implementing the laws
and judgements that would ensure Dalit women's socio-economic
rights in practice. The state must also create equitable and effective
institutional arrangements for the delivery of land reforms, education,
health care, and so on (Yamin 2005). It is this latter form of political accountability which, arguably, deserves greater attention within
rights-based strategies. Dalit women like those in Kovilur, then, would
not have to balance severe economic constraints against continual petitioning for over three years to receive housing land title.

Political accountability in this sense requires political transformation.
The conflicting interests embedded in state laws and policies, and the
myriad of contradictory or complementary state practices at the local,
state, and national levels, must be transformed. The agenda then becomes
about structurally reforming corrupt and clientelist state institutions
(Tarrow 1996). This would promote stronger state institutions and practices better capable of challenging the dominant interests in society. These
reformed institutions would be more accountable, and be able to enforce
redistributive policies to bring about more equitable development
(Crook 2001). The unsuccessful outcome in the Mallibakkam shrimp
farm struggle is testimony to the limitations of collective action in the
absence of responsive state policies and practices. Political accountability,
moreover, highlights the need to examine not only state practices but
also state discourses. It is important to make sure that state discourses of
'empowerment' and 'entitlements' align with rights-based formulations
and strategies that focus on facilitating people's agency to realize their
rights. At the same time, it is necessary to create active citizens by promoting their civil and political rights. This will prevent the reinforcement
of dominant social and economic structures.

The accountability gaps, however, do not stop with the state as duty holder vis-à-vis Dalit women's claims. Extreme inequalities of resources and power in caste society point to the need to complement the focus on state accountability by a consideration of horizontal claim–duty relationships. International human rights law has taken steps in this direction with the creation of legally enforceable obligations against non-state actors, which apply in gradually widening circumstances. There is growing jurisprudence on the state's duty to protect the rights of non-state actors even within the 'private' domain of the family,[3] and more broadly, to protect women against discrimination by any non-state actors (Committee on the Elimination of Discrimination against Women [CEDAW] 2010: paras 9–10, 13). Sen (1999), however, argues for an even broader, more flexible notion of 'imperfect obligation' that conceptually ties in with rights viewed in terms of socio-political processes. Imperfect obligations exist where rights–claims are addressed generally to anyone who can help, even though no particular person or agency may be legally charged with bringing about the fulfilment of the right(s) involved (Sen 1999: 230). Dalit women's claims to housing and agricultural land in Kovilur and Vettriyur villages, respectively, thus imply imperfect obligations on dominant castes vis-à-vis the women's claims. In Kovilur, this is an obligation to allow the government to acquire the housing land; in Vettriyur, an obligation not to contest the women's legitimate claim to land title. This obligation could be extended to women's claims against their families. The families would be obliged to accept that women should have control over livelihood resources and enjoy equal property rights. In contrast to the perfect obligations of the state, which retains centre stage as duty holder, imperfect obligations illustrate how multiple actions or duties by different stakeholders are required to fulfil a right (Gready and Ensor 2005).

In summary, the practice of human rights requires that one strengthens the conceptual link between human rights and power by incorporating an understanding of productive power alongside repressive power. This strengthening uses intersectionality as a tool to analyse the complex interactions of multiple structural axes of difference, which are embedded in social norms and institutions that shape Dalit women's agency. Praxis also points to the indeterminate nature of power relations and processes of exclusion, and allows for women's capacity to navigate around these multiple relations and processes to secure entitlements.

This capacity is built and supported through the introduction of new discourses on caste and gender equality, which women adapt into their lifeworlds in the light of relations of power. These discourses generate a sense of entitlement and motivate collective action to claim resources. The other side of the claim–duty relationship speaks of a greater focus on the state's political accountability. There should be a widening in the range of actors who have obligations in claims processes.

The Enduring Bind of Gender Norms and Relations

The understanding of structural power relations, developed in the preceding section, draws specific attention to differences in voice, decision making, power, and status within family and kinship relations. This subsection seeks to explain why collective struggles by Dalit women to secure livelihood entitlements left gender relations relatively untouched. First, an intersectional analysis of social relations reveals how gender becomes subsumed by other interests and why acquired rights do not necessarily translate into actualized rights. Second, an examination of power in more intimate social relations reveals how gender norms lead to women having conflicting needs. Gender norms also construct the life cycle of women's political agency. They alter the ways in which women might achieve power and autonomy.

In order to unravel gender relations and their impact on Dalit women's collective action, Dalit male discourses regarding the women's agency are first outlined. Three male discourses concern gender differences and power relations. One is Dalit women's duties within the gender division of labour as well as duties to earn a livelihood that their caste–class status imposes on them. The second concerns female inferiority caused by their being less knowledgeable and powerful. The third relates to patriarchal caste norms of male protection and control of female chastity. Dalit women's roles are thereby prescribed based on adaptation of dominant caste-based gender norms. This preserves privilege for Dalit men in the family and community, whereas such privilege is denied by the wider caste society. Concurrently, gender norms buttress the power of dominant castes to prevent horizontal ties forming among Dalits, which might displace vertical social relations. This is evident from dominant caste men inciting Dalit men to 'control your women' in Vettriyur village.

The instrumentality of collective action by women, however, changes what men allow them to do in public. This exposes the fluidity of
the public/private division of gender roles within a framework of male
dominance, leadership, and authority. Hence, Kovilur Dalit men modified their notions of what constituted private, family issues in order to
accommodate Dalit women's public actions therein, while reinforcing
the public–political domain as a male space. Mallibakkam men similarly reframed the shrimp farm struggle as male led, while allocating
to women a subordinate, supportive role, one reinforced by gendered
kinship norms that represent stability and security. This demarcation
led Dalit men to disparage the women, especially in the initial stages of
collective action, as 'space invaders' (Puwar 2004) lacking any political
capacity. At the same time, in Vettriyur village, women pointed to their
roles as mothers as intimately connected to their public roles in collective action. They collapsed any gendered separation of their roles. In
this sense, Dalit women's collective action on entitlements is simultaneously a struggle to remodel gender relationships and claim a place in
the public sphere. This involves subverting gender norms, which exalt
motherhood and female duties to their families.

Dalit women's negotiations of gender relations within their families
and communities reinforce contemporary feminist thinking about gender. That is, their actions reveal the need to acknowledge that gender
is not always *the* primary axis of difference or foundational set of relations (Moore 1994), though it is certainly *a* primary way of signifying
relations of power (Scott 1986). Gender interests cannot be separated
out from other, sometimes conflicting interests produced by these
women's intersecting identities and social position. Power holders in
a society influence the arena in which people struggle for livelihood
entitlements. In Indian society, they define the livelihood security of
the Dalit community, and what family and community life mean for
Dalit women. Women in the villages thus fought for the livelihood
and physical security of their communities against caste–class forces
that have a history of wielding power to threaten or control their
security. The clearest case is the Vettriyur Dalit women's representations of land entitlement as central to their being able to disengage
from nādu governance mechanisms and caste power relations that
define their exclusion. Community, therefore, became the strongest
identity through which to challenge caste–class structures.[4] Women's

spaces to manoeuvre around power relations then involved a degree of dependence on, and negotiation of power with, family and community (Villarreal 1992). This precluded the securing of entitlements as exclusively or even primarily women's interests.

In addition, adopting an intersectional understanding of gender relations helps explain the divergence produced between acquired rights and actualized or effective rights. To recap, the former means that one has protected access to resources as entitlements, while the latter implies control over a resource in its use as a form of enfranchisement (Appadurai 1984). While entitlement systems analysis tends to combine these aspects, this research shows that they should be considered separately because one does not automatically lead to the other. On one level, the distinction can emerge through state practices vis-à-vis state entitlement arrangements. Thus, Kovilur Dalit women continued their collective action when they witnessed government officials grant land title in their names without actually allotting plots for them to start building their homes. On another level, as seen in Vettriyur village, development interventions may shape Dalit women's willingness to secure land title in their names. The interventions thereby displaced caste and gender norms excluding their entitlement. As yet, however, the women have not moved to confront gender inequalities in decision making on agricultural inputs and control over the returns from cultivation. Further, in both Vettriyur and Kovilur villages, women reproduced caste and gender norms governing property rights by insisting on following patrilineal inheritance norms. This was despite their recognizing the security that landownership provides women.

Actualizing rights is therefore a further process beyond acquirement. Informal institutions reflecting gender norms may still affect how rights and resources are distributed within households. This may occur even when access is legitimized through other entitlement systems such as state arrangements. Sen (1990) might argue that women's participation in gainful employment outside the household will improve their bargaining power for resources within it. A more complicated picture emerges, however, if one examines what equitable shares mean in the context of certain social practices, and what force they command when viewed in light of the acquired–effective rights distinction. In the case of land, these practices relate to dowry and old-age social security systems. First, one must understand the cultural meanings attached to various livelihood resources from the perspective of Dalit women's intersectional identities. Then only can one determine which resources offer the best leverage for realizing effective rights for different groups of women (Jackson 1999).

The seeming intractability of gender power relations and inequalities is explained by the way in which power circulates through more intimate social interactions and gender is constructed as a normative category. Durable gender relations arise from women being defined in relation to, and not separately from, both their caste community and family/kinship group. They are implicated in perpetuating these identity groupings. Concomitantly, Dalit women's relationships with Dalit men are marked by shifting dynamics of autonomy and dependence, because the women have conflicting needs. They want power over their lives (through exercising agency) *and* intimacy and security (through kinship and familial relationships). This is no clearer than in the case of many Mallibakkam women's downplaying their contribution to the shrimp farm struggle in order to uphold the image of their male kin. Hence, women may counter some inequalities while seeming to accept others. Which ones they accept depends on how possible it is for them to challenge gender relations and how much security and sense of self or belonging are provided by family and community against dominant caste society.

The idea that needs might conflict counters arguments that women's bargaining power within the family is weaker because they do not perceive their economic contribution or what is in their self-interest (Sen 1990), or have a socio-biological trait of greater altruism. Many Dalit women villagers recognized their often larger contribution to household maintenance and children's welfare as a consequence of the gender inequality built into household economic relations (cf. Kapadia 1995). In addition, they expressed a sense of entitlement to life without domestic violence or male alcoholism. Just because they know their interests, however, does not mean that they choose to act on them, especially where sacrificing certain interests ensures their future security (Agarwal 1994a). Hence, it becomes imperative to understand the material contexts in which women may appear to consent to gender inequalities. One must also take into account the norms and institutions that pressurize women to maintain particular social arrangements, and that do not leave women a lot of choice (Goetz 2006).

Dalit women, thus, constantly negotiate gender norms that construct the terms on which they are permitted to participate in public life through their sangams (Kabeer 1994). These norms also affect resource distribution and control. If one examines the intersections of gender with caste and class axes, one can map the life cycle of Dalit women's engagement in collective action, and reveal ways in which they might achieve power and autonomy. The non-availability of disposable or surplus time beyond that used to sustain livelihoods and families is a key constraint on rural Dalit women's collective action. Friedmann (1992) terms this time factor the second most important form of social power, after a secure place of residence and before even knowledge and skills. Its importance is evident from Dalit women's lives in the villages, bounded as they are by long hours of both productive and reproductive labour. The period of child bearing and child rearing creates a gap in women's political participation (Phillips 1999), which is exacerbated in the case of Dalit women by a caste–class gap caused by their having to do waged labour. Male control over women's sexuality compounds the prevailing divisions of labour. This control makes itself felt in restrictions on women's freedom of movement outside waged labour. In all the villages, Dalit women negotiated their participation in politics by conceding to gender norms regarding labour and male control. At the same time, by spending more time on public–political action, they started the process of creating alternative norms of appropriate Dalit female behaviour (Wilson 2008). This aspect of time thus highlights the critical need to build strategies that negotiate changes to, and ultimately transform, the gender divisions of labour. The transformation of these divisions is key to strengthening women's public–political action in the long term.

Their life cycle of political participation also revolves around intragender household power dynamics. This reveals further intersections of age and marital status. Research on South Asian household dynamics notes how mothers-in-law are granted control over the labour of their daughters-in-law as compensatory power due to their senior status in households (Kandiyoti 1988, 1998). This power often entails mothers-in-laws withdrawing into the household. Sometimes, though, as evident in Kovilur village, they participate in the sangams by taking advantage of the presence of younger daughters-in-law to unburden themselves of household duties. A similar trend can be seen among the large numbers of Mallibakkam widows, though this is balanced by their relying on a wider network of female relatives to enable their political participation. These trends show that certain household positions give women power over other women, which means they have a stake in maintaining certain patriarchal arrangements (Kandiyoti 1998). This includes the power of mothers over their teenage daughters. In patrilineal cultural systems, daughters are expected to undertake household duties while they are attached to their natal family. This, again, reinforces how women's collective action both challenges and reproduces gender norms and practices. This is particularly true of those practices that confer (albeit limited) powers on women through gender relations.

This analysis regarding the construction and durability of gender norms has significant bearing on rights-based development strategies that target women. It complicates assumptions that Dalit women's autonomous organizing and collective agency will challenge the reproduction of gender norms (for example, Guru 1995). This is not necessarily true, even if the organizing is founded on discourses of women's power, greater solidarity, and political agency. Instead, one sees incremental changes in structural gender inequalities within an overall continuity. This suggests the need to look at resistance to gender norms in different forms outside the overt or direct. Women often reject direct resistance in favour of seeming acquiescence to male dominance so as to negotiate spaces to manoeuvre within family relations (Liddle and Joshi 1986). Strategic gender interests that challenge gender subordination and enhance women's power relative to men, therefore, are not always priorities for Dalit women's emancipation. This is especially the case when such emancipation might disempower women on other axes or even threaten their short-term practical interests (such as security within the marital home). Instead, one should build women's political consciousness, their collective identities, and their self-confidence. One should inspire them with the awareness of what they can achieve through collective strategies to secure entitlements. All these measures can be viewed as steps towards establishing spaces for Dalit women within the political arena. Alongside these measures, must be deeper engagement with the cultural norms that construct female identity and subjectivity. The enormity of the challenge to transform gender inequalities requires strengthening solidarity among women. They must be linked to wider

networks to gain social legitimacy for their entitlements and ensure
that their strategies have a broad appeal.

Strategies for Redistribution, Recognition, and Freedom

The previous sections highlight how outcomes that further the realization of rights are dependent on rights-based processes that are attuned
to constantly evolving conditions and power relations. This subsection
examines the forms of external intervention and the strategies that
strengthen the ability of Dalit women to secure entitlements. First, I
look at the power dynamics between Dalit women and external development brokers, and the roles that are constructed for the brokers in
the process. Second, based on the data in this research, I propose key
features of rights-based development strategies. These strategies are
built around the links between entitlements and freedoms, between
power and knowledge, and between an egalitarian politics of redistribution and an emancipatory politics of recognition.

Throughout the collective action processes described in this book, a
model of external development intervention is being showcased. This
model is in keeping with a bottom-up approach to human rights, in
which external development brokers should play a catalytic rather than
directive role. Their function is to provide political conscientization,
capacitation, and guidance on collective action strategies. The question
is, as Mies (1986: 146) suggested, 'not whether outsiders are necessary to start this process of collective action; rather, it is to define the
contribution of outsiders in such a way that it furthers the initiative and
autonomy of the women'. In the present study, this is the autonomy to
secure entitlements and transform power relations. The answer lies in
considering the power of development brokers and the social construction of their roles. Development brokers in the three villages played a
bridging role between state actors and Dalit women. They compensat-
ed for the women's exclusion from formal institutional processes and
politics. At the same time, they introduced women to new discourses
on their entitlements and collective power to act. They were able to
translate, simultaneously, formal institutional processes for the women,
while shaping the women's demands into viable claims on the state.
This influenced the women's social interfaces with the state and the
structural discontinuities produced therein. In this sense, development

brokers contributed towards reshaping how women understood their agency and livelihood entitlements as well as how the state understood them. The brokers thereby supported the institutional legitimation of Dalit women's entitlement.

However, Indian villages have a history of being governed by hierarchical patron–client relations. Development brokers, thus, often tread a fine line between directing and facilitating collective action. This was evident in Kovilur Dalit women's interactions with the local non-governmental organization (NGO). The women sought to replicate a previous patronage relationship of loyalty in exchange for protection and development. Alternative, more equitable models of leadership and facilitation therefore need to be built. A new sort of leadership would broaden Dalit women's perceptions beyond hierarchical relations and promote their equal voice and independent decision making. In all three villages, this shift in perceptions is incomplete, which causes a divide in sangam participation between leaders who have some ability to set sangam priorities and members who only participate in activities. Part of this process is continually emphasizing alternative discourses such as equality and promoting discursive consciousness of structural inequalities. Another part is promoting accountability among women as well as between women and development brokers. Everyone must be accountable for finances, roles, and responsibilities, as well as for information sharing. The dangers of not attending to these various processes were exposed in Kovilur village, where the sangams fell apart because of a lack of financial accountability. In Mallibakkam village, problems of information sharing among the large group of women served to weaken their collective political identity. Particular attention is thereby drawn to strategies that build Dalit women's leadership, while legitimizing the claims that arise with their growing sense of entitlement and for which they exercise agency.

From this perspective, there are three intertwined aspects of promoting entitlement strategies. It is necessary to enhance Dalit women's freedoms so that they can exercise agency, support the redistribution of resources, including knowledge resources, and generate positive recognition of identities. Before examining each of these aspects in turn, I shall recap the actual strategies that Dalit women deployed under the guidance-cum-direction of the two external development interveners. The targets were primarily higher government officials, because the women wanted to overcome their socially institutionalized disentitlement to resources. The tactics were both institutional (petitions, court cases) and non-institutional (public protests, road blockages). The strategies constantly evolved during the course of collective action, in response to the opposition faced or the support gained. The women were helped to exercise their agency by interventions, which increased their freedoms of voice, organization and movement, knowledge, and positive self-identity.

Interventions that build freedoms to act collectively to secure livelihood entitlements emphasize the indivisibility and interdependence of rights.[5] The practice of human rights exposes the artificial hierarchy often argued to exist between civil–political and socio-economic rights. This argument is based primarily on the non-justiciability of socio-economic rights the idea that the law should not intrude into democratic processes by which resources are distributed (Neier 2006). The counterargument makes socio-economic rights for subsistence a prerequisite for exercising civil–political freedoms. Freedoms of association, expression, and movement, however, are critical civil–political rights that Dalit women exercise in order to realize socio-economic rights, while enjoyment of socio-economic rights promotes the exercise of civil–political rights. These freedoms thus form the basis of external interventions, which are aimed at enabling women to voice their livelihood needs as well as realize their right to information. They, therefore, become key personal gains to which Dalit women attached value as resulting from collective action. Women constantly focused on their enhanced voice, freedom of movement, and the power they felt from being part of the collective. Conversely, violations of civil–political rights, such as violence and the use of false cases in Mallibakkam village, function to curtail other civil rights such as freedom of expression, as well as to entrench non-enjoyment or violations of socio-economic rights. In this sense, both sets of rights share a causal link as they relate to the different forms of security Dalit women desire in their lives—livelihood security and physical security—and are instrumental to one another in promoting agency.[6]

Linked to enhanced freedoms supporting their agency, women must also be told about the sort of claims that are possible and how they should go about making them. The women must have the confidence to exercise their freedom to speak up. Promoting access to quality education, therefore, becomes a vital tool. Education in a caste context implies not only knowledge but also, more symbolically, a 'permissible' or 'authentic' voice with the authority and confidence to speak. As such, education is a crucial force, one that affects inter-caste relations and social hierarchy (Dreze and Sen 2002; Mencher 1972). According to Foucault (1980a), both the pursuit of information and power relations comprise knowledge, with knowledge forming an integral part of making a claim to power (see Mills 2003). This includes both the production of knowledge about excluded people and restrictions on their access to knowledge, which maintain their exclusion. If one applies this idea to the situation of Dalit women, one can see that their caste- and gender-based exclusion from knowledge has been instrumental in perpetuating caste, class, and gender power hierarchies. Their subordinated social status is thus 'fixed' through a discourse of ignorance and 'unskilled' labour extraction, which effectively silences their political voice. The silencing was obvious in interactions with the women: they constantly added provisos to their comments along the lines of: 'I'm not an educated person, what can I say?'

Apart from the utility of education in enabling people to escape from traditional caste occupations, the strategic significance of education lies in potentially enabling subordinated groups to transform their social status. Education, in this sense, functions as a form of cultural capital which engenders self-respect and enables the challenging of caste (and gender) as bases for socio-structural inequalities (Jeffrey *et al.* 2005). Education as escape and as capital plays a big part in the stories of Dalits in this research. It was often cited as important for building self-awareness, dignity, and entitlement in order to overcome agrestic servitude. As Roja from Kovilur village recalled, education led to their voicing claims to equality. The emphasis, though, was on challenging caste–class and not gender differences in power; hence, even today, Dalit women are less well educated than their male counterparts. With the strengthening of Dalit women's education, there would be greater voice, which is an integral factor in influencing their capacity to aspire for change and to negotiate the socio-cultural norms and institutions which circumscribe their lives (Appadurai 2004, 2007).

Freedoms and education/knowledge aside, the process of positive identification is the third aspect of promoting Dalit women's power and capacity to act strategically. Dalit women's identity-based organization to secure entitlements necessarily draws identity into the claim-making process. Hence, Kovilur Dalit women's struggle for housing land cannot be separated from the concurrent temple struggle, which saw the emergence of a dignified Dalit identity premised on equality in religion. Nor can the land struggle in Vettriyur be separated from the women's constructing a gender identity as primary providers for their families, which they associated with having the power to take political action. Vettriyur Dalits' separation from nādu patron–client relations also hinges on both economic independence and positive identity formation. In all three villages, identification processes were divergent but complementary. Caste identities were primarily (re)formed through religious conflict, because 'low-caste' identity and status is maintained by symbolic resources such as religion and ritual status (Dube 1996). Meanwhile, gender identities were disturbed by the construction of positive gender roles within the sangams. Struggles over resource entitlements, moreover, encompassed struggles over the meanings attached to Dalit women's identity, which included their capacities for voicing claims, for political agency, and for control over resources.

These processes of identification affirm the argument that an egalitarian politics of resource redistribution necessarily involves an emancipatory politics of cultural recognition. However, Fraser's (1995) analytical distinction between economic–political and cultural injustice, by which she separates these forms of politics, is not accepted by this research. The distinction advocates an additive approach, one that does not take into account the fact that issues of culture, identity, and social institutions are inextricably intertwined with economic and political issues. Each is embedded in and has implications for the other (Lykke 2011; Young 1997).[7] The processes of identification in the villages, discussed earlier, demonstrate this link between the two politics. Power relations produce Dalit women's 'low' caste–class–gender identity, which is marked by their resource disentitlement and economic dependence on others. Disturbing these identity constructions, therefore, is vital, because it creates structural discontinuities that support entitlement processes and lead to social change.

Dalit women's collective agency thus can be conceived as holding instrumental value, due to its securing institutionally legitimized entitlements, as well as expressive value, due to its affirming the identity and human dignity (and thus moral right to resources) of these women (Rajagopal 2003). Positive caste and gender identification both strengthened their ingrained sense that they should have equality of status and resources, as evidenced in discussions on religious rights and developments in other villages to which they felt equally entitled. In this sense, the goal of cultural empowerment is not solely to elevate the social status of Dalit women to that of full partners in social life. It is also to challenge the dominant cultural ideology, which seeks to strip women of access to and control over resources. What is required, therefore, is a sustained effort to generate a social consensus on new structural norms and entitlements for Dalit women, in order to ensure durable social change. In sum, instead of rating one of these two political strategies above the other, one should consider them mutually reinforcing in removing structural inequalities. Taken individually, each is insufficient to ensure that Dalit women get the resources they are entitled to, and insufficient to ensure their wider emancipation.

The Challenges Ahead

Overall, this research seeks to reinstate an understanding of human rights that is founded on the actual sites of resistance and struggle by individuals and communities. In calling for the eradication of 'narrative monopolies' in human rights theory and practice, Baxi (1998: 148) reminded us that it is the local and not the global that is 'the crucial locus of struggles for the enunciation, implementation and enjoyment of human rights'. To acknowledge this is to recognize Dalit women in ways that move beyond abstractions of 'poor, low-caste females' that do not touch upon the terms of resource distribution. It is to recognize them as people with dignity, entitlements, and freedoms. It is also to recognize that while human rights may be universal, the risk of rights violations is not (Farmer 1999). Hence, there is a need to understand the structuring of social difference in local contexts. This focus on the local becomes even more critical in the context of economic globalization, which is exacerbating socio-economic inequalities and exclusion. The forging of critical linkages between these local and universal narratives of human rights demands that those who pronounce on human rights standards are self-reflexive regarding the power relations between them and those experiencing rights violations and struggling for their rights. It also means recognizing that building 'up' from local practices of rights and translating them into national and international human rights discourses often may not be a seamless process, because the purpose of human rights activism at these various levels is different. The challenge, then, becomes to ensure that actions at other levels always support local processes. It is also to reframe the debate on international human rights norms by examining struggles against social exclusion and subordination in light of wider economic and political processes.

This research has argued that human rights law and practice will begin to converge only if rights struggles are placed within specific socio-historical contexts. The interests that a right represents for people positioned differently within multiple power relations must be investigated. This will necessarily entail overcoming divisions between state and non-state power holders; between economy and politics; between civil–political and socio-economic rights; and between redistribution and recognition. It will require viewing human rights as equally about processes of collective action as about legal standards, as well as about outcomes that guarantee substantive equality to excluded social groups. A focus on collective action to secure entitlements also emphasizes that while human rights are primarily the rights of individuals; these individuals are located within relational and situational contexts. Strategies, accordingly, need to be based on an understanding of the ways in which these relationships and conditions shape people's sense of, as well as their actual choices, rights, and entitlements. They also need to be grounded in an intersectional perspective. Such a perspective offers a dynamic view of agency based on a person's position within her life cycle and her ability to manoeuvre within multiple power relations. Developing strategies from this perspective strengthens a rights-based development approach. At the heart of its conceptualization is the transformation of inequitable power relations that perpetuate structural injustices.

The focus on Dalit women's collective action, on agency as simultaneously shaping and being shaped by power relations, also brings into crisis the current development frameworks operative through international agencies and the Indian state, especially the latter's rubric of 'inclusive growth'. These frameworks, in emphasizing economic growth and service delivery to reduce poverty and encourage social mobility, increasingly displace more political strategies focused on social exclusion, power structures, and relations. Terms like empowerment and agency, under these frameworks, are implicitly viewed as the choices of free-willed agents, with women expected to foster their own and their families' development through gaining assets and accessing opportunities. Instead, this research shows that agency is constructed and enacted through power relations, which implies a need to focus on structural inequalities that ensure enduring deprivation for certain social groups such as Dalit women. This re-politicizes development strategies involving law, structures, institutions, power, and agency, in order to achieve social and economic justice.

Translated into an operational strategy, this means building flexible, long-term, and sustained development interventions that combine three key strategies aiming at structural, cultural, and institutional change. One is facilitating collective action in order for Dalit women to secure the entitlements and freedoms that they make priorities in their lives. This should take into account their continually evolving definitions of livelihood interests and opportunities as they gain access to information and alternative discourses. A second strategy is countering the socio-cultural norms that silence Dalit women and naturalize their lesser access to resources and power. This requires tackling both caste and gender norms. It is necessary to address the power, prejudices, and discrimination inherent in these norms, and build social relations based on equality. These two strategies call attention to the intertwining of struggles for economic redistribution with those of cultural recognition in removing structural inequalities. The third strategy is the promotion of wider institutional reforms that socially and formally legitimize Dalit women's entitlements and freedoms. Reforms should simultaneously establish an impartial and corruption-free political environment that is conducive to the women pressing their claims. These three strategies take precedence over those enhancing economic productivity and economic self-reliance, such as government microcredit schemes. These three strategies are premised on a comprehensive mapping of power relations and wider political and economic conditions, which identifies both opportunities as well as potential risks.[8] These strategies should take account of the women's spaces for manoeuvre in fluid power contexts, rather than basing interventions solely on an analysis of their structural subordination or their livelihood needs. Security should also be seen from their viewpoint, and attention paid to livelihood security as well as physical security.

Taking into account power relations and their relational autonomy, effective strategies to transform gender inequalities may then require that Dalit women's individual rights be addressed 'in relation to' the broader Dalit community's rights (Khare 1998; Nyamu-Musembi 2005). Dalit women's gender interests can be framed as contributing to the realization of the goal of caste liberation, in which Dalit men have a stake. This strategy of solidarity should be combined with helping Dalit men to interrogate how Dalit masculinity is co-constructed by caste and gender. These forms of resistance to gender norms rely on negotiation and dialogue as opposed to confrontation. The realization of Dalit women's rights should be seen as a matter both of individual rights and of community interest and commitment (Franco *et al.* 2000; Goonesekere undated). This means forming greater interlinkages between Dalit women's sangams and wider Dalit movements, something that was missing in the three villages studied, on terms that do not displace gender concerns. At the same time, this does not mean stopping the search for possible strategies to secure gender interests in particular contexts, by expanding women's perceptions of their own realizable interests in relation to those institutionalized in family and social relations. This includes but is not limited to strengthening women's 'fallback position' (Sen 1990) in household bargaining over resource control. This fallback position becomes stronger as women acquire more resources, knowledge, skills, and support networks on which to rely in securing livelihood entitlements. Concurrently, institutional rules and practices should be changed to reflect women's socio-political interests and what constitutes legitimate resource claims (Goetz 2006).

Furthermore, a change in the nature of state obligations is a necessary outcome of accepting intersectionality into rights discourse. Difference and the inequalities of power and forms of subordination that result are placed at the heart of struggles, rather than formal equality. Recent interpretations of international human rights norms support this move. They call for state measures to prevent, diminish, and eliminate conditions and attitudes which cause or perpetuate substantive, multiple discrimination, as well as specific measures to attenuate or suppress conditions that reproduce this discrimination (Committee on Economic, Social and Cultural Rights [CESCR] 2009: paras 9–10). These rights norms have implications for state development policy and planning. They signal the need to move beyond treating caste, class ('the poor'), and gender as discrete categories for sectoral planning, as has so far been the case in India's Five Year Plans. The argument is that separate categorization fails to meet the specific development needs and priorities of Dalit women and other groups at the intersections of multiple social categories. Instead, development strategies and programmes must examine the intersections of the caste category with other key identities such as gender. As for gender mainstreaming, greater inclusion necessarily means recognizing the differences among women, and integrating caste concerns into gender policy in India. A positive step in this direction came from the Working Group on Women's Empowerment (2006: 80) for the Eleventh Five Year Plan, which stated that intersectionality should be incorporated as a guiding principle of gender planning. The final Plan (Planning Commission 2008: 195), however, did not go so far in its wording. Instead, it introduced a section on marginalized women, including Scheduled Caste (SC) women, in recognition of their vulnerability and the multiple discriminations they face.

The first challenge of incorporating intersectionality into development planning is to broaden conceptual understanding. Gender is not the only category that intersects with others, and so policy should deal with all intersecting categories. Second, policies and mechanisms need to be evolved to ensure increasing participation by currently 'invisible' intersectional identity groups in agenda setting and decision making on development. Third, emphasis should be placed on development interventions, to foster political consciousness and empowerment among these groups. These interventions must transcend the narrow focus on economic empowerment in the government's microcredit sangam/self-help group (SHG) model. This would re-politicize and deepen notions of participation and empowerment in ways that challenge inequitable relations of power.

In this manner, the boundaries of human rights work expand beyond remedying rights violations to transforming the inequitable power relations and structures underlying such violations. At the heart of this work must be contextualized rights-based development strategies. These strategies should aim to enable socially excluded actors to develop a sense of entitlement and exercise their agency to secure the entitlements and concomitant freedoms that they themselves have made priorities. These strategies must envisage and operationalize changes at the structural, cultural, and institutional levels, so as to ensure substantive equality. All this further aids the project of legitimizing human rights as a transcultural framework that is grounded in a common ethic of human dignity and that encompasses a committed human rights practice.

Notes

1. The SRED promotes people's movements among the unorganized sector, empowering especially rural Dalits, Adivasis, and women to assert their political rights, access economic opportunities, and gain equal status in Tamil society.

2. In this regard, Khare (1998) referred to discourses of faith—that is, Hindu karma and dharma principles interpreted/reinterpreted in accordance with human rights-based notions of equality and justice—which, in certain situations, might bolster the strength and legitimacy of women's claims, instead of secular human rights.

3. For example, case law on forced disappearances has used the notion of a state's failure to exercise due diligence to prevent or investigate and punish acts of violence (see *Velasquez-Rodriguez* vs *Honduras*, (1988) 4 Inter. Am. Ct. HR, Ser. C, No. 4). Similarly, state accountability has been extended to the failure to protect women from domestic violence by male family members (see *Maria da Penha* vs *Brazil*, (2000), Case 12.051, Report No. 54/01, OEA/Ser.L/V/II.111 Doc. 20 rev., 704).

4. Collins (1990: 226) suggests that unlike race (caste) and class, fewer comparable institutional bases for challenging gender norms exist because gender cross-cuts these other structures.

5. The indivisibility and interdependence of rights have been affirmed inter alia in the Vienna Declaration on human rights (World Conference on Human Rights 1993) and General Comment 9 of the Committee on Economic, Social and Cultural Rights (CESCR 1998a).

6. This corresponds to feminist legal arguments based on the links between structural discrimination against women in socio-economic development and civil–political rights violations in the form of violence against women. There is, therefore, a need to collapse both sets of rights in order to emancipate women (Sullivan 1995).

7. Fraser herself seems to shift towards acknowledging this interlinkage in her later writing, which conceptualizes struggles for recognition in such a way that they can be integrated with struggles for redistribution, rather than displacing or undermining them (Fraser 2000).

8. Rai (2008) argued for power mapping based on the often-quoted case of the Women's Development Programme in Rajasthan, northern India, which aimed to empower marginalized women to act as agents of change in their communities. Physical threats and resistance to their work aside, local worker Bhanwari Devi was gang-raped by dominant caste men after undertaking a campaign against child marriages in her village. Similarly, Irudayam *et al.* (2006) also note retaliatory violence against Dalit women for collectively asserting their rights.

GLOSSARY

Adimai vēlai	Literally, slavery, agrestic servitude
Adivasi	Tribal or indigenous person in India
Agamudaiyar	Tamil caste of cultivators, also known as Servai and officially listed as backward class, who are one of three castes comprising the Mukkulathor community
Ambalam/ambalar	Headman
Arunthathiyar	Formerly known as Chakkiliyar caste
Atrocity	Term that, according to the Ministry of Home Affairs, Government of India, implies offences under the Indian Penal Code perpetrated against Scheduled Castes and Scheduled Tribes by those not belonging to either community, where caste consideration is the root cause of the crime even though caste consciousness may not be the immediate motive
backward class/caste	Castes other than Scheduled Castes and Scheduled Tribes listed by the Government of India as socially and economically underdeveloped; castes which hold position below forward castes in the social hierarchy of the caste system

Cent	Measurement of land; 100 cents equates to 1 acre
Chakkiliyar	Tamil Dalit caste that traditionally engaged in leather work and today is concentrated in sweeping/cleaning works
Chettiyar	Tamil merchant and moneylending caste
Chief Minister	Head of state government
Crore	(Hindi) 10,000,000
Dalit	Literally, broken people (Sanskrit), term used to define persons, irrespective of religion, belonging to the lowest group in the social hierarchy of the caste system who face discrimination and 'untouchability' on the basis of their birth into specific castes to which degrading occupations are attached
District Collector	Revenue administrative head of a district with quasi-judicial law and order powers
District Revenue Officer	Supervisor of revenue administration in a district
Dominant caste	Castes, irrespective of any religious affiliation, which are socially, politically, and economically dominant from the perspective of Dalits. In most cases, everyone who is not a Dalit or Adivasi in a village or town is dominant vis-à-vis Dalits
forward caste	All 'high' castes that are not classified by the Government of India as backward class, Scheduled Caste, or Scheduled Tribe
irāl	prawns
Jāti	Caste, kind
Kali yuga	Last of the four stages that the world goes through as described in the Hindu scriptures. During this stage, human civilization is said to degenerate spiritually in terms of increased human strife, sin, and discord, and rulers stopping protection of their subjects

Kallar	Warrior caste who are mostly cultivators, officially classified as backward class, who are one of three castes comprising the Mukkulathor community
Kanmāi	Natural reservoir, irrigation tank
Kāttu poramboke	Government forest land
Kattupādu	Order, discipline
Kollakādu	Another term for *puncai* land
Lakh	(Hindi) 100,000
Manusmriti	Civil and criminal code comprising religio-legal rules which constitutes the chief authority on Hindu jurisprudence
Mēchal poramboke	Government grazing land
Member of Legislative Assembly (MLA)	Member of lower house of Tamil Nadu state government
most backward class/ caste	Castes listed by the State Government of Tamil Nadu separately as a subcategory within the backward class list who are especially socially and economically underdeveloped
nandu	crabs
Nādu	Region, tract, division of a country
Nāttukkottai Chettiyar	Major trading and moneylending Tamil caste, especially during the period 1870–1930, many accumulating wealth from trade in Ceylon (Sri Lanka), Malaya (Malaysia), and Burma (Myanmar), and living in one of Chettinad region's 96 villages; officially considered as forward caste
Nancai	Land classified by the Revenue Department as tank-irrigated
Padiyāl	Non-permanent farm worker
Pallar	Tamil Dalit caste who traditionally engaged in cultivation, agricultural labour, and animal husbandry. They are said to have migrated to the southern Tamil region after 1565, as a consequence of military operations in then Ramnad Kingdom

Panchayat	Unit of local governance sanctioned under the 73rd and 74th Constitutional Amendment Acts 1992
Panchayat union	Intermediate panchayat tier comprising group of village panchayats
Pannaiyāl	Permanent farm worker
Paraiyar	Literally, drum beaters; Tamil Dalit caste who traditionally beat leather drums at functions or to spread news
Public distribution system	System of government distribution of essential food and other goods at fixed, subsidized rates to Indian citizens
Puncai	Non-tank irrigated dry land
Puthirai Vannar	Tamil Dalit caste of *dhobis* or washer people for Dalits
ration shop	Shop in which government subsidized rations are sold
Reddiyar	Telugu-speaking forward caste of cultivators enjoying a high status in the caste hierarchy
Reservations	Quotas allowing for increased representation in education, government jobs, and political bodies for Sheduled Castes
Revenue Divisional Officer	Revenue head of a division within a district with quasi-judicial powers
Sangam	Association
sarukkai	water sluice
Scheduled Caste (SC)	Official term used to denote castes of Hindu, Sikh, and Buddhist confession listed in the schedule to the Constitution of India 1949 as extremely socially, educationally, and economically backward due to the practice of 'untouchability', for the purpose of establishing entitlement to government benefits of special development, legal protection, and affirmative action schemes

Scheduled Tribe (ST)	Official term used to denote tribes listed in the schedule to the Constitution of India 1949, for the purpose of establishing entitlement to government benefits of special development, legal protection, and affirmative action schemes
Sub-Collector	Deputy administrative head of subdivision of district
Suya Udhavi Kuzhu	Self-help group established for microcredit and micro-entrepreneurial activities
Tahsildar	Head of a revenue *taluk* administration
Taluk	Revenue subdivision of a district
Tharisu poramboke	Wasteland, fallow or uncultivable land
Untouchability	The imposition of social disabilities by reason of their birth into certain 'polluted', 'low' castes
Ūrani	Pond, usually for drinking water
Valluvar	Tamil Dalit caste of priests who perform life cycle ceremonies for Dalits
Vayalkādu	Another term for *nancai* land
Vazhvādhāram	Livelihood, livelihood resources
Village administrative officer	Village-level administrative functionary
Zamindari system	Landholding system formalized by the British colonial administration, whereby the landlords became the legal intermediaries between the actual cultivators and the state. In contrast, under the *ryotwari* system, the cultivators directly paid taxes to the state.

BIBLIOGRAPHY

Ackerly, B. and J. True. 2010. *Doing Feminist Research in Political and Social Science*. Basingstoke: Palgrave Macmillan.

Agarwal, B. 1994a. *A Field of One's Own: Gender and Land Rights in South Asia*. Cambridge: Cambridge University Press.

———. 1994b. 'Gender and Command over Property: A Critical Gap in Economic Analysis and Policy in South Asia', *World Development*, 22(10): 1455–78.

———. 1997. '"Bargaining" and Gender Relations: Within and Beyond the Household', *Feminist Economics*, 3(1): 1–51.

———. 2003. 'Gender and Land Rights Revisited: Exploring New Prospects via the State, Family and Market', *Journal of Agrarian Change*, 3(1–2): 184–224.

Akerkar, S. 2007. 'Disaster Mitigation and Furthering Women's Rights: Learning from the Tsunami', *Gender, Technology and Development*, 11(3): 357–88.

Aldrich, D.P. 2010. 'Separate and Unequal: Post-tsunami Aid Distribution in Southern India', *Social Science Quarterly*, 91(5): 1369–89.

Allen, A. 1998. 'Rethinking Power', *Hypatia*, 13(1): 21–40.

———. 2002. 'Power, Subjectivity, and Agency: Between Arendt and Foucault', *International Journal of Philosophical Studies*, 10(2): 131–49.

———. 2005. 'Feminist Perspectives on Power', available at plato.stanford.edu/entries/feminist-power/ (accessed 21 June 2010).

Ambedkar, B.R. 1949. 'Third Reading of the Draft Constitution, 17–26 November 1949', *Constituent Assembly of India Proceedings*, available at www.ambedkar.org/ambcd/63F1.Third%20Reading%20of%20Draft%20Const17.11.1949%20to%2026.11.1949.htm (accessed 21 September 2010).

———. 2002. 'Castes in India: Their Mechanism, Genesis and Development', in V. Rodrigues (ed.), *The Essential Writings of B.R. Ambedkar*. New Delhi: Oxford University Press, pp. 241–62.

Anandhi, S. 2003. 'The Women's Question in the Dravidian Movement c. 1925–1948', in A. Rao (ed.), *Gender and Caste*. New Delhi: Kali for Women, pp. 141–63.

Andersen, M. 2005. 'Thinking about Women: A Quarter Century's View', *Gender and Society*, 19(4): 437–55.

Andersen, M.L. and P.H. Collins (eds). 2007/2010. *Race, Class and Gender: An Anthology*. Belmont, CA: Wadsworth Cengage Learning.

Apffel-Marglin, F. and S.L. Simon. 1994. 'Feminist Orientalism and Development', in W. Harcourt (ed.), *Feminist Perspectives on Sustainable Development*. London: Zed Books, pp. 26–45.

Appadurai, A. 1984. 'How Moral is South Asia's Economy?—A Review Article', *Journal of Asian Studies*, 43(3): 481–97.

———. 2004. 'The Capacity to Aspire: Culture and the Terms of Recognition', in V. Rao and M. Walton (eds), *Culture and Public Action*. Stanford: Stanford University Press, pp. 59–84.

———. 2007. 'The Capacity to Aspire: Culture and the Terms of Recognition', in D. Held and H.L. Moore (eds), *Cultural Politics in a Global Age: Uncertainty, Solidarity and Innovation*. Oxford: Oneworld, pp. 29–35.

Appadurai, A. & C.A. Breckenridge. 1976. 'The South Indian Temple: Authority, Honour and Redistribution', *Contributions to Indian Sociology*, 10(2): 187–211.

Appasamy, P., S. Guhan, R. Hema, Manabi Majumdar, and A. Vaidyanathan (1995). 'Social Exclusion in Respect of Basic Needs in India'. *Social Exclusion: Rhetoric, Reality, Responses*. G. Rodgers, C. Gore and J. B. Figueiredo. Geneva, International Institute for Labour Studies, UNDP.

Asian Development Bank, United Nations, and World Bank. 2005. *India Post-Tsunami Recovery Program: Preliminary Damage and Needs Assessment*. New Delhi: Asian Development Bank, United Nations, and World Bank.

Asian Human Rights Commission (AHRC). 2010. *The State of Human Rights in India in 2010*. AHRC-SPR-004-2010. Hong Kong: Asian Human Rights Commission.

Asian NGOs Network on National Institutions (ANNNI). 2008. *Report on the Performance and Establishment of National Human Rights Institutions in Asia*. Bangkok: Asian Forum for Human Rights and Development.

Association for Women's Rights in Development (AWID). 2002. *A Rights-based Approach to Development*. Women's Rights and Economic Change 1. Toronto: Association for Women's Rights in Development.

Athreya, V. and R. Chandra. 2000. 'Dalits and Land Issues', *Frontline*, vol. 17, no. 2, 10–23 June, available at http://www.frontline.in/navigation/?type=static&page=archive (accessed 4 August 2013).

Auyero, J. 1999. '"From the Client's Point(s) of View": How Poor People Perceive and Evaluate Political Clientelism', *Theory and Society*, 28(2): 297–334.

Association for Women's Rights in Development (AWID). 2004. 'Inter-sectionality: A Tool for Gender and Economic Justice'. *Women's Rights and Economic Change 9.* Toronto: Association for Women's Rights in Development.

Balasubramaniam, J. 2011. 'Dalits and Lack of Diversity in the Newsroom', *Economic and Political Weekly*, 46(11): 21–23.

Bastiaensen, J., T. de Herdt, and B. D'Exelle. 2005. 'Poverty Reduction as a Local Institutional Process', *World Development*, 33(6): 979–93.

Basu, S. 2000. 'The Bleeding Edge: Resistance as Strength and Paralysis', *Indian Journal of Gender Studies*, 7(2): 185–202.

Batliwala, S. 1994. 'The Meaning of Women's Empowerment: New Concepts for Action', in G. Sen, A. Germain, and L.C. Chen (eds), *Population Policies Reconsidered: Health, Empowerment, and Rights*. Boston, MA: Harvard University Press, pp. 127–38.

———. 2007. 'Putting Power Back into Empowerment', *Open Democracy News Analysis*, available at www.opendemocracy.net/article/putting_power_back_into_empowerment_0 (accessed 10 October 2010).

Baxi, U. 1998. 'Voices of Suffering and the Future of Human Rights', *Transnational Law and Contemporary Problems*, 8, 125–69.

———. 2007. 'The Rule of Law in India', *SUR International Journal on Human Rights*, 6(4): 7–25.

Baxter, P. and S. Jack. 2008. 'Qualitative Case Study Methodology: Study Design and Implementation for Novice Researchers', *The Qualitative Report*, 13(4): 544–59.

Bebbington, A. 1999. 'Capitals and Capabilities: A Framework for Analyzing Peasant Viability, Rural Livelihoods and Poverty', *World Development*, 27(12): 2021–44.

Bertaux, D. 1981. 'From the Life-History Approach to the Transformation of Sociological Practice', in D. Bertaux (ed.), *Biography and Society: The Life History Approach in the Social Sciences*. London: Sage Publications, pp. 29–46.

Betancourt, R. and S. Gleason. 2000. 'The Allocation of Publicly-provided Goods to Rural Households in India: On Some Consequences of Caste, Religion and Democracy', *World Development*, 28(12): 169–82.

Beteille, A. 1999. 'Empowerment', *Economic and Political Weekly*, 34(10): 589–97.

Bhalla, A. and F. Lapeyre. 1997. 'Social Exclusion: Towards an Analytical and Operational Framework', *Development and Change*, 28(3): 413–33.

Borooah, V.R. 2010. 'Social Exclusion and Jobs Reservation in India', *Economic and Political Weekly*, 45(52): 31–5.

Bradshaw, S. 2006. 'Is the Rights Focus the Right Focus? Nicaraguan Responses to the Rights Agenda', *Third World Quarterly*, 27(7): 1329–41.

Brah, A. and A. Phoenix. 2004. 'Ain't I a Woman? Revisiting Intersectionality', *Journal of International Women's Studies*, 5(3): 75–86.

Breman, J. 1974. *Patronage and Exploitation: Changing Agrarian Relations in South Gujarat, India*. Berkeley: University of California Press.

Bunch, C. 2002. 'Human Rights at the Intersection of Race and Gender', in R. Raj, in collaboration with C. Bunch and E. Nazombe (eds), *Women at the Intersection: Indivisible Rights, Identities, and Oppressions*. New Brunswick, NJ: Centre for Women's Global Leadership, Rutgers State University of New Jersey, pp. 111–18.

Burchardt, T., J. le Grand, and D. Piachaud. 2002. 'Degrees of Exclusion: Development a Dynamic, Multidimensional Measure', in J. Hills, J. le Grand, and D. Piachaud (eds), *Understanding Social Exclusion*. Oxford: Oxford University Press, pp. 30–43.

Burnad, F. and Society for Rural Education and Development (SRED) Team. 2006. *Tsunami Aftermath: Violations of Human Rights of Dalit Women, Tamil Nadu, India*. Chiang Mai: Tamil Nadu Dalit Women's Movement & Asia-Pacific Forum on Women, Law and Development.

Centre for Human Rights and Global Justice (CHRGJ) and Human Rights Watch (HRW). 2007. *Hidden Apartheid: Caste Discrimination against India's 'Untouchables'*. New York: Human Rights Watch.

Chakravarti, U. 2003. *Gendering Caste: Through a Feminist Lens*. Calcutta: Stree.
————. 2008. 'Beyond the Mantra of Empowerment: Time to Return to Poverty, Violence and Struggle', *IDS Bulletin*, 39(6): 10–17.

Chapman, J., in collaboration with V. Miller, A. Campolina Soares, and J. Samuel. 2005. 'Rights-based Development: The Challenge of Change and Power', GPRG Working Paper No. 27, Oxford and Manchester: Global Poverty Work Group.

Charrad, M.M. 2010. 'Women's Agency across Cultures: Conceptualizing Strengths and Boundaries', *Women's Studies International Forum*, 33(6): 517–22.

Clark, C., M. Reilly, and J. Wheeler. 2005. 'Living Rights: Reflections from Women's Movements about Gender and Rights in Practice', *IDS Bulletin*, 36(1): 76–81.

Clert, C. 1999. 'Evaluating the Concept of Social Exclusion in Development Discourse', *European Journal of Development Research*, 11(2): 176–99.

Coastal Aquaculture Authority. 2006. *Coastal Aquaculture Authority Compendium of Act, Rules, Guidelines and Notifications*. New Delhi: Coastal Aquaculture Authority, Government of India.

Colatei, D. and B. Harriss-White. 2004. 'Social Stratification and Rural Households', in B. Harriss-White and S. Janakarajan. *Rural India Facing the Twenty-first Century*. London: Anthem Press, pp. 115–58.

Collins, P.H. 1990. *Black Feminist Thought: Knowledge, Consciousness, and the Politics of Empowerment*. New York: Routledge.

Commins, P. 2004. 'Poverty and Social Exclusion in Rural Areas: Characteristics, Processes and Research Issues'. *Sociologia Ruralis*, 44(1): 60–75.

Committee on Economic, Social and Cultural Rights (CESCR). 1990. *General Comment No. 3: The Nature of States Parties Obligations*. UN Doc. E/1991/23. Geneva: United Nations.

———. 1991. *General Comment No. 4: The Right to Adequate Housing*. UN Doc. E/1992/23. Geneva: United Nations.

———. 1998a. *General Comment No. 9: The Domestic Application of the Covenant*. UN Doc. E/C.12/1998/24. Geneva: United Nations.

———. 1998b. *General Comment No. 10: The Role of National Human Rights Institutions in the Protection of Economic, Social and Cultural Rights*. UN Doc. E/C.12/1998/25. Geneva: United Nations.

———. 2002. *General Comment No. 15: The Right to Water*. UN Doc. E/C.12/2002/11. Geneva: United Nations.

———. 2008. *Concluding Observations, Report of India*. UN Doc. E/C.12/IND/CO/5. Geneva: United Nations.

———. 2009. *General Comment No. 20: Non-discrimination in Economic, Social and Cultural Rights*. UN Doc. E/C.12/GC/20. Geneva: United Nations.

Committee on the Elimination of Discrimination against Women (CEDAW). 2010. *General Recommendation No. 28: Core Obligations of States Parties under Article 2 of the Convention on the Elimination of All Forms of Discrimination against Women*. UN Doc. CEDAW/C/2010/47/GC.2. Geneva: United Nations.

Committee on the Elimination of Racial Discrimination (CERD). 2002. *General Recommendation No. 29: Article 1, Paragraph 1 of the Convention (Descent)*. UN Doc. A/57/18. Geneva: United Nations.

———. 2007. *Concluding Observations, Report of India*. UN Doc. CERD/C/IND/CO/19. Geneva: United Nations.

Corbidge, S., G. Williams, M. Srivastava, and R. Veron. 2005. *Seeing the State: Governance and Governmentality in India*. Cambridge: Cambridge University Press.

Cornwall, A. 2002. 'Making Spaces, Changing Places: Situating Participation in Development', IDS Working Paper No. 170, Brighton: Institute of Development Studies, University of Sussex.

———. 2007. 'Myths to Live By? Female Solidarity and Female Autonomy Reconsidered', *Development and Change*, 38(1): 149–68.

Cornwall, A. and C. Nyamu-Musembi. 2004. 'Putting the "Rights-based Approach" to Development in Perspective', *Third World Quarterly*, 25(8): 1415–37.

Crenshaw, K. 2000. 'The Intersectionality of Race and Gender Discrimination', Position Paper on Intersectionality of Race and Gender Discrimination, New York: African-American Policy Forum.

Crenshaw Williams, K. 1994. 'Mapping the Margins: Intersectionality, Identity Politics, and Violence against Women of Color', in A. Albertson Fineman and R. Mykitiuk (eds), *The Public Nature of Private Violence*. New York: Routledge.

Crook, R. 2001. 'Strengthening Democratic Governance in Conflict-torn Societies: Civic Organisations, Democratic Effectiveness and Political Conflict', IDS Working Paper No. 129, Brighton: Institute for Development Studies, University of Sussex.

Daly, M. and C. Saraceno. 2002. 'Social Exclusion and Gender Relations', in B. Hobson, J. Lewis, and B. Siim (eds), *Contested Concepts in Gender and Social Politics*. Cheltenham: Edward Elgar Publishing, pp. 84–104.

Daniel, S.B. 1983. 'The Tool Box Approach of the Tamil to the Issues of Moral Responsibility and Human Destiny', in C.F. Keyes and E.V. Daniel (eds), *Karma: An Anthropological Inquiry*. Berkeley: University of California Press, pp. 27–62.

Das, M.B. 2006. 'Do Traditional Axes of Exclusion Affect Labor Market Outcomes in India?', Social Development Papers, South Asian Series No. 97, Washington, DC: The World Bank.

Das, R.J. 2007. 'Looking, but Not Seeing: The State and/as Class in Rural India', *Journal of Peasant Studies*, 34(3–4): 408–40.

de Gaay Fortman, B. 1990. 'Entitlement and Development: An Institutional Approach to the Acquirement Problem', ISS Working Paper No. 87, The Hague: Institute of Social Studies.

———. 1999. 'Beyond Income Distribution: An Entitlement Systems Approach to the Acquirement Problem', in J.T.J.M. van der Linden and A.J.C. Manders (eds), *The Economics of Income Distribution: Heterodox Approaches*. Cheltenham: Edward Elgar Publishing, pp. 29–76.

———. 2006a. 'Human Rights', in D.A. Clark (ed.), *The Elgar Companion to Development Studies*. Cheltenham: Edward Elgar Publishing, pp. 260–5.

———. 2006b. 'Poverty as a Failure of Entitlement: Do Rights-based Approaches Make Sense?', in L. Williams (ed.), *International Poverty Law: An Emerging Discourse*. London: Zed Books, pp. 34–48.

———. 2011. *Political Economy of Human Rights: Rights, Realities and Realization*. Abingdon and New York: Routledge.

de Haan, A. 1999. 'Social Exclusion: Towards an Holistic Understanding of Deprivation', Paper prepared for the World Development Report 2001 Forum on 'Inclusion, Justice, and Poverty Reduction', available at www.dfid.gov.uk/pubs/files/sdd9socex.pdf (accessed 30 October 2008).

Deliege, R. 1997. *The World of the 'Untouchables': Paraiyars in Tamil Nadu*. New Delhi: Oxford University Press.

della Porta, D. and M. Diani. 1999. *Social Movements: An Introduction*. Oxford: Blackwell Publishers.

Department of Agriculture and Cooperation. 2001. *Agricultural Census 2000–01*. New Delhi: Ministry of Agriculture, Government of India.

Department for International Development (DFID). undated. 'Sustainable Livelihoods Framework', available at www.livelihoods.org/info/info_guidancesheets.html (accessed 20 April 2005).

Desai, S., A. Dubey, B.L. Joshi, M. Sen, A. Sharif, and R. Vanneman. 2010. *Human Development in India: Challenges for a Society in Transition*. New Delhi: Oxford University Press.

Deshpande, A. 2002. 'Assets versus Autonomy? The Changing Face of the Gender–Caste Overlap in India', *Feminist Economics*, 8(2): 19–35.

———. 2007. 'Overlapping Identities under Liberalization: Gender and Caste in India', *Economic Development and Cultural Change*, 55(4): 735–60.

Deshpande, S. 2003. *Contemporary India: A Sociological View*. New Delhi: Penguin.

Deveaux, M. 1994. 'Feminism and Empowerment: A Critical Reading of Foucault', *Feminist Studies*, 20(2): 223–47.

Devlin, R. 1993. 'Solidarity of Solipsistic Tunnel Vision? Reminiscences of a Renegade Rapporteur', in K.E. Mahoney and P. Mahoney (eds), *Human Rights in the Twenty-first Century: A Global Challenge*. Dordrecht: Martinus Nijhoff Publishers, pp. 991–1003.

Dietrich, G. 2003. 'Dalit Movements and Women's Movements', in A. Rao (ed.), *Gender and Caste*. New Delhi: Kali for Women, pp. 57–79.

Dirks, N.B. 1990. 'The Original Caste: Power, History and Hierarchy in South Asia', in M. Marriott (ed.), *India through Hindu Categories*. New Delhi: Sage Publications, pp. 59–77.

———. 1993. *The Hollow Crown: Ethnohistory of an Indian Kingdom*. Michigan: University of Michigan Press.

Dorairaj, S. 2010. 'Facing Flak: The National Commission for Scheduled Castes Criticises Tamil Nadu for Poor Implementation of Dalit Welfare Measures', *Frontline*, vol. 27, no. 6, 13–26 March, available at http://www.flonnet.com/fl2706/stories/20100326270603800.htm (accessed 4 August 2013).

Downey, D.J. and D.A. Rohlinger. 2008. 'Linking Strategic Choice with Macro-organizational Dynamics: Strategy and Social Movement Articulation', *Research in Social Movements, Conflicts and Change*, 28: 3–38.

Dreze, J. and A. Sen. 1989. *Hunger and Public Action*. Oxford: Clarendon Press.

———. 2002. *India: Development and Participation* (2nd edition). New Delhi: Oxford University Press.

Dube, L. 1996. 'Caste and Women', in M.N. Srinivas (ed.), *Caste: Its Twentieth Century Avatar*. New Delhi: Penguin Books, pp. 1–27.

———. 2003. 'Caste and Women', in A. Rao (ed.), *Gender and Caste*. New Delhi: Kali for Women, pp. 223–48.

Dutt, S.C. 2004. 'Working for Women's Empowerment: Issues before the Agency that Catalyses Change', *Indian Journal of Gender Studies*, 11(2): 157–77.

Ellis, F. 2006. Livelihoods Approach. In *The Elgar Companion to Development Studies* (ed.) D.A. Clark. Cheltenham: Edward Elgar Publishing.

Ensor, J. 2005. Linking Rights and Culture—Implications for Rights-Based Approaches. In *Reinventing Development? Translating Rights Based-Approaches from Theory into Practice* (eds) P. Gready & J. Ensor. London: Zed Books.

Expert Group. 2000. *Gender and Racial Discrimination: Report of Expert Group Meeting*. Expert Group Meeting, Zagreb: United Nations Division for the Advancement of Women, Office of the High Commissioner for Human Rights, and United Nations Development Fund for Women, 21–4 November.

Eyben, R., C. Harris, and J. Pettit. 2006. 'Introduction: Exploring Power and Change', *IDS Bulletin*, 37(6): 1–10.

Falk Moore, S. 1978. *Law as Process: An Anthropological Approach*. London: Routledge & Kegan Paul.

Farmer, P. 1999. 'Pathologies of Power: Rethinking Health and Human Rights', *American Journal of Public Health*, 89(10): 1486–96.

Ferguson, A. 2004. 'Can Development Create Empowerment and Women's Liberation?', Paper presented at Center for Global Justice Workshop, 'Alter Globalizations: Another World is Possible', San Miguel de Allende, Mexico, 4–12 August.

Figueroa, A., T. Altamirano, and D. Sulmont. 1995. 'Social Exclusion and Social Inequality in Peru', in G. Rodgers, C. Gore, and J.B. Figueiredo (eds), *Social Exclusion: Rhetoric, Reality, Responses*. Geneva: International Institute for Labour Studies, United Nations Development Programme, pp. 201–14.

Fine, B. 1997. 'Entitlement Failure?', *Development and Change*, 28(4): 617–47.

Food and Agricultural Organization (FAO). 2002. *Aquaculture Production 2002. Yearbook of Fishery Statistics*. Rome: Food and Agriculture Organization.

———. 2003. *Women in Agriculture, Environment and Rural Production: Factsheet India*. Bangkok: FAO Regional Office for Asia and the Pacific.

Foucault, M. 1980a. 'Questions in Geography', in C.Gordon (ed.) *Power/ Knowledge: Selected Interviews and Other Writings 1972–1977*. Brighton: The Harvester Press, pp. 78–108.

———. 1980b. 'Two Lectures', in C. Gordon (ed.), *Power/Knowledge: Selected Interviews and Other Writings 1972–1977*. Brighton: Harvester Press, pp. 109–33.

———. 1980c. 'Truth and Power', in C. Gordon (ed.), *Power/Knowledge: Selected Interviews and Other Writings 1972–1977*. Brighton: Harvester Press, 146–65.

Foucault, M. 1980d. 'The Eye of Power', in C. Gordon (ed.), *Power/Knowledge: Selected Interviews and Other Writings 1972–1977*. Brighton: Harvester Press.

————. 1994. 'The Subject and Power', in J.D. Faubion (ed.), *Power: The Essential Works of Foucault 1954–1984, Vol. 3*. London: Penguin, pp. 326–48.

Foweraker, J. 1995. *Theorizing Social Movements*. London: Pluto Press.

Fox, J. 2005. 'Empowerment and Institutional Change: Mapping "Virtuous Circles" of State–Society Interaction', in R. Alsop (ed.), *Power, Rights, and Poverty: Concepts and Connections*. Washington, DC: The World Bank, pp. 68–92.

Franco, F., J. Macwan, and S. Ramanathan. 2000. *The Silken Swing: The Cultural Universe of Dalit Women*. Calcutta: Stree.

Fraser, N. 1989. *Unruly Practices: Power, Discourse and Gender in Contemporary Social Theory*. Cambridge: Polity Press.

————. 1995. 'From Redistribution to Recognition? Dilemmas of Justice in a "Post-Socialist" Age', *New Left Review*, 212: 68–93.

————. 2000. 'Rethinking Recognition', *New Left Review*, 3: 107–20.

Friedmann, J. 1992. *Empowerment: The Politics of Alternative Development*. Cambridge, MA: Blackwell Publishers.

Gaiha, R., G. Thapa, K. Imai, and V.S. Kulkarni. 2007. 'Disparity, Deprivation and Discrimination in Rural India', BWPI Working Paper No. 13, Manchester: Brooks World Poverty Institute, University of Manchester.

Galtung, J. 1969. 'Violence, Peace and Peace Research', *Journal of Peace Research*, 6(3): 167–91.

————. 1990. 'Cultural Violence', *Journal of Peace Research*, 27(3): 291–305.

Gamson, W.A. 1992. 'The Social Psychology of Collective Action', in A.D. Morris and C. Mclurg Mueller (eds), *Frontiers of Social Movement Theory*. New Haven and London: Yale University Press, pp. 53–76.

Ganz, M. 2000. 'Resources and Resourcefulness: Strategic Capacity in the Unionization of California Agriculture, 1959–1966', *American Journal of Sociology*, 105(4): 1003–62.

Gedalof, I. 1999. *Against Purity: Rethinking Identity with Indian and Western Feminisms*. London and New York: Routledge.

Geertz, C. 1994. 'Thick Description: Towards and Interpretive Theory of Culture', in M. Martin and L.C. McIntyre (eds), *Readings in the Philosophy of Social Science*. Cambridge, MA: Massachusetts Institute of Technology, pp. 213–32.

Geetha, V. 2007. *Patriarchy*. Calcutta: Stree.

George, G. 2002. 'Four Makes Society: Women's Organisation, Dravidian Nationalism and Women's Interpretation of Caste, Gender and Change in South India', *Contributions to Indian Sociology*, 36(3): 495–24.

Giddens, A. 1984. *The Constitution of Society: Outline of the Theory of Structuration*. Cambridge: Polity Press.

Gill, T. 2007. *Making Things Worse: How 'Caste-blindness' in Indian Post-tsunami Disaster Recovery has Exacerbated Vulnerability and Exclusion*. Utrecht: Dalit Network Netherlands.

Gledhill, J. 2000. *Power and its Disguises: Anthropological Analysis of Political Practice*. Sterling, VA: Pluto Press.

Goetz, A.M. 2006. 'Institutionalising Women's Interests and Accountability to Women in Development: Introduction', *IDS Bulletin*, 37(4): 71–81.

Goodale, M. and S.E. Merry. 2007. *The Practice of Human Rights: Tracking Law between the Global and the Local*. Cambridge: Cambridge University Press.

Goodwin, J. and J.M. Jasper. 1999. 'Caught in a Winding, Snarling Vine: The Structural Bias in Political Process Theory', *Sociological Forum*, 14(1): 27–54.

Goonesekere, S. undated. 'A Rights-based Approach to Realizing Gender Equality', Paper for United Nations Division for Advancement of Women, available at www.un.org/womenwatch/daw/news/savitri.htm (accessed 21 June 2011).

Gore, C. 1993. 'Entitlement Relations and "Unruly" Social Practices: A Comment on the Work of Amartya Sen', *Journal of Development Studies*, 29(3): 429–60.

Gorringe, H. 2005. *Untouchable Citizens: Dalit Movements and Democratisation in Tamil Nadu*. New Delhi: Sage Publications.

Gorringe, H. and I. Rafanell. 2007. 'The Embodiment of Caste: Oppression, Protest and Change', *Sociology*, 41(1): 97–114.

Government of India. 2001. *National Census of India*. New Delhi: Government of India.

———. 2006. *Fifteenth to Nineteenth Periodic Reports of the Republic of India to the Committee on the Elimination of Racial Discrimination*. UN Doc. CERD/C/IND/19. Geneva: United Nations.

Government of Tamil Nadu. 2003. *Tamil Nadu Human Development Report*. Chennai: Government of Tamil Nadu.

Govinda, R. 2009. 'In the Name of the "Poor and Marginalised"? Politics of NGO Activism with Dalit Women in Rural North India', *Journal of South Asian Development*, 4(1): 45–64.

Gready, P. and J. Ensor. 2005. 'Introduction', in P. Gready and J. Ensor (eds), *Reinventing Development? Translating Rights-based Approaches from Theory into Practice*. London: Zed Books, pp. 1–46.

Grey, M. 2005. 'Dalit Women and the Struggle for Justice in a World of Global Capitalism', *Feminist Theology*, 14(1): 127–49.

Griffiths, A.M.O. 2005. 'Academic Narratives: Models and Methods in the Search for Meanings', in S. Falk Moore (ed.), *Law and Anthropology: A Reader*. Oxford: Blackwell Publishing, pp. 221–34.

Guijt, I. 2007. 'Assessing and Learning for Social Change'. Discussion Paper, Brighton: Institute of Development Studies, University of Sussex.

Gupta, A. 1995. 'Blurred Boundaries: The Discourse of Corruption, the Culture of Politics, and the Imagined State', *American Ethnologist*, 22(2): 375–402.

Guru, G. 1995. 'Dalit Women Talk Differently', *Economic and Political Weekly*, 30(41–2): 2548–50.

Hadiprayitno, I. 2009. *Hazard or Right? The Dialectics of Development Practice and the Internationally Declared Right to Development with Special Reference to Indonesia*. Antwerp: Intersentia.

Hamadeh-Banerjee, L. 2000. *Women's Agency in Governance*. New York: United Nations Development Programme.

Hammersley, M. and P. Atkinson. 2007. *Ethnography: Principles in Practice*. London and New York: Routledge.

Harding, S. and K. Norberg. 2005. 'New Feminist Approaches to Social Science Methodologies: An Introduction', *Signs: Journal of Women in Culture and Society*, 30(4): 2009–15.

Harriss-White, B. 2004a. 'Labour, Gender Relations and the Rural Economy', in B. Harriss-White and S. Janakarajan (eds), *Rural India Facing the Twenty-first Century*. London: Anthem Press, pp. 159–74.

————. 2004b. 'So What for Policy? Rural Development in a Poor State', in B. Harriss-White and S. Janakarajan (eds), *Rural India Facing the Twenty-first Century*. London: Anthem Press, pp 447–66.

Hart, G. 1991. 'Engendering Everyday Resistance: Gender, Patronage and Production Politics in Rural Malaysia', *Journal of Peasant Studies*, 19(1): 93–121.

Haynes, D. and G. Prakash (eds). 1991. *Contesting Power: Resistance and Everyday Social Relations in South Asia*. Berkeley, LA: University of California Press.

Hayward, C. and S. Lukes. 2008. 'Nobody to Shoot? Power, Structure and Agency: A Dialogue', *Journal of Power*, 1(1): 5–20.

Hayward, C.R. 1998. 'De-facing Power', *Polity*, 31(1): 1–22.

Heller, K.J. 1996. 'Power, Subjectification and Resistance in Foucault', *SubStance*, 25(1): 78–110.

Helmke, G. and S. Levitsky. 2004.' Informal Institutions and Comparative Politics: A Research Agenda', *Perspectives on Politics*, 2(4): 725–40.

Herbert, S. 2000. 'For Ethnography', *Progress in Human Geography*, 24(4): 550–68.

Heyer, J. 2007. 'The Marginalisation of Dalits in a Modernising Economy', Research paper, Queen Elizabeth House, University of Oxford, available at www.qeh.ox.ac.uk/pdf/pdf-heyer07/heyer07-heyer-workshop.pdf (accessed 21 January 2012).

Hickey, S. and A. du Toit. 2007. 'Adverse Incorporation, Social Exclusion and Chronic Poverty', CPRC Working Paper No. 81, Chronic Poverty Research Centre.

Hilhorst, D. 1997. 'Discourse Formation in Social Movements. Issues of Collective Action', in H. de Haan and N. Long (eds), *Images and Realities of Rural Life*. Assen: Van Gorcum, pp. 121–49.

———. 2000. 'Records and Reputations: Everyday Politics of a Philippines Development NGO', PhD Thesis, Wageningen University, Wageningen.

———. 2001. 'Village Experts and Development Discourse: "Progress" in a Philippine Igorot Village', *Human Organization*, 60(4): 401–13.

Hoff, K. and P. Pandey. 2004. 'Belief Systems and Durable Inequalities: An Experimental Investigation of Indian Caste', Policy Research Working Paper No. 0-2875, Washington, DC: The World Bank.

———. 2005. 'Opportunity is Not Everything: How Belief Systems and Mistrust Shape Responses to Economic Interests', *Economics of Transition*, 13(3): 445–72.

Hopkin, J. 2006. 'Conceptualising Political Clientelism: Political Exchange and Democratic Theory', Paper presented at APSA Annual Meeting, Philadelphia, 31 August–3 September.

Human Rights Committee. 2000. *General Comment No. 28: Equality of Rights between Men and Women*. UN Doc. CCPR/C/21/Rev.1/Add.10. Geneva: United Nations.

Human Rights Watch. 2005. *After the Deluge: India's Reconstruction Following the 2004 Tsunami*. New York: Human Rights Watch.

Hunt, A. 1993. 'Rights and Social Movements: Counterhegemonic Strategies', in A. Hunt (ed.), *Explorations in Law and Society: Towards a Constitutive Theory of Law*. London and New York: Routledge, pp. 227–48.

Ilangumaran. 1996. *Kizharnthelukirathu Kizhukku Mugavai ('East Ramnad Erupting')*. Devakottai: Tamizhamudan Vezhiyedu.

Institute of Development Studies (IDS). 2003. 'The Rise of Rights: Rights-based Approaches to Development', IDS Policy Briefing Issue No. 17, Brighton: Institute of Development Studies, University of Sussex.

International Commission of Jurists (ICJ). 1998. 'The Maastricht Guidelines on Violations of Economic, Social and Cultural Rights', *Human Rights Quarterly*, 20(3): 691–704.

International Council on Human Rights Policy (ICHRP). 2010. *Integrating Human Rights in the Anti-corruption Agenda: Challenges, Possibilities and Opportunities*. Geneva: International Council on Human Rights Policy.

International Human Rights Internship Programme (IHRIP) and Asian Forum for Human Rights and Development (AFHRD). 2000. *Circle of Rights: Economic, Social and Cultural Rights Activism: A Training Resource*. Washington, DC: International Human Rights Internship Programme.

International Institute for Population Sciences (IIPS) and Macro International. 2007. *National Family Health Survey (NFHS-3) India 2005–06*. Mumbai: International Institute for Population Sciences.

International Institute for Population Sciences (IIPS) and Population Council. 2009. *Youth in India: Situation and Needs 2006–07, Tamil Nadu.* Mumbai: International Institute for Population Sciences.

Irudayam, A., J. Mangubhai, and J. Lee. 2006. *Dalit Women Speak Out: Violence against Dalit Women in India.* Chennai: National Campaign on Dalit Human Rights, National Federation of Dalit Women, Institute of Development Education, Action and Studies.

———. 2011. *Dalit Women Speak Out: Caste, Class and Gender Violence in India.* New Delhi: Zubaan.

Islam, S., J. Mangalam, and N. Sharma. 2001. *Untouchables in Manu's India.* Delhi: Media House.

Jackson, C. 1999. 'Social Exclusion and Gender: Does One Size Fit All?', *The European Journal of Development Research*, 11(1): 125–46.

Jacob, T.G. and P. Bandhu. 2009. *Reflections on the Caste Question: The Dalit Situation in South India.* Ootacamund: Odyssey.

Jakimow, T. and P. Kilby. 2006. 'Empowering Women: A Critique of the Blueprint for Self-Help Groups in India', *Indian Journal of Gender Studies*, 13(3): 375–400.

Jasper, J.M. 2004. 'A Strategic Approach to Collective Action: Looking for Agency in Social Movement Choices', *Mobilization*, 9(1): 1–16.

———. 2008. 'Strategic Marginalizations, Emotional Marginalities: The Dilemma of Stigmatized Identities', paper presented at the Conference on Social Development, Social Movements and the Marginalized, Indira Gandhi National Open University (IGNOU), New Delhi, 17 February.

Jeffrey, C. 2002. 'Caste, Class and Clientelism: A Political Economy of Everyday Corruption in Rural North India', *Economic Geography*, 78(1): 21–41.

Jeffrey, C., P. Jeffery, and R. Jeffery. 2005. 'When Schooling Fails: Young Men, Education and Low-caste Politics in Rural North India', *Contributions to Indian Sociology*, 39(1): 1–38.

Jeffrey, C. and J. Lerche. 2000. 'Stating the Difference: State, Discourse and Class Reproduction in Uttar Pradesh, India', *Development and Change*, 31(4): 857–78.

Joe Arun, C. 2007. *Constructing Dalit Identity.* Jaipur: Rawat Publications.

Kabeer, N. 1994. *Reversed Realities: Gender Hierarchies in Development Thought.* London: Verso.

———. 1999. 'Resources, Agency, Achievements: Reflections on the Measurement of Women's Empowerment', *Development and Change*, 30(3): 435–64.

———. 2000. 'Social Exclusion, Poverty and Discrimination: Towards an Analytical Framework', *IDS Bulletin*, 31(4): 83–97.

———. 2001. 'Resources, Agency, Achievements: Reflections on the Measurement of Women's Empowerment', in A. Sisask (ed.), *Discussing Women's Empowerment: Theory and Practice.* Stockholm: Sida, pp. 17–57.

Kabeer, N. 2002. 'Citizenship, Affiliation and Exclusion: Perspectives from the South', *IDS Bulletin*, 33(2): 12–23.

———. 2005. '"Growing" Citizenship from the Grassroots: Nijera Kori and Social Mobilization in Bangladesh', in N. Kabeer (ed.), *Inclusive Citizenship: Meanings and Expressions*. London: Zed Books, pp. 181–98.

———. 2006a. 'Citizenship, Affiliation and Exclusion: Perspectives from the South', *IDS Bulletin*, 37(4): 91–101.

———. 2006b. 'Poverty, Social Exclusion and the MDGs: The Challenge of "Durable Inequalities" in the Asian Context', *IDS Bulletin*, 37(3): 64–78.

Kabeer, N. and R. Subrahmanian (eds). 1999. *Institutions, Relations and Outcomes: A Framework and Case Studies for Gender-aware Planning*. New Delhi: Kali for Women.

Kalpana, K. 2008. 'The Vulnerability of "Self-help": Women and Microfinance in South India', IDS Working Paper No. 303, Brighton: Institute of Development Studies, University of Sussex.

Kambhampati, U.S. and R. Rajan. 2007. 'The "Nowhere" Children: Patriarchy and the Role of Girls in India's Rural Economy', *Journal of Development Studies*, 44(9): 1309–41.

Kandiyoti, D. 1988. 'Bargaining with Patriarchy', *Gender and Society*, 2(3): 274–90.

———. 1998. 'Gender, Power and Contestation: Rethinking Bargaining with Patriarchy', in C. Jackson and R. Pearson (eds), *Feminist Visions of Development: Gender Analysis and Policy*. London and New York: Routledge, pp. 135–51.

Kannabiran, V. 2005. 'Marketing Self-help, Managing Poverty', *Economic and Political Weekly*, 40(34): 3716–19.

Kannabiran, V. and K. Kannabiran. 2003. 'Caste and Gender: Understanding Dynamics of Power and Violence', in A. Rao (ed.), *Gender and Caste*. New Delhi: Kali for Women, pp. 249–60.

Kannan, K.P. 2008. 'Dualism, Informality and Social Inequality: An Informal Economy Perspective of the Challenge of Inclusive Development in India', Paper presented at 50th Annual Conference, The Indian Society of Labour Economics, Lucknow, 13–15 December.

Kapadia, K. 1991. 'Discourses of Gender and Caste in Rural South India: An Analysis of the Ideology of Impurity', Working Paper D 1991: 4, Bergen: Chr. Michelsen Institute.

———. 1995. *Siva and Her Sisters: Gender, Caste and Class in Rural South India*. Boulder: Westview Press.

———. 1997. 'Mediating the Meaning of Market Opportunities', *Economic and Political Weekly*, 32(52): 3329–35.

Kapur, A. and N. Duvvury. 2006. *A Rights-based Approach to Realizing the Economic and Social Rights of Poor and Marginalized Women: A Synthesis of Lessons Learned.* Washington, DC: International Center for Research on Women.

Kapur, D., C.B. Prasad, L. Pritchett, and D. Shyam Babu. 2010. 'Rethinking Inequality: Dalits in Uttar Pradesh in the Market Reform Era', *Economic and Political Weekly*, 45(35): 39–49.

Kasturi, K. 2010. 'Coastal Regulations Flip-Flip', *Infochange News and Features*, available at infochangeindia.org/Agenda/Coastal-communities/Coastal-regulations-flip-flop.html (accessed 2 March 2011).

Kelly, C. and S. Breinlinger. 1996. *The Social Psychology of Collective Action: Identity, Injustice and Gender.* London: Taylor & Francis.

Khan, A. 2006. 'Indian Media Caught in Time Warp', *IBN Live*, available at ibnlive.in.com/news/indian-media-caught-in-a-caste-warp/12213-3.html (accessed 21 November 2011).

Khare, R.S. 1998. 'Elusive Social Justice, Distant Human Rights: Untouchable Women's Struggles and Dilemmas in Changing India', in M.R. Anderson and S. Guha (eds), *Changing Concepts of Rights and Justice in South Asia.* New Delhi: Oxford University Press, pp. 198–219.

King, B.G. and M. Cornwall. 2005. 'Specialists and Generalists: Learning Strategies in the Women's Suffrage Movement 1988–1918', *Research in Social Movements, Conflicts and Change*, 26: 3–34.

Klandermans, B. 1992. 'The Social Construction of Protest and Multi-organizational Fields', in A.D. Morrise and C. McClurg Mueller (eds), *Frontiers of Social Movement Theory.* New Haven and London: Yale University Press, pp. 77–103.

Klein Goldewijk, B. and B. de Gaay Fortman. 1999. *Where Needs Meet Rights: Economic, Social and Cultural Rights in a New Perspective.* Dindigul: Vaigarai Publications.

Kothari, R. 2004[1970]. 'Introduction', in R. Kothari (ed.), *Caste in Indian Politics.* Hyderabad: Orient Longman, pp. 3–26.

Krishna, S. 2007. 'Recasting Citizenship for Women's Livelihood and Development: An Overview', in S. Krishna (ed.), *Women's Livelihood Rights: Recasting Citizenship for Development.* New Delhi: Sage Publications, pp. 1–38.

Kruks-Wisner, G. 2011. 'Seeking the Local State: Gender, Caste, and the Pursuit of Public Services in Post-tsunami India', *World Development*, 39(7): 1143–54.

Kumar, D. 1992. *Land and Caste in South India.* Delhi: Manohar Publishers.

Kumar, N. and M. Rai. 2006. *Dalit Leadership in Panchayats: A Comparative Study of Four States.* New Delhi: Indian Institute of Dalit Studies and Rawat Publications.

Kumaran, K. 2002. *People's Report on the Status of Untouchability in India: Tamil Nadu.* Chennai: Actionaid.

Lahiri-Dutt, K. and G. Samanta. 2002. 'State Initiatives for the Empowerment of Women in Rural India: Experiences from Eastern India', *Community Development Journal*, 37(2): 137–56.

Lairap-Fonderson, J. 2002. 'The Disciplinary Power of Micro-credit: Examples from Kenya and Cameroon', in J.L. Parpart, S.M. Rai, and K. Staudt (eds), *Rethinking Empowerment: Gender and Development in the Global/Local World*. London and New York: Routledge, pp. 182–98.

Lang, K. and G.E. Lang. 1978. 'The Dynamics of Social Movements', in L.E. Generie (ed.), *Collective Behaviour and Social Movements*. Itasca, IL: F.E. Peacock Publishers.

Leach, M., R. Mearns, and I. Scoones. 1997. 'Environmental Entitlements: A Framework for Understanding the Institutional Dynamics of Environmental Change', Discussion Paper No. 359, Brighton: Institute of Development Studies, University of Sussex.

Leonard, D.K., J.N. Brass, M. Nelson, Sophal Ear, Dan Fahey, Tasha Fairfield, Martha Johnson Gning, Michael Halderman, Brendan McSherry, Devra C. Moehler, Wilson Prichard, Robin Turner, Tuong Vu, and Jeroen Dijkman. 2010. 'Does Patronage still Drive Politics for the Rural Poor in the Development World? A Comparative Perspective from the Livestock Sector', *Development and Change*, 41(3): 475–94.

Liddle, J. and R. Joshi. 1986. *Daughters of Independence: Gender, Caste and Class in India*. New Delhi and London: Kali for Women and Zed Books.

Lindberg, S., V.B. Athreya, G. Djurfeldt, and A. Rajagopal. 2011. 'A Silent "Revolution"? Women's Empowerment in Rural Tamil Nadu', *Economic and Political Weekly*, 46(13): 111–20.

Lingam, L. 1994. 'Women-headed Households: Coping with Caste, Class and Gender Hierarchies', *Economic and Political Weekly*, 29(12): 699–704.

Lipton, M. and N. Maxwell. 1992. 'The New Poverty Agenda: An Overview', IDS Discussion Paper No. 306, Brighton: Institute of Development Studies, University of Sussex.

Long, N. 1992. 'From Paradigm Lost to Paradigm Regained?', in A. Long & N. Long (eds), *Battlefields of Knowledge: The Interlocking of Theory and Practice in Social Research and Development*. London/ New York: Routledge, pp. 16–43.

———. 1997. 'Agency and Constraint, Perceptions and Practice: A Theoretical Position', in H. de Haan and N. Long (eds), *Images and Realities of Rural Life*. Assen: Van Gorcum, pp. 1–20.

———. 2001. *Development Sociology: Actor Perspectives*. London and New York: Routledge.

Long, N. and J.D. van der Ploeg. 1989. 'Demythologized Planned Intervention: An Actor Perspective', *Sociologica Ruralis*, 29(3–4): 226–49.

Louis, P. undated. 'Social Exclusion: A Conceptual and Theoretical Framework', PACS Programme Backgrounder paper, available at www.empowerpoor.org/downloads/Social_Exclusion_PACS_final.pdf (accessed 31 July 2008).

Lovell, T. 2003. 'Resisting with Authority: Historical Specificity, Agency and the Performative Self', *Theory, Culture and Society*, 20(1): 1–17.

Ludden, D. 1989. *Peasant History in South India*. New Delhi: Oxford University Press.

Lykke, N. 2011. 'Intersectional Analysis: Black Box or Useful Critical Feminist Thinking Technology?', in H. Lutz, M.T. Herrera Vivar, and L. Supik (eds), *Framing Intersectionality*. London: Ashgate, pp. 207–20.

Madhok, S. 2007. 'Autonomy, Gendered Subordination and Transcultural Dialogue', *Journal of Global Ethics*, 3(3): 335–57.

Madison, D.S. 2005. *Critical Ethnography*. Thousand Oaks, CA: Sage Publications.

Mahmood, S. 2001. 'Feminist Theory, Embodiment, and the Docile Agent: Some Reflections on the Egyptian Islamic Revival', *Cultural Anthropology*, 16(2): 202–36.

————. 2009. 'Agency, Performativity, and the Feminist Subject', in L. Sjørup and H.R. Christensen (eds), *Pieties and Gender*. Leiden: Brill, pp. 13–45.

Makkonen, T. 2002. *Multiple, Compound and Intersectional Discrimination: Bringing the Experiences of the Most Marginalised to the Fore*. Turku: Institute for Human Rights, Abo Akademi University.

Mangubhai, J.P. 2004. *New Economic Reforms: Hope or Mirage for Dalit Livelihoods*. Hyderabad: Sakshi Human Rights Watch Andhra Pradesh.

Mangubhai, J.P. and A. Irudayam. 2003. 'Water Battlegrounds on Caste', available at www.dalit.de/details/dsid_hintergrund_wasser_recht.pdf (accessed 9 March 2010).

Mangubhai, J.P., A. Irudayam, and E. Sydenham. 2009. *Dalit Women's Right to Political Participation in Rural Panchayati Raj: A Study of Gujarat and Tamil Nadu*. Madurai: Justitia et Pax, Institute of Development Education, Action and Studies, and Equalinrights.

Marine Products Export Development Authority (MPEDA). 2007. *Vision Document for Marine Products Export Development Authority*. Cochin: Marine Products Export Development Authority.

Mason, J. 1996. *Qualitative Researching*. London: Sage Publications.

Mayers, J. 2005. *Stakeholder Power Analysis*. Power Tools Series. London: International Institute for Environment and Development.

Mayoux, L. 2000. 'Micro-finance and the Empowerment of Women: A Review of the Key Issues', Social Finance Working Paper No. 23, Geneva: International Labour Organization.

McAdam, D. 1983. 'Tactical Innovation and the Pace of Insurgency', *American Sociological Review*, 48(December): 735–54.

McCall, L. 2005. 'The Complexity of Intersectionality', *Signs: Journal of Women in Culture and Society*, 30(3): 1771–800.

McClintock, A. 1995. *Imperial Leather: Race, Gender and Sexuality in the Colonial Conquest*. New York: Routledge.

McDougal, T.L. 2007. *Law of the Landless: The Dalit Bid for Land Distribution in Gujarat, India*. Cambridge MA: International Development Group, Massachusetts Institute of Technology.

Melucci, A. 1988. 'Getting Involved: Identity and Mobilization in Social Movements', in B. Klandermans, H. Kriesi, and S. Tarrow (eds), *From Structure to Action: Comparing Social Movement Research across Cultures*. Greenwich: JAI Press, pp. 329–48.

Mencher, J.P. 1972. 'Continuity and Change in an Ex-untouchable Community in South India', in J.M. Mahar (ed.), *The Untouchable in Contemporary India*. Tucson, AZ: University of Arizona Press, pp. 37–56.

Mencher, J.P. and K. Saradamoni. 1982. 'Muddy Feet, Dirty Hands: Rice Production and Female Agricultural Labour', *Economic and Political Weekly*, 17(52): A149–67.

Mendelsohn, O. and M. Vicziany. 1994. 'The Untouchables', in O. Mendelsohn and U. Baxi (eds), *The Rights of Subordinated Peoples*. New Delhi: Oxford University Press, pp. 64–116.

Merry, S.E. 2005. 'Transnational Human Rights and Local Activism: Mapping the Middle', *American Anthropologist*, 108(1): 38–51.

Midgal, J.S. 2004. *State in Society: Studying How States and Societies Transform and Constitute One Another*. Cambridge: Cambridge University Press.

Mies, M. 1986. *Indian Women in Subsistence and Agricultural Labour*. New Delhi: Vistaar Publications.

Miller, V., L. VeneKlasen, M. Reilly, and C. Clark. 2006. *Making Change Happen: Power*. Washington, DC: Just Associates.

Mills, S. 2003. *Michel Foucault*. London: Routledge.

Ministry of Human Resource Development (MHRD). 2006. *Selected Educational Statistics 2005–2006*. New Delhi: Ministry of Human Resource Development, Government of India.

Ministry of Personnel, Public Grievances and Pensions (MPPGP). 2006. *Annual Report 2005–2006*. New Delhi: Government of India.

Ministry of Rural Development (MRD). 2010. *MGNREGA Statistics: Tamil Nadu*. New Delhi: Ministry of Rural Development, Government of India.

Ministry of Social Justice and Empowerment (MSJE). 2010. *Annual Report 2009–2010*. New Delhi: Ministry of Social Justice and Empowerment, Government of India.

———. 2011. 'Atrocity Prone Areas Identified by the State Governments under the Scheduled Castes and Scheduled Tribes (Prevention of Atrocities)

Act 1989', Website data, available at http://socialjustice.nic.in/pronearea. php?pageid=3 (accessed 27 October 2011).

Ministry of Women and Child Development (MWCD). 2010. *Annual Report 2009–2010*. New Delhi: Ministry of Women and Child Development, Government of India.

Mitchell, S. 1996. 'Gender and Development: A SAFE Recipe', *Development in Practice*, 6(2): 140–3.

Molyneux, M. 1985. 'Mobilization without Emancipation? Women's Interests, the State, and Revolution in Nicaragua', *Feminist Studies*, 11(2): 227–54.

———. 1998. 'Analysing Women's Movements', *Development and Change*, 29(2): 219–45.

Moore, H.L. 1994. *A Passion for Difference*. Cambridge: Polity Press.

Morgen, S. 1988. '"It's the Whole Power of the City against Us!": The Development of Political Consciousness in the Women's Health Care Coalition', in A. Bookman and S. Morgen (eds), *Women and the Politics of Empowerment*. Philadelphia: Temple University Press, pp. 97–115.

Moser, C.O.N. 1993. *Gender Planning and Development: Theory, Practice and Training*. London and New York: Routledge.

Mosse, D. 1994. 'Idioms of Subordination and Styles of Protest among Christian and Hindu Harijan Castes in Tamil Nadu', *Contributions to Indian Sociology*, 27(1): 67–104.

———. 1999. 'Responding to Subordination: The Politics of Identity Change among South Indian Untouchable Castes', in J.R. Campbell and A. Rew (eds), *Identity and Affect: Experiences of Identity in a Globalising World*. Sterling, VA: Pluto Press, pp. 64–104.

———. 2003a. 'The Making and Marketing of Participatory Development', in P. Quarles van Uffard and A. Giri (eds), *A Moral Critique of Development: In Search of Global Responsibilities*. London and New York: Routledge, pp. 43–75.

———. 2003b. *The Rule of Water: Statecraft, Ecology and Collective Action in South India*. New Delhi: Oxford University Press.

Munday, J. 2006. 'Identity in Focus: The Use of Focus Groups to Study the Construction of Collective Identity', *Sociology*, 40(1): 89–105.

Murthy, R.K. 2004. 'Organisational Strategy in India and Diverse Identities of Women: Bridging the Gap', *Gender and Development*, 12(1): 10–18.

Narasimha Reddy, D., R. Tankha, C. Upendranadh, and A.N. Sharma. 2010. 'National Rural Employment Guarantee as Social Protection', *IDS Bulletin*, 41(4): 63–76.

Narula, S. 2008. 'Equal by Law, Unequal by Caste: The "Untouchable" Condition in Critical Race Perspective', *Wisconsin International Law Journal*, 26(2): 255–343.

National Commission for Enterprises in the Unorganized Sector (NCEUS). 2007. *Report on Conditions of Work and Promotion of Livelihoods in the Unorganised Sector.* New Delhi: National Commission for Enterprises in the Unorganised Sector.

National Crimes Records Bureau (NCRB). 2010. *Crimes in India 2009.* New Delhi: National Crimes Records Bureau, Ministry of Home Affairs.

National Human Rights Commission (NHRC). 2004. *Report on Prevention of Atrocities against Scheduled Castes: Policy and Performance, Suggested Interventions and Initiatives for NHRC.* New Delhi: National Human Rights Commission.

National Sample Survey Organization (NSSO). 2005. *Employment and Unemployment Situation among Social Groups in India 2004–05.* New Delhi: National Sample Survey Organization, Government of India.

Nayak, P. 1995. 'Economic Development and Social Exclusion in India', in A. De Haan and P. Nayak (eds), *Social Exclusion and South Asia.* Geneva: International Institute for Labour Studies. Available at http://ilomirror.library.cornell.edu/public/english/bureau/inst/papers/1994/dp77/ch2.htm (accessed 4 August 2013).

Neier, A. 2006. 'Social and Economic Rights: A Critique', *Human Rights Brief,* 13(2): 1–3.

Nelson, S.C. 2007. *Small-scale Aid's Contribution to Long-term Tsunami Recovery.* Chapel Hill, NC: Centre for Global Initiatives.

Norris, A.N., A. Zajicek, and Y. Murphy-Erby. 2010. 'Intersectional Perspective and Rural Poverty Research: Benefits, Challenges and Policy Implications', *Journal of Poverty,* 14(1): 55–75.

Nyamu-Musembi, C. 2002. 'Towards an Actor-oriented Perspective on Human Rights', IDS Working Paper No. 169, Brighton: Institute of Development Studies, University of Sussex.

———. 2005. 'Towards an Actor-oriented Perspective on Human Rights', in N. Kabeer (ed.), *Inclusive Citizenship: Meanings and Expressions.* London: Zed Books, pp. 31–49.

O'Donoghue, T. 2007. *Planning your Qualitative Research Proposal: An Introduction to Interpretivist Research in Education.* London: Routledge.

Office of the High Commissioner for Human Rights (OHCHR). 2004. *Human Rights and Poverty Reduction: A Conceptual Framework.* New York and Geneva: United Nations.

———. undated. 'What is a Rights-based Approach to Development?', Human Rights in Development webpages, available at www.unhchr.ch/development/approaches-04.html (accessed 30 April 2006).

Okely, J. 1991. 'Defiant Moments: Gender, Resistance and Individuals', *Man (New Series),* 26(1): 3–22.

Omvedt, G. 1979. 'On the Participant Study of Women's Movements: Methodological, Definitional and Action Considerations', in G. Huizer and B. Mannheim (eds), *The Politics of Anthropology: From Colonialism and Sexism towards a View from Below*. The Hague: Mouton Publishers, pp. 373–93.

———. 1993. *Reinventing Revolution: New Social Movements and the Socialist Tradition in India*. Armonk, NY: M.E. Sharpe.

———. 1995. *Dalit Visions: The Anti-caste Movement and the Construction of an Indian Identity*. New Delhi: Orient Longman.

Osmani, S.R. 1988. 'Food and the History of India—An Entitlement "Approach"'. WIDER Working Paper No. 50, Helsinki: World Institute for Development Economics Research.

Paik, S. 2009. 'Chhadi Lage Chham Chham, Vidya Yeyi Gham Gham (The Harder the Stick Beats, the Faster the Flow of Knowledge): Dalit Women's Struggle for Education', *Indian Journal of Gender Studies*, 16(2): 175–204.

Pandey, G. 2010. 'Politics of Difference: Reflections on Dalit and African American Struggles', *Economic and Political Weekly*, 45(19): 62–84.

Pandian, J. 1987. *Caste Nationalism and Ethnicity: An Interpretation of Tamil Cultural History and Social Order*. Bombay: Popular Prakashan

Pankaj, A. and R. Tankha. 2010. 'Empowerment Effects of NREGS on Women Workers: A Study of Four States', *Economic and Political Weekly*, 45(30): 45–55.

Pant, M. 2000. 'Intra-household Allocation Patterns: A Study of Female Autonomy', *Indian Journal of Gender Studies*, 7(1): 93–100.

Papanek, H. 1990. 'To Each Less than She Needs, From Each More than She Can Do: Allocations, Entitlements, and Value', in I. Tinker (ed.), *Persistent Inequalities: Women and World Development*. Oxford: Oxford University Press, pp. 162–81.

Parliamentary Committee on the Welfare of Scheduled Castes and Scheduled Tribes. 2005. *Fourth Report on Ministry of Home Affairs, Ministry of Social Justice and Empowerment and Ministry of Tribal Affairs (14th Lok Sabha): Atrocities on Scheduled Castes and Scheduled Tribes and Pattern of Social Crimes towards Them, 2004–2005*. New Delhi: Government of India.

Paterson, R. 2008. 'Women's Empowerment in Challenging Environments: A Case Study from Balochistan', *Development in Practice*, 18(3): 333–44.

Pattendon, J. 2011. 'Social Protection and Class Relations: Evidence from Scheduled Caste Women's Associations in Rural South India', *Development and Change*, 42(2): 469–98.

Petchesky, R.P. 1998. 'Introduction', in R.P. Petchesky and K. Judd (eds), *Negotiating Reproductive Rights: Women's Perspectives across Countries and Cultures*. London: Zed Books, pp. 1–30.

Phillips, A. 1999. *Which Equalities Matter?* Cambridge: Polity Press.

Planning Commission. 2002. *Tenth Five Year Plan (2002–2007), Volume 2: Sectoral Policies and Programmes.* New Delhi: National Planning Commission, Government of India.

———. 2005. *Percentage of Population below Poverty Line of Social Groups by States 2004–05.* New Delhi: National Planning Commission, Government of India.

———. 2008. *Eleventh Five Year Plan (2007–2012): Inclusive Growth.* New Delhi: Oxford University Press.

Polletta, F. and J.M. Jasper. 2001. 'Collective Identity and Social Movements', *Annual Review of Sociology*, 27: 283–305.

Posani, B. and Y. Aiyar. 2009. 'State of Accountability: Evolution, Practice and Emerging Questions in Public Accountability in India', AI Working Paper No. 2, New Delhi: Accountability Initiative.

Pösö, T., P. Konkatukia, and L. Nyqvist. 2008. 'Focus Groups and the Study of Violence', *Qualitative Research*, 8(1): 73–89.

Press Trust of India. 2010. 'Corruption and Irregularities in Implementation of NREGA: Study', *Business Standard*, 23 May, available at www.business-standard.com/india/news/corruptionirregularities-in-implementationnrega-study/21/18/95288/on (accessed 23 May 2010).

Programme on Women's Economic, Social and Cultural Rights (PWESCR). 2007. *Dalit Women in Rajasthan: Status of Economic, Social and Cultural Rights.* New Delhi: Programme on Women's Economic, Social and Cultural Rights.

Purushothaman, S. 1998. *The Empowerment of Women in India: Grassroots Women's Networks and the State.* New Delhi: Sage Publications.

Puwar, N. 2004. *Space Invaders: Race, Gender and Bodies Out of Place.* Oxford: Berg.

Rai, S.M. 2008. 'Civic Driven Change: Opportunities and Risks', in A. Fowler and K. Biekart (eds), *Civil Driven Change: Citizen's Imagination in Action.* The Hague: Institute of Social Studies, pp. 103–118.

Rajagopal, B. 2003. *International Law from Below: Development, Social Movements and Third World Resistance.* Cambridge: Cambridge University Press.

Ramasamy, K. 2005. 'Attitude and Approach', Paper presented to the National Judicial Colloquium on Dalits and the Law, New Delhi, 18 December.

Rana, R. 2009. 'Could Domestic Courts Enforce International Human Rights Norms? An Empirical Study of the Enforcement of Human Rights Norms by the Indian Supreme Court since 1997', *Indian Journal of International Law*, 49(4): 533–75.

Rao, A. 2003a. 'Introduction', in A. Rao (ed.), *Gender and Caste.* New Delhi: Kali for Women, pp. 1–47.

———. 2003b. 'Understanding Sirasgaon', in A. Rao (ed.), *Gender and Caste.* New Delhi: Kali for Women, pp. 276–309.

Rao, N. 2005. 'Questioning Women's Solidarity: The Case of Land Rights, Santal Parganas, Jharkhand, India', *Journal of Development Studies*, 41(3): 353–75.

Ravikumar. 2005. 'Waiting to Lose their Patience', in S. Viswanathan (ed.), *Dalits in Dravidian Land: Frontline Reports on Anti-Dalit Violence in Tamil Nadu (1995–2004)*. Chennai: Navayana Publishing, pp. xi–xxxviii.

Rege, S. 1998. 'Dalit Women Talk Differently: A Critique of "Difference" and towards a Dalit Feminist Standpoint Position', *Economic and Political Weekly*, 33(44): WS39–46.

————. 2000. '"Real Feminism"' and Dalit Women: Scripts of Denial and Accusation', *Economic and Political Weekly*, 46(6): 492–5.

Revenue Department. 2010. *Revenue Department Policy Note 2010–2011*. Chennai: Government of Tamil Nadu.

Rew, A. and M. Rew. 2003. 'Development Models "Out-of-Place": Social Research on Methods to Improve Livelihoods in Eastern India', *Community Development Journal*, 38(3): 213–24.

Ringrose, J. 2007. 'Troubling Agency and "Choice": A Psychological Analysis of Students' Negotiations of Black Feminist "Intersectionality" Discourses in Women's Studies', *Women's Studies International Forum*, 30(3): 264–78.

Robinson, M. 1998. 'Corruption and Development: An Introduction', *European Journal of Development Research*, 10(1): 1–14.

Rodgers, G. 1995. 'What is Special about a "Social Exclusion" Approach?', in G. Rodgers, C. Gore, and J.B. Figueiredo (eds), *Social Exclusion: Rhetoric, Reality, Responses*. Geneva: International Institute for Labour Studies, pp. 43–56.

Rudha, A. 1984. 'Local Power and Farm-level Decision-making', in M. Desai, S. Hoeber, and A. Rudha (eds), *Agrarian Power and Agricultural Productivity in South Asia*. New Delhi: Oxford University Press, pp. 250–80.

Rudolph, L.I. and S.H. Rudolph. 1984. 'Determinants and Varieties of Agrarian Mobilization', in M. Desai, S. Hoeber, and A. Rudha (eds), *Agrarian Power and Agricultural Productivity in South Asia*. New Delhi: Oxford University Press, pp. 281–344.

Ruggeri Laderchi, C., R. Saith, and F. Stewart. 2003. 'Does it Matter that We Do Not Agree on the Definition of Poverty? A Comparison of Four Approaches', *Oxford Development Studies*, 31(3): 243–74.

Rural Development and Panchayati Raj Department (RDPRD). 2010. *Policy Note 2010–2011*. Chennai: Rural Development and Panchayati Raj Department, Government of Tamil Nadu.

Ryan, C. and W.A. Gamson. 2006. 'The Art of Reframing Political Debates', *Contexts*, 5(1): 13–18.

Saith, R. 2001. 'Social Exclusion: The Concept and Application to Developing Countries', QEH Working Paper No. 72, Oxford: Queen Elizabeth House.

Sakshi Human Rights Watch. 2007. *Dalit Human Rights Monitor 2003–2006*. Hyderabad: Sakshi Human Rights Watch, Andhra Pradesh.

Sangari, K. 1995. 'Politics of Diversity: Religious Communities and Multiple Patriarchies', *Economic and Political Weekly*, 30(52): 3287–310.

———. 1996. 'Consent, Agency, and the Rhetorics of Incitement', in T.V. Sathyamurthy (ed.), *Social Change and Political Discourse in India: Structures of Power, Movements of Resistance*. New Delhi: Oxford University Press, pp. 463–502.

Sardenberg, C.M.B. 2007. *Liberal vs Liberating Empowerment: Conceptualising Women's Empowerment from a Latin American Feminist Perspective*. Brighton: Institute of Development Studies, University of Sussex.

Satya Babu Bose, B. 2007. 'Land Entitlements—A Historical Development', in T. Pallinatham Sdb (ed.), *Rekindling Hope? Access, Retention and Development of Land: A Dalit Perspective*. Hyderabad: Dalit Bahujan Shramik Union, pp. 11–34.

Sawicki, J. 1991. *Disciplining Foucault: Feminism, Power, and the Body*. London and New York: Routlege.

Scoones, I. 1998. 'Sustainable Rural Livelihoods: A Framework for Analysis', Working Paper No. 72, Brighton: Institute of Development Studies, University of Sussex.

Scott, J.C. 1985. *Weapons of the Weak: Everyday Forms of Peasant Resistance*. New Haven: Yale University Press.

Scott, J.W. 1986. 'Gender: A Useful Category of Historical Analysis', *The American Historical Review*, 91(5): 1053–75.

Sen, A. 1981. *Poverty and Famines: An Essay on Entitlement and Deprivation*. New Delhi: Oxford University Press.

———. 1990. 'Gender and Cooperative Conflicts', in I. Tinker (ed.), *Persistent Inequalities: Women and World Development*. New York: Oxford University Press, pp. 123–49.

———. 1999. *Development as Freedom*. Oxford: Oxford University Press.

———. 2000. 'Social Exclusion: Concept, Application and Scrutiny', Social Development Papers 1, Manila: Asian Development Bank.

Sengupta, A., K.P. Kannan, and G. Raveendran. 2008. 'India's Common People: Who are They, How Many are They and How do They Live?', *Economic and Political Weekly*, 43(11): 49–63.

Shah, G. 1990. *Social Movements in India: Review of Literature*. New Delhi: Sage Publications.

Shah, G., H. Mander, S. Thorat, S. Deshpande, and A. Baviskar. 2006. *Untouchability in Rural India*. New Delhi: Sage Publications.

Sharma, K. 2011. 'Small Loans, Big Dreams: Women and Microcredit in a Globalising Economy', *Economic and Political Weekly*, 46(43): 58–63.

Silver, H. 1995. 'Reconceptualizing Social Disadvantage: Three Paradigms of Social Exclusion', in G. Rodgers, C. Gore, and J.B. Figueiredo (eds), *Social Exclusion: Rhetoric, Reality, Responses*. Geneva: International Institute for Labour Studies, pp. 57–80.

Singh, M. 2006a. 'Prime Minister's Address, 10th Meeting of the Inter-State Council', Press Information Bureau, Government of India, New Delhi, 9 December.

———. 2006b. 'Prime Minister's Address, Dalit–Minority International Conference', Press Information Bureau, Government of India, New Delhi, 27 December.

Sivakumar, R., 2009. 'A Study of Dalit Women's Movements in Tamil Nadu', available at www.articlesbase.com/womens-issues-articles/a-study-on-dalit-women-movement-in-tamilnadu-753088.html (accessed 21 October 2010).

Sivaraman, R. 2011. 'Women thank EC for Ban on Liquor Sales', *The Times of India*, Madurai/Trichy edition, 18 October.

SLSA Team. 2003. 'Rights Talk and Rights Practice: Challenges for Southern Africa', *IDS Bulletin*, 34(3): 97–111.

Smith, D. 2005. *Institutional Ethnography: A Sociology for People*. Lanham, MD: AltaMira.

Smith, P.J. 2008. 'From Beijing 1995 to the Hague 2006—The Transnational Activism of the Dalit Women's Movement', Paper presented at Canadian Political Science Association Annual Meeting, Vancouver, British Columbia, 3–6 June.

Snow, D.A. and R.D. Benford. 1988. 'Ideology, Frame Resonance, and Participant Mobilization', in B. Klandermans, H. Kriesi, and S. Tarrow (eds), *From Structure to Action: Comparing Social Movement Research Across Cultures*. Greenwich: JAI Press, pp. 197–217.

Social Watch Tamil Nadu. 2004. *Special Component Plan: Dalit Hopes Betrayed?* Chennai: Social Watch Tamil Nadu.

Special Rapporteur on Adequate Housing. 2005. *Report of the Special Rapporteur on Adequate Housing as a Component of the Right to an Adequate standard of Living*. Commission on Human Rights 61st Session. UN Doc. E/CN.4/2005/48. Geneva: United Nations.

Srinivas, M.N. 1987. *The Dominant Caste and Other Essays*. Oxford: Oxford University Press.

Srivastava, P. 2005. 'Microfinance in India: Odysseus or Interloper?', *Economic and Political Weekly*, 40(33): 3626–8.

Stammers, N. 1993. 'Human Rights and Power', *Political Studies*, 41(1): 70–82.

———. 1999. 'Social Movements and the Social Construction of Human Rights', *Human Rights Quarterly*, 21(4): 980–1008.

Staun's, D. 2003. 'Where have All the Subjects Gone? Bringing together the Concepts of Intersectionality and Subjectification', *NORA Nordic Journal of Feminist and Gender Research*, 11(2): 101–10.

Stein, B. 1994. *Peasant State and Society in Medieval South India*. Oxford: Oxford University Press.

Steinar, K. and S. Brinkmann. 2009. *Interviews: Learning the Craft of Qualitative Research Interviewing* (2nd edition). Thousand Oaks, CA: Sage Publications.

Steiner, H.J. and P. Alston. 2007. *International Human Rights in Context: Law, Politics, Morals* (3rd edition). Oxford: Oxford University Press.

Strauss, A. and J. Corbin. 1990. *Basics of Qualitative Research: Grounded Theory Procedures and Techniques*. London: Sage Publications.

Strauss, J. and K. Beegle. 1996. 'Intrahousehold Allocations: A Review of Theories, Empirical Evidence and Policy Issues', MSU International Development Working Paper 62, East Lansing, MI: Department of Agricultural Economics, Michigan State University.

Subramaniam, M. 2003. 'Capacity Building and Change: Women and Development in India', *Women's Studies Quarterly*, 31(3–4): 192–211.

———. 2006. *The Power of Women's Organizing: Gender, Caste, and Class in India*. Lanham: Lexington Books.

Sudhakar Rao, N. 2001. 'The Structure of South Indian Untouchable Castes: A View', in G. Shah (ed.), *Dalit Identity and Politics*. New Delhi: Sage Publications, pp. 74–96.

Sullivan, D. 1995. 'The Public/Private Distinction in International Human Rights Law', in J. Peters and A. Wolper (eds), *Women's Rights, Human Rights: International Feminist Perspectives*. New York: Routledge, pp. 126–34.

Sunstein, B.S. and E. Chiseri-Slater. 2007. *Fieldworking: Reading and Writing Research* (3rd edition). Boston and New York: Bedford and St Martin's.

Suresh, V. 2005. 'Constitutional Agenda, Institutional Indifference, Official Subversion: The Tragedy of Protection of the Rights of India's Dalits', Paper presented to the National Judicial Colloquium on Dalits and the Law, New Delhi, 18 December.

Tamil Nadu Corporation for the Development of Women (TNCDW). 2011. 'Mahalir Thittam', available at www.tamilnaduwomen.org (accessed 1 November 2011).

Tanner, C.L. 1995. 'Class, Caste and Gender in Collective Action: Agricultural Labour Unions in Two Indian Villages', *Journal of Peasant Studies*, 22(4): 672–98.

Tarrow, S. 1994. *Power in Movement: Social Movements, Collective Action and Politics*. Cambridge: Cambridge University Press.

———. 1996. 'Making Social Science Work across Space and Time: A Critical Reflection on Robert Putnam's *Making Democracy Work*', *American Political Science Review*, 90(2): 389–95.

Taylor, C. 1992. *Multiculturalism and 'The Politics of Recognition'*. Princeton, NJ: Princeton University Press.

Taylor, V. and N. van Dyke. 2007. '"Get Up, Stand Up": Tactical Repertoires of Social Movements', in D.A. Snow, S.A. Soule, and H. Kriesi (eds), *Blackwell Companion to Social Movements*. Malden, MA, and Oxford: Blackwell Publishing, pp. 262–93.

Teltumbde, A. 1999. 'Globalization and the Dalits', available at http://ambedkar.org/research/GLOBALISATIONANDTHEDALITS.pdf (accessed 21 January 2013).

———. 2012. SC/STs and the State in the Indian Constitution. Available at http://www.countercurrents.org/teltumbde060212.pdf (accessed 5 August 2013).

Thorat, S. 2002. 'Inequality and Caste Based Discrimination: Reflection on Theory and Empirical Facts with respect to Scheduled Caste Wage Labour in India', Paper presented at the Workshop on Economic Development of the Scheduled Castes with special reference to Agricultural Labourers, Gokhale Institute of Politics and Economics, Pune, 16–17 March.

———. 2007. 'Human Poverty and Socially Disadvantaged Groups in India', Discussion Paper Series No. 18, New Delhi: Human Development Resource Centre/UNDP India Office.

Thorat, S. and P. Attewell. 2007. 'The Legacy of Social Exclusion: A Correspondence Study of Job Discrimination in India', *Economic and Political Weekly*, 42(41): 4141–5.

Thorat, S. and J. Lee. 2006. 'Dalits and the Right to Food: Discrimination and Exclusion in Food-related Government Programmes', IIDS Working Paper 1(3), New Delhi: Indian Institute of Dalit Studies.

Thorat, S. and K.S. Newman. 2007. 'Caste and Economic Discrimination: Causes, Consequences and Remedies', *Economic and Political Weekly*, 42(41): 4121–4.

Thorat, S. and N. Sadana. 2009. 'Discrimination and Children's Nutritional Status in India', *IDS Bulletin*, 40(4): 25–9.

Thorat, S. and N. Sabharwal. 2010. 'Caste and Social Exclusion: Issues Related to Concept, Indicators and Measurement', Working Paper 2(1), New Delhi: Indian Institute of Dalit Studies and UNICEF.

Thorat, V. 2001. 'Dalit Women have been Left Behind by the Dalit Movement and the Women's Movement', *Communalism Combat*, vol. 69, p. 12.

Thorp, R., F. Stewart, and A. Heyer. 2005. 'When and How Far is Group Formation a Route Out of Poverty', *World Development*, 33(6): 907–20.

United Nations (UN) Conference on Environment and Development. 1992. *Rio Declaration on Environment and Development*. Rio de Janeiro: United Nations Conference on Environment and Development, New York: United Nations..

United Nations Development Programme (UNDP). 2000. *Human Development Report 2000*. New York: United Nations Development Programme.

Uvin, P. 2002. 'On High Moral Ground: The Incorporation of Human Rights by the Development Enterprise', *Praxis: The Fletcher Journal of Development Studies*, 17: 1–11.

van Velsen, J. 1967. 'The Extended-case Method and Situational Analysis', in A.L. Epstein (ed.), *The Craft of Social Anthropology*. London: Tavistock Publishers, pp. 129–49.

Vasavi, A.R. 2003. 'Schooling for a New Society? The Social and Political Bases of Education Deprivation in India', *IDS Bulletin*, 34(1): 72–80.

VeneKlasen, L., V. Miller, C. Clark, and M. Reilly. 2004. 'Rights-based Approaches and Beyond: Challenges of Linking Power and Participation', IDS Working Paper No. 235, Brighton: Institute of Development Studies, University of Sussex.

Verloo, M. 2006. 'Multiple Inequalities, Intersectionality and the European Union', *European Journal of Women's Studies*, 13(3): 211–28.

Vijayalakshmi, V. 2004. 'Citizenship, Differences and Identity: Dalit Women and Political Inclusion', ISEC Working Paper No. 147, Bangalore: Institute for Social and Economic Change.

Villarreal, M. 1992. 'Power, Gender and Intervention from an Actor-oriented Perspective', in N. Long and A. Long (eds), *Battlefields of Knowledge: The Interlocking of Theory and Practice in Social Research and Development*. London and New York: Routledge, pp. 247–67.

———. 1994. 'Wielding and Yielding: Power, Subordination and Gender Identity in the Context of a Mexican Development Project', PhD Thesis, Wageningen University, Wageningen.

Visvanathan, S. and C. Parmar. 2005. 'Life, Life World, and Life Chances: Vulnerability and Survival in Indian Constitutional Law', in B. de Sousa Santos and C.A. Rodriguez-Garavito (eds), *Law and Globalization from Below: Towards a Cosmopolitan Legality*. Cambridge: Cambridge University Press, pp. 339–62.

Viswanathan, S. 2002. 'A Law against Workers', *Frontline*, vol. 19, no. 11, 25 May–7 June. Available at http: //www.frontline.in/static/html/fl1911/19110400.htm (accessed 4 August 2013).

———. 2003. 'States within a State', *Frontline*, vol. 20, no. 16, 2–15 August. Available at http://www.frontline.in/static/html/fl2016/stories/20030815004703800.htm (accessed 4 August 2013).

———. 2004. 'Land of Inequalities', *Frontline*, vol. 21, no. 21, 9–22 October. Available at http://www.frontline.in/static/html/fl2121/stories/20041022003004300.htm (accessed 4 August 2013).

Walby, S. 1990. *Theorizing Patriarchy*. Oxford: Basil Blackwell.

Webster, N. 2004. 'Understanding the Evolving Diversities and Originalities of Rural Social Movements in the Age of Globalization', Civil Society and Social Movements Programme Paper No. 7, Geneva: United Nations Research Institute for Social Development.

White, S. 2003. 'The "Gender Lens": A Racial Blinder?', Paper presented at seminar on Gender Myths and Feminist Fables: Repositioning Gender in Development Policy and Practice, Institute of Development Studies, University of Sussex, Brighton, 2–4 July.

White, S.C. 1996. 'Depoliticising Development: The Uses and Abuses of Participation', *Development in Practice*, 6(1): 6–15.

Wierenga, S. 1994. 'Women's Interests and Empowerment: Gender Planning Revisited'. *Development and Change*, 25(4): 829–48.

Wilson, C. 2004. 'Understanding the Dynamics of Socio-economic Mobility: Tales from Two Indian Villages', Working Paper No. 236, London: Overseas Development Institute.

Wilson, J. 1973. *Introduction to Social Movements*. New York: Basic Books Inc.

Wilson, K. 2008. 'Reclaiming "Agency", Reasserting Resistance', *IDS Bulletin*, 39(6): 83–91.

Winter, D.D. and D.C. Leighton. 2001. 'Structural Violence', in D.J. Christie, R.V. Wagner, and D.D. Winter (eds), *Peace, Conflict, and Violence: Peace Psychology in the 21st Century*. New York: Prentice-Hall, pp. 99–101.

Working Group on Women's Empowerment. 2006. *Report of the Working Group on Empowerment of Women for the XI Five-Year Plan*. New Delhi: Ministry of Women and Child Development, Government of India.

World Bank. 1990. *World Development Report 1990: Poverty*. Washington, DC: The World Bank.

World Conference on Human Rights. 1993. *Vienna Declaration and Programme of Action*. Geneva: World Conference on Human Rights.

Yamin, A.E. 2005. 'The Future in the Mirror: Incorporating Strategies for the Defense and Promotion of Economic, Social, and Cultural Rights into the Mainstream Human Rights Agend', *Human Rights Quarterly*, 27(4): 1200–44.

Yin, R.K. 1993. *Applications of Case Study Research*. Newbury Park, CA: Sage Publications.

Young, I.M. 1997. 'Unruly Categories: A Critique of Nancy Fraser's Dual Systems Theory', *New Left Review*, I/222: 147–60.

Yuval-Davis, N. 2006. 'Intersectionality and Feminist Politics', *European Journal of Women's Studies*, 13(3): 193–209.

Case Law

Apparel Export Promotion Council vs *A.K. Chopra*, (1999) 1 SCC, 759.

C.E.S.C. Ltd vs *S.C. Bose*, (1992) 1 SCC, 441.

Consumer Education and Research vs *Union of India*, (1995) 3 SCC, 42.

Francis Coralie Mullin vs *The Administrator, Union Territory of Delhi and Others*, (1981) 2 SCR, 516.

Maria da Penha vs *Brazil*, (2000), Case 12.051, Report No. 54/01, OEA/Ser.L/V/II.111 Doc. 20 rev., 704.

M.C. Mehta vs *Union of India*, (1987) 1 SCC, 395.

Olga Tellis vs *Bombay Municipal Corporation*, AIR (1986) SC, 180.

People's Union for Civil Liberties vs *Union of India and others*, (1997) 3 SCC, 433.

S. Jagannath vs *Union of India and Others*, (1997) 2 SCC, 87.

State of Karnataka vs *Appa Balu Ingale and Others*, AIR (1993) SC, 1146.

Unni Krishnan J.P. and Others vs *State of Andhra Pradesh*, (1993) SCC (1), 645.

Velasquez-Rodriguez vs *Honduras*, (1988) 4 Inter. Am. Ct. HR, Ser. C, No. 4.

Vishakha vs *State of Rajasthan*, (1997) 6 SCC, 241.

INDEX

collective agency and politics of
securing entitlements, for Dalit
women
collective action strategies and
outcomes 148–60
external intervention of NGOs
143–8
motivation of actions 141–3
comprises of Muthu nādu 139
Dalits
caste interdependence,
diminishing trend of 140
establishment of self-
governance 139
as permanent farm labourers
139
power relations embedded in
resilient and enduring nādu
institutional rules 140
women need support from
higher officials to counter
political influence 225
Hindu Dalit SC families in 138
land and socio-political status
connected with rural Tamil
Nadu 139
landownership, importance
given to 141

socio-historical features of
138–9
Viduthalai Chiruthaigal Katchi
(VCK), Dalit political party 20
village administrative officer 111,
116, 118, 137, 142, 150, 154,
156, 189
violence, against Dalit women 2, 69
appeal for legal protection 70
causes of 70
cultural 4
physical 4
sexual 49
structural 3

Water (Prevention and Control of
Pollution) Act 1974 184–5
women's movements, Indian
recognition of difference and
focus on processes 5–6
women's savings, opportunities for 4
women's sexuality 28
male control over 235
Working Group on Women's
Empowerment 201, 246

zamindari abolition law 139
zero-sum game 44

ABOUT THE AUTHOR

Jayshree P. Mangubhai is Research Programme Director at the Centre for Social Equity and Inclusion in New Delhi. She has worked as a consultant in human rights and development in India for over a decade, with a particular focus on the rights of Dalits and Adivasis, especially women of these communities. She completed her PhD from the Netherlands Institute of Human Rights, University of Utrecht, The Netherlands in 2012. Her books include: *Dalit Women Speak Out: Caste, Class and Gender Violence in India* (2011, co-author); *Dalit Women's Right to Political Participation in Rural Panchayati Raj: A Study of Gujarat and Tamil Nadu* (2009; co-author); *New Economic Reforms: Hope or Mirage for Dalit Livelihoods?* (2004).